AF522622

INTELLECTUAL DISABILITY AND LANGUAGE INTERVENTION

INTELLECTUAL DISABILITY AND LANGUAGE INTERVENTION

By

Dr. Mary P.V. (Sister Glory)

Associate Professor in Special Education
Nirmala Sadan Training College for Special Education
Muvattupuzha - 686661
Kerala

Published by:

DISCOVERY PUBLISHING HOUSE
4383/4B, Ansari Road, Darya Ganj
New Delhi-110 002 (India)
Phone : +91-11-23279245; 23253475; 43596065
E-mail : discoverybooksindia@gmail.com
discoverypublishinghouse@gmail.com
namitwasan9@gmail.com
web : www.discoverypublishinggroup.com

First Edition: **2023**

ISBN: 978-81-958210-8-2

Intellectual Disability and Language Intervention

Printed at:
Infinity Imaging Systems
Delhi

DEDICATION

Dedicated to my Lord Jesus Christ, the great teacher, and the very special children, who struggle hard every day to improve their language and literacy skills.

Foreword

It is a matter of pleasure and pride to present foreword for the book written by Dr. Mary P.V. (Sister Glory) on 'Intellectual Disability and Language Intervention". It becomes a pleasure because Sister Glory has done her research work leading to doctoral degree with me. It becomes a pride as she deals with a very important theme, that too in a scientific manner. Her immense experience as a teacher educator in the field of education of students with intellectual disability, coupled with dedicated hard work and painstaking research is the basis of this text. Moreover, being a clergywoman, she is always concerned with the welfare of others. Sister Glory is the first person to organize B.Ed. and M.Ed. Special Education programmes in Kerala State of South India. I can confidently state that this work is the outcome of concrete experiences, scientific knowledge, empathetic attitude, well designed research, and clear vision of a person with a passion for all round development of individuals with intellectual disability.

Intellectual disability is a multidisciplinary phenomenon which affects all aspects of life of an individual. This global developmental deficit demands the attention and intervention from various professionals. Among these professionals the role of a special educationist is very unique in many respects. Growth and development of a person with intellectual disability can be ensured only through the implementation of appropriate individualized educational programme. Quality research is essential to develop appropriate educational programmes and this work is a very good attempt towards this goal.

This book addresses an important developmental area of special education. The author focusses on the development of reading vocabulary, reading comprehension, phonological awareness, reading fluency and writing skills. The different chapters of this book will give the reader very useful information regarding the theoretical overview of literacy rich approach, description of the experimental method followed in the study, development of the instruments of data collection, statistical techniques used for analysis of data, systematic presentation of the results and discussion, and also a very good list of references as well. It discusses the implications of the findings of the study and lists thought provoking suggestions also. I congratulate Rev. Dr. Mary P.V. (Sister Glory) for this excellent venture and wish her to continue to write further by blending academic, social and research aspects of topic like this.

Dr. P.S. Sukumaran

Professor

School of Behavioural Sciences

Mahatma Gandhi University

Kottayam, Kerala

Preface

The researcher is delighted to bring out the results of the study entitled "Intellectual Disability and Language Intervention". This research report contains five chapters and focuses on how to teach language (reading and writing) to children with intellectual disability.

The aim of providing education to children with intellectual disability is to make them independent as much as possible. Many of these children have problems in understanding abstract concepts and therefore it is difficult for them to learn reading and writing. But personal independence requires at least functional literacy. Academic learning of all subjects depends on the mastery of literacy skills. In work place, community surroundings and social gatherings the literacy level decides one's grasping of concepts and speed of functioning. Several factors influence these children's low level of literacy. Some of them are problems in memory and attention, difficulty in understanding abstraction and inability to generalize.

Having several years of experience in teaching reading and writing to children with intellectual disability, I found it very difficult to teach them effectively. With present methods and procedures initial acquisition of skills was possible. But students experience difficulty in maintaining and generalizing learned skills. Therefore I looked for something more effective and Literacy Rich Approach (LRA) came to mind.

Using the prior teaching experience and literature review, I combined several factors together and made this Literacy Rich approach. With this a reading writing package was prepared and investigated its effect on children with mild intellectual disability. The instructional content involves development of reading vocabulary, reading comprehension, phonological awareness, reading fluency, and writing skills. The components of LRA are small group practice, ongoing monitoring, positive feedback, continuous reinforcement, class room library and writing centre. The result of the study shows that LRA is highly effective in acquiring, generalizing and maintaining literacy skills of children with intellectual disability compared to the conventional approach. Although LRA is implemented in reading and writing of Malayalam language, this approach can be used with any language and in any time.

Dr. Mary P.V. (Sister Glory)

Acknowledgement

I wish to express my immense gratitude to God Almighty for His loving presence, providential care, and showering of blessings during the time of my research.

I am deeply grateful to my supervising teacher, Professor (Dr.) P.S. Sukumaran, Dean, Faculty of Behavioural Sciences, Mahatma Gandhi University, Kottayam, Kerala, for his scholarly guidance, continuous support, constant encouragement, and above all his superb modelling to complete this work successfully. His immense knowledge and experience encouraged me in all times of this research. I would like to extent my sincere thanks to the Director and staff of School of Behavioural Sciences, Mahatma Gandhi University.

I am deeply indebted to my provincial superiors of Franciscan Clarist Congregation, Vimala province, Sr. Joviet, Sr. Grace Mary, Sr. Rincy, Sr. Lucitta and present provincial Sr. Merlin for completing my Ph.D and publishing this book. Without their encouragement, support and prayers it would not have been possible for me to do this. I would like to express my thanks to Dr. Sr. Divya, Principal and all staff members of Nirmala Sadan Training College for Special Education, Muvattupuzha for their timely support. Sr. Jancy George, Principal and all staff members of Nirmala Sadan special school are remembered with gratitude for making arrangements to conduct the experimental study. Teachers and students participated in the study are also specially remembered.

I extend sincere thanks to all experts who spent their valuable time and expertise for validating the research instrument. Dr. T.M. Jacob, Professor in Statistics in Nirmala College, Muvattupuzha is specially remembered. Rev. Dr. Jose Kodamullil, late Principal of Nirmala Higher Secondary School is greatly appreciated for doing the editing and proof reading of the research work. Many thanks are due to Sr. Tancy, office in charge of Nirmala Sadan Training College, for typing the manuscript and providing timely support. I am also indebted to Swamy's DTP centre and SIMS computer centre for helping in preparing the manuscript.

Library staff of School of Behavioural Sciences, Mahatma Gandhi University, Kottayam; Nirmala College, Muvattupuzha; National Insitute for the Empowerment of Persons with Intellectual Disabilities, Secunderabad; All India Institute for Speech and Hearing, Nirmala Sadan Training College for Special Education, Muvattupuzha are greatly remembered for their help in retrieving the information needed for the study. Sisters of Nirmala Sadan convent, Lourd Matha convent, and my family members are specially remembered.

I express my thanks to all those who directly and indirectly helped me in the development of this research and writing of this book.

Finally I wholeheartedly thank Discovery Publishing House, New Delhi for undertaking the publication of this thesis. Mr. Wasan's quick response, dedication, interest are superb.

Dr. Mary P.V. (Sister Glory)

Contents

Abstract

This study investigated the effectiveness of Literacy-Rich Approach (LRA) in the language development of children with Intellectual Disability. Specifically effectiveness of LRA was assessed with respect to development of reading vocabulary, reading comprehension, phonological awareness, reading fluency and writing skills. Sample constitutes 60 children with mild Intellectual Disability, (30 experimental and 30 control) who were studying in special school. Pre test – post test – control- group design was used. The study was done in three stages. Stage I was pre test stage in which students were tested on language development. Stage II was the conduct of experiment (Intervention). During this stage instruction through conventional approach was given to experimental and control groups and then experimental group was given additional intervention using Literacy- Rich- Approach (LRA). In stage III students were retested using parallel test (to measure acquisition), post test (to measure generalization) and retention test (to measure maintenance). The retention test was given after six months of intervention. Analysis of Covariance was the major statistical technique employed for analysis of data. The results showed that LRA was highly effective for overall literacy development. (total reading-writing) Objective wise analysis showed conventional approach was adequate for acquiring majority of skills, while LRA was needed for generalizing and maintaining learned skills. The results are discussed and implications and suggestions are also given.

Keywords: *Children with Intellectual Disability, language (literacy) development. Literacy-rich approach, Components of literacy– vocabulary, reading comprehension, phonological awareness, reading fluency, writing skills.*

Introduction

CONTEXT OF THE STUDY

Persons with intellectual disability form a heterogeneous group who differ in their levels of intelligence and proficiency in adaptive behaviour. As AAIDD defines, intellectual disability is characterized by significant limitations both in intellectual functioning and adaptive behaviour as expressed in conceptual, social and practical adaptive skills. These limitations originate before age 18 (Schalock, *et al.*, 2010).

The most common feature of intellectual disability is the failure to achieve age appropriate developmental tasks. These tasks involve processes of maturation in learning and social adjustment. These are commonly known as adaptive behaviour deficits. In the preschool years a slower rate of maturation is reflected in the delay seen in acquiring skill in the areas of motor, language, cognition, self-help, and socialization. At school age the learning difficulty inherent in persons with intellectual disability is expressed in their poor academic achievement. In adulthood this disability may affect capacities for self-management, employment and fulfilment of adult interpersonal roles. Intellectual disability is classified into four levels of severity – mild, moderate, severe and profound. More than 80 percent of all persons with intellectual disability appear in mild category. Persons with intellectual disability have considerable inter individual differences. Many factors influence individual behaviour and functioning – chronological age, the severity of disability, its etiology and educational opportunities.

While providing education and training to children with intellectual disability, our aim is to improve their adaptive behaviour and enable them to live in the most independent way possible. Therefore their curriculum areas should include conceptual, social, and practical adaptive skills as mentioned by AAIDD. The conceptual skills have four main areas –language (receptive and expressive), reading and writing, money concepts, and self direction. Of these, reading and writing (literacy) becomes an essential component of curriculum.

As the ability to read and write is essential for living today's world, personal independence requires at least functional literacy. Failure to read restricts academic progress of normal school age population because proficiency in Maths, English or Social Studies depends on ability to read. Students who cannot read probably cannot spell, and both of these deficiencies will affect their writing activities. Reading is a skill very much related to a student's self-concept. Proficiency in reading will help to avoid experiences that result in diminished self worth. At the same time this proficiency provides opportunities for good experiences within the activity of daily school life.

Adults who read well are regarded as intelligent, and educated. Adult who is deficient in reading ability may have serious adult adjustment problems. Faced with persistent failure and disapproval from family and peers and subjected to discrimination by employees, poor readers experience less self-satisfaction and lower opinion of themselves. Most jobs in our society also require at least minimal reading skills. Reading may even be the key to personal/social adjustment and to successful involvement in community activities.

Mackay (2007) listed some reasons why adults need reading : getting a license and driving a car, going on a trip, ordering food at a restaurant, buying something on time, getting a job, going to a doctor, and reading instructions on a medicine bottle.

Like all persons successful progress in literacy is crucial for children with intellectual disability. Perhaps in no other area does the teacher need to place greater emphasis on skill development than in reading. Smith (1968) listed many noteworthy reasons to emphasize reading for children with intellectual disability.

(1) Inability to read will adversely affects other areas of instruction-arithmetic, social and personal development, communication and vocational placement. (2) Reading is a means of acquiring general information. If the youngsters have developed the basic skills of word identification and continue to expand their reading vocabulary, the additional information, acquired through independent reading allows for the generation of alternative solution to problems. (3) Reading' requires transfer, generalization and elaboration and this will enable children to solve problems in other areas of life. (4) Reading provides opportunities for pleasurable out-of-school activities. (5) The skill in reading decreases the possibility of the child experiencing physical harm and provides an insulation against severe social and emotional difficulties.

Langone (1986) stated that the major reason for teaching intellectually disabled learners reading and language arts skill is that these skills can help them to be more independent in home, work, leisure/recreation and community environments.

Although instruction in reading is essential for children with intellectual disability to become independent, there has been so little work and interest in problems surrounding the teaching of reading to these children.

Review of literature on literacy development and intellectual disability (for example Singh & Singh, 1986; and Westling, 1986) found people with intellectual disability read well below their mental age. This is true even for children with mild intellectual disability. Carter (1975) observed that majority of students with mild intellectual disability read at lower levels than expected for their mental age. The reasons for this type of reading mentioned in the literature (Katims, 2000; 1996) are twofold. (1) Many practitioners de-emphasize literacy learning and concentrate more heavily on social, personal and vocational related curriculum domains for students with intellectual disability. (2) Traditional approach to literacy education for this population generally focused on the teaching of isolated sub skills, which rarely engage students with well constructed, connected texts containing multiple sentences. Since people with disabilities have great difficulty in mastering this isolated sub skills they do not gain access to participation in the higher processes of using literacy as a tool for communication, obtaining information or reading for pleasure (Pikulski, 1994).

Some researchers (Browder, Trela, Gibbs, Wakeman & Harris, 2007) found reading is not a target of instruction for learners with intellectual disability because educators incorrectly assumed that they cannot learn to read or benefit from such instruction.

Conners (1992) noted that in regular education the focus of reading instruction is on gaining meaning from print, while the research on reading instruction for students with intellectual disability focuses almost exclusively on the identification of individual words. Lev Vygotsky observed this trend earlier, that is, teach youngsters with intellectual disability using only concrete methods which eliminated anything associated with abstract, symbolic, or constructivist thinking. Vygotsky called for instruction which advanced the development of symbolic and meaningful thought in these people (Vygotsky, 1978).

The goal of schooling for students with intellectual disability may not have be to centre exclusively around social, vocational and daily living skills while limiting literacy instruction to a set of functional words. An increasing number of investigators have demonstrated that children with intellectual disability can move toward more advanced literacy if presented with opportunities to interact with words in context, and construct meaning from text (Katims, 1991; 1994; 1996; Hedrick, Katims, Curr, 1999; Katims and Pierce, 1995). Programmes of students can be designed from pre primary to transition into adulthood in a way that balances necessary daily skills, vocational skills with literacy instruction that emphasize reading and writing with meaning.

The avoidance of higher level skills for children with intellectual disability may due to several reasons. The complexity of reading process itself might have influenced special educators who are reluctant to teach these skills. As Mann, Suiter, McClung, (1992) explained the student must master a series of complex skills effectively to perform and receive the maximum advantage from reading. These skills are: auditory-visual sensory input, auditory-visual perception, auditory-visual memory, language-symbolization, and input-output relationships. Reading is a dynamic process in which perception, memory, and language, must function harmoniously with each other.

Although the reading process seems complicated for persons with Intellectual Disability, many authors recognized the potential of this group of children. Langone (1986) clearly listed the reading potentials of mild intellectually disabled learner in English language. According to him children with mild intellectual disability can exhibit the following decoding skills: (1) Identifies and pronounces blends commonly found in words at the first, second and third grade levels. (2) Identifies and pronounces consonants when found in initial, medial, and final positions in words. (3) Identifies and pronounces both short and long vowels when found in words. (4) Identifies and pronounces digraphs and diphthongs when found in words at first, second and third grade levels. (5) Identifies and pronounces root words prefixes and suffixes. In the comprehension area they can: (1) demonstrate the meaning of a wide variety of words, (2) locate and describes the main idea of a story and can recall details, (3) follow written directions, (4) sequence events in logical order and (5) make basic inferences and evaluations.

Carney (1979) reported, children with mild intellectual disability can achieve a level of literacy commensurate with their mental ages, if instruction is designed specifically to meet the child's individual needs. Algozzine and Wood (1994) argued that instruction for students with intellectual disability should include an early active focus on comprehension, use of wide variety of texts and cooperative grouping practices.

Alnadhi (2015) did a systematic review of literature related to instructional strategies to improve reading skills for students with intellectual disability. It was concluded that these students are in need to receive very intense practice and instruction to improve their reading skills and it should be provided explicitly, systematically and consistently.

Considering the remarks of the authors mentioned above and evaluating the present practices in literacy instruction of children with intellectual disability, the investigator felt that a detailed content is required in this area. This felt need is reflected in the preparation of content and tools and reading package for this research.

In western literature , many strategies are explained for reading instruction of intellectually disabled children. Many of these are explained in chapter 2 (review of related literature).

It is a well known fact that anything taught (acquired) in the classroom or training situation need to be generalized for a student with intellectual disability so that he/she will be able to apply the skill learnt to any appropriate situation. Similarly the student should be able to maintain the skill overtime even after training procedures are withdrawn. Therefore this study aims at development of literacy skills with special reference to generalization and maintenance.

Alberto and Troutman (1995) explained the terms acquisition, generalization and maintenance clearly. Acquisition is the basic level of students' response competence. Maintenance is the ability to perform a response overtime without reteaching. It is the ability to perform a response overtime even after systematic behavoiur procedures have been withdrawn. Generalization is the expansion of student's capability of performance beyond for those conditions set for initial acquisition. Two types of generalizations are (i) stimulus generalization and (ii) response generalization. Stimulus generalization occurs when responses that have been reinforced in the presence of specific stimulus occur in the presence of different but similar stimuli. A group of stimuli that should occasion the same response may be considered members of stimulus class. Response generalization occurs when changing one behaviour will result in changes in other similar behaviors. Such similar behaviours are often referred to as response class, and changes in untrained members of the response class, as response generalization.

The usual procedure for maintenance are providing opportunity for over learning trials and repeated practice (Alberto and Troutman, 1995). In this study it is planned to use a method- Literacy Rich Approach (LRA), which is a combination of several factors. For designing this approach the investigator adopted the three components of literacy rich environment mentioned in a study by Katims (1991), that is, classroom library, writing centre, and daily story reading. This was the first empirical study in the research literature to investigate effects of literacy–rich environment on a group of young students with disabilities including intellectual disability and found this approach to be quiet promising. With these three components investigator added few more.

Literacy Rich Approach (LRA)

Literacy Rich Approach is an approach used for teaching, reading and writing. When using this approach, instead of large group, students will be taught in small groups. Classroom library with age and level appropriate books will be provided. Stories will be read daily by the teacher or other adults. In the classroom there will be a writing center where the students can practice writing. Students' progress will be monitored continuously and positive feedback and continuous reinforcement will be given by the teacher.

NEED AND SIGNIFICANCE OF THE STUDY

Special education of children with intellectual disability has come a long way at the turn of this century. From total rejection from school system in the pre-independent India, movement towards acceptance of children with intellectual disability in education stream with various educational provisions is an achievement in recent years. But the changes have not occurred as it should be. Even though eight decades have completed since the first school for children with Intellectual Disability established in India, special education that gives weightage to academic skills, especially literacy instruction is still in its infancy. Majority of the special educators and special schools give weightage to personal, social and vocational skills in their curriculum.

Many special educators set minimal learning expectations about literacy skills. Further these educators hold the conviction that teaching reading and writing to children with intellectual disability is an unrewarding and unrealistic goal. They feel that the time invested in this area could be put to better use in developing needed daily-living, vocational, and social skills. Reading and writing skills that could be acquired with great difficulty, and at the expense of more practical skills, would have little value in aiding these children's life.

Instruction in daily living skills should be given due importance. Vocational and social skills are also essential to make the person self-dependent. At the same time academic instruction including literacy training, should not be ignored. Although there are many eminent educators in India, (e.g. Myreddy & Narayan, 1998) who have written textbooks on functional academics which give systematic guidelines on teaching literacy skills, majority of schools limit reading and writing instruction to functional words. Sight vocabulary is the main area of instruction. Skills such as reading and writing protective words (stop, walk, wait etc.) conventional signs (e.g. toilet, men, women etc.) cautionary words (e.g. danger, do not enter etc.) and names of common objects are some examples. In sight word approach, objects/pictures were paired with corresponding words and thus auditory and visual modalities are provided.

While looking at the education and training of children with intellectual disability in Indian context, with proper instruction and coaching these children can exhibit outstanding performance in co-curricular activities such as yoga, music, dance sports and games. These students are winners of various cultural programmes, games and athletics at national and international levels. The systematic training, high motivation, and immediate reinforcement help them to become outstanders. If this is possible, it is sure that children with intellectual disability have the potential to progress in academic subjects especially in the area of literacy. In many textbooks of special education and intellectual disability it is mentioned that children with mild intellectual disability have the academic potential of successfully completing 4th grade (Langone, 1986). But reflecting on the past experience, effective instruction in this area is not done as it should be and thus academic area is not improved much. Many children who have completed schooling have problems to adjust to community activities due to the low literacy level. Considering the above facts, it is necessary to stress on the development of functional literacy for the children with mild intellectual disability. Special educators should gain confidence to teach higher-level literacy skills (e.g. comprehension, phonological awareness, fluency etc.) to children especially those who are in the mild category. They should also develop the perseverance and willingness to take this as a challenge.

The conventional method used for literacy instruction is inadequate for proper maintenance and generalization of skills learnt. Therefore alternative methods for increasing the rate of maintenance and generalization are to be developed. Since reading - writing process itself is complicated for students with intellectual disability, conventional approach plus some effective procedure, which has the power to provide high motivation, is needed for retention and application of learned skills. Using a Literacy Rich Approach (LRA), which has many components, may found effective. In India, especially in the state of Kerala, no study in this regard is done so far.

STATEMENT OF THE PROBLEM

The present study is designed to find out the effect of Literacy Rich Approach (LRA) in the language (reading & writing) development of children with mild intellectual disability. The study aims to find out the effect of this approach in the following areas – vocabulary development, reading comprehension, phonological awareness, reading fluency, and writing skill development. Therefore the study is entitled *"Intellectual Disability and Language Intervention."*

OBJECTIVES

1. To find out the effect of literacy – rich approach in the vocabulary development of children with intellectual disability.

2. To compare the vocabulary scores of children with intellectual disability of the control and experimental groups in pre, post, parallel, and retention tests.
3. To find out the effect of literacy – rich approach in developing reading comprehension in children with intellectual disability.
4. To compare the reading comprehension scores of children with intellectual disability of the control and experimental groups in pre, post, parallel, and retention tests.
5. To find out the effect of literacy – rich approach in the phonological awareness of children with intellectual disability.
6. To compare the phonological awareness scores of children with intellectual disability of the control and experimental groups in pre, post, parallel, and retention tests.
7. To find out the effect of literacy – rich approach in developing reading fluency in children with intellectual disability.
8. To compare the reading fluency scores of children with intellectual disability of the control and experimental groups in pre, post, parallel, and retention tests.
9. To find out the effect of literacy – rich approach in the development of writing skill of children with intellectual disability.
10. To compare the writing skill scores of children with intellectual disability of the control and experimental groups in pre, post, parallel, and retention tests.

HYPOTHESES

The following major research hypotheses are stated:

1. There will be significant difference between the experimental and control groups in vocabulary development.
2. There will be significant difference among the vocabulary scores of children with intellectual disability of the control and experimental groups in pre, post, parallel and retention tests.
3. There will be significant difference between the experimental and control groups in developing reading comprehension.
4. There will be significant difference among the reading comprehension scores of children with intellectual disability of the control and experimental groups in pre, post, parallel and retention tests.
5. There will be significant difference between the experimental and control groups in developing phonological awareness.
6. There will be significant difference among the phonological awareness scores of children with intellectual disability of the control and experimental groups in pre, post, parallel and retention tests.

7. There will be significant difference between the experimental and control groups in developing reading fluency.
8. There will be significant difference among the reading fluency scores of children with intellectual disability of the control and experimental groups in pre, post, parallel and retention tests.
9. There will be significant difference between the experimental and control groups in developing writing skills.
10. There will be significant difference among the writing scores of children with intellectual disability of the control and experimental groups in pre, post, parallel and retention tests.

INCLUSION/EXCLUSION CRITERIA

Inclusion Criteria

Children with mild intellectual disability who belong to the age group of 7-20 are included in this study.

Exclusion Criteria

This study excludes children who have associated handicaps such as cerebral palsy, hearing impairment, visual impairment and autism.

OPERATIONAL DEFINITION OF KEY TERMS

Literacy Rich Approach (LRA): It is an approach for teaching reading and writing using small group practices, ongoing monitoring, positive feedback, continuous reinforcement, classroom library, writing centre and daily story reading.

Language development: Language is the application of meaning to words and other symbols based on one's experience. It is the act of expressing oneself through a motor act or through clear sequential verbal thought patterns (Mann, Suiter, McClung, (1992). Major components of language arts are listening, speaking, reading, and writing (Rubin 1997).

In this study language development means acquisition, maintenance and generalization of reading and writing skills in Malayalam language.

Intellectual Disability: Intellectual disability is a disability characterized by significant limitations both in intellectual functioning and in adaptive behaviour as expressed in conceptual, social and practical adaptive skills. The disability originate before the age of 18.

Five assumptions essential to the application of the definition are:

1. Limitation in the present functioning must be considered within the context of community environments typical of the individuals' age, peers and culture.
2. Valid assessment considers cultural and linguistic diversity as well as differences in communication, sensory, motor, and behavioural factors.

3. Within an individual, limitations often coexist with strengths.
4. An important purpose of describing limitation is to develop a profile of needed supports.
5. With appropriate personalized supports over a sustained period the life functioning of the person may generally improve.

Children with intellectual disability: In this study children with intellectual disability means children who belong to the 'mild' category, that is, with an IQ between 50-70 (up to 75) and attending special schools.

Reading: Reading is a dynamic complex act that involves the bringing of meaning to and getting of meaning from the written page (Rubin, 1997).

Reading comprehension: Reading comprehension is constructing meaning by integrating the information provided by the author with the reader's background knowledge. It requires that the reader interact with text to construct meaning (Bos & Vaughn, 1994).

Writing skills: In this study writing skill means student learn to print Malayalam alphabets, letters with symbols, words, sentences, and able to use them meaningfully. In higher level students need to use various aspects of language in their written expression.

Vocabulary development: Vocabulary is the total number of words in a language a person knows. In this study vocabulary development means the number of words students learn to identify and read from given list of words.

Phonological awareness: It is the ability to detect the separate phonemes in a word (Gunning, 1998).

Phoneme: Smallest unit of sound distinguishes one word from another word.

Reading fluency: Ability to read easily, smoothly and correctly with no hesitation or inaccuracy.

METHODOLOGY IN BRIEF

This study is conducted to find out the effect of Literacy Rich Approach (LRA) in the language development of children with intellectual disability. Experimental design (pre-test - post-test – control-design) is used for this study. The study population is composed of children with mild intellectual disability. The sample of the study consists of 60 children with mild intellectual disability who belong to the age group 7-20 (30 experimental and 30 control) who are studying in the special school-Nirmala sadan Muvattupuzha, Ernakulam District, Kerala. Their IQ were assessed by using the intelligence test, MISIC (Malin's Intelligence Scale for Indian Children). Random sampling method was used to select the sample. The tools used are:

1. Functional Reading Assessment Test (FRAT) for standard I

2. Functional Writing Assessment Test (FWAT) for standard I
3. Functional Reading Assessment Test (FRAT) for standard III
4. Functional Writing Assessment Test (FWAT) for standard III
5. Parallel Functional Reading Assessment Test (PFRAT) for standard I
6. Parallel Functional Writing Assessment Test (PFWAT) for standard I
7. Parallel Functional Reading Assessment Test (PFRAT) for standard III, and
8. Parallel Functional Writing Assessment Test (PFWAT) for standard III.

All these tools are developed by the investigator.

The investigator developed a reading writing package for standard I and III which includes all the components of Literacy Rich Approach (LRA), that is, (1) small group practice, (2) classroom library, (3) daily story reading, (4) writing centre, (5) on-going monitoring, (6) positive feedback, and (7) continuous reinforcement.

Data was collected in four stages- entry assessment (pretest), parallel test, post test and retention test. The collected data are analyzed using appropriate statistical techniques and the results obtained are interpreted accordingly.

SCOPE OF THE STUDY

It is hoped that finding of this study will help in improving the existing special education, especially literacy instruction practices. Once the educators who teach special children get enough empirical data on the effectiveness of instructional procedures and suitable methodology, they will attempt to utilize the literacy curriculum relevant to the needs and lives of children with intellectual disability. The children will be the direct beneficiaries of the study. Since the aim of education for children with intellectual disability is to make them independent, any possible change in this regard will help them to become more fruitful members of the community.

It is also expected that finding of this study will enable parents of children with intellectual disability to involve actively in the literacy training of their children. In a study (Sukumaran, 2000) on parental involvement in reading and writing skills of their intellectually disabled children, it was found that only 24.70% had highly involved. Average involvement was found in 27.60% and 47.70% had only low level involvement.

SUMMARY

This chapter deals with the back ground of the study, need and significance of the study, objectives, hypotheses, operational definitions, methodology in brief, and scope of the study.

Review of Related Literature

INTRODUCTION

The review involves systematic identification, location and analysis of documents containing information related to research problem (Gay, 1996). Since a good research is founded upon the complete academic knowledge that is known in the area of research, the review section provides a testimony and confirmation to that effect (Khan, 2007).

A careful review always aims at interpreting prior studies and indicating their usefulness for the study to be undertaken. Thus prior studies serve as the foundation for the present study. The review also gives an idea about the variables of the problem under investigation. Through review a researcher can identify variables relevant for the research and determine meaning and relationship among variables.

The review for the present study was done on research and non-research literature. The literature reviewed is organized and presented under appropriate headings.

VOCABULARY DEVELOPMENT IN CHILDREN WITH INTELLECTUAL DISABILITY

The importance of vocabulary knowledge to school success, in general, and reading comprehension in particular, is widely documented (Baker, Simmons, Kame'enui, 1998; Cunningham & Stanovich, 1998). Snow (2002) suggests that vocabulary and word knowledge can contribute to improved comprehension, and it provides a sound rationale for increased emphasis on vocabulary instruction.

Vocabulary instruction focuses on words and word meanings. Fluency in word recognition and in understanding words contribute to increased reading comprehension. So vocabulary instruction for students with intellectual disability is an important aspect of their literacy programme. Words and concepts are interrelated. Therefore understanding vocabulary helps to lay the foundation for understanding concepts.

Maria (1990) noted that the reader's level of vocabulary is the best predictor of his/her ability to understand text, and the number of difficult words in a text is the best measure of its level of difficulty.

Fuchs, Fuchs, Hosp, Jenkins, (2001) noted that fluent word recognition allows the reader to allocate increased attention to key comprehension process, such as making meaningful connection between sentences within a passage or relating text meaning to prior experiences and information. Thus learning how to decode text provides a requisite foundation not only for reading fluency but also for higher level comprehension processes.

Share and Stanovich (1995) observed that evidence from 20 years of research points the development of fluent word recognition skills as the biggest difficulty that students face in learning to read. Theories of word recognition (Ehri, 1998, Fuchs & Deno, 1991, Share & Stanovich, 1995) suggest that struggling readers have difficulty in learning to recognize words as whole orthographic units or by phonetic cues.

Significant amount of student's vocabulary growth may develop through independent reading. Unfortunately students who struggle with reading often fail to engage in independent reading necessary to improve vocabulary development. Over all differences in the amount of independent reading, lack of strategies to learn words from context, and diffuse word knowledge appear to be the most critical obstacles to vocabulary development of students with disabilities (Stahl & Shiel, 1999).

Research on vocabulary instruction for students with intellectual disability is mainly in the area of sight word instruction. The reason may be that sight word identification is an important early phase in reading acquisition for children with and without intellectual disability (Conners, 2003). This may be the first step in comprehensive reading instruction programme for learners with moderate to mild intellectual disability. Sight word instruction leads to rapid acquisition of the skill to identify essential and functional words. In the literature review by Conners (1992), three areas of research on reading instruction for children with moderate intellectual disability were reviewed: sight word instruction, word analysis instruction, and oral reading error-correction. The report indicates that (a) among sight word instruction methods, those that use picture integration, constant delay, and Edmark errorless discrimination methods seem strongest, (b) word analysis instruction is viable option for many students with moderate intellectual disability and (c) word analysis is the most effective method for oral reading error correction.

Didden, Graaff, Nelemans, Vooran and Lancioni (2006) investigated the effects of three training procedures to teach sight words to 13 children with moderate to mild intellectual disability. The training procedures were (1) word alone (word was presented without picture), (2) integrated picture (word was presented with integrated picture – no fading) and (3) picture fading (integrated picture was faded out). Results show that most children learn to identify sight words faster in word alone condition. Effects were largely maintained during follow-up 2 to 5 weeks after training. Using pictorial prompts during reading instruction to these children may hinder learning. The causes of these hindering effects of pictorial cues have not yet been determined, though several hypotheses have been generated. (1) This result may be explained by a blocking effect, whereby previous conditioning of a verbal response to a picture may block conditioning of the verbal response to its written equivalent when the picture and written sight word are presented as a compound stimulus (Didden, Princen, & Sigafoos, 2000, Singh & Solman, 1990). (2) Selective attention to picture may hinder learning. For example, according to Dorry and Zeaman (1975) the pictorial cue is the most meaningful stimulus for a child when presented with an unknown written word.

Browder and Minarovic (2000) examined the effect of teaching three employees with moderate intellectual disability who were non-readers to use sight words to self-initiate job tasks in competitive employment settings. The training package was composed of (a) a progressive time delay procedure to teach sight word recognition, (b) a verbalized "Did-Next-Now" self instruction technique and (c) a written work routine checklist for self-monitoring. Use of this combined package resulted in the acquisition of reading job specific sight words, and increase in several work related behaviours. This was the first study to focus on sight words for employment settings and this contributed to the literature on sight word by demonstrating a method for teaching word comprehension.

Browder, Huyyetters, and Karol, (1998) conducted an evaluation of transfer of stimulus control and of comprehension in sight word reading for children classified as mildly intellectually disabled and severely emotionally disturbed. The children received sight word instruction that included time delay to transfer stimulus control from a verbal prompt to printed word. Out of five children, four mastered the words without direct instruction.

Noble and Merrill (1989) conducted sight word vocabulary instruction in 16 moderately intellectually disabled children aged 9-13 by manipulating pictorial stimuli (fading versus non fading), relationship to the word stimulus location (superimposition versus juxtaposition of picture and word), to orient the learners attention to the word. Subjects who were trained in using super imposition methods significantly outperformed others.

Carlton (1985) examined the effects of an interclass peer tutoring programme on the sight word recognition ability of students who are mildly intellectually disabled (ages 11-13 years old). Results showed higher gain scores (pretest-posttest) on both vocabulary and reading subtests than did 62 controls.

Lally (1981) examined computer assisted teaching of word recognition for intellectually disabled school children. Eight children were taught associations between the written and spoken versions words by a talking computer. These children increased their sight vocabularies by an average of 128 percent, a comparison group had a 34 percent increase.

Several authors expressed the idea that sight word recognition alone is inadequate in the vocabulary development of children with intellectual disability. With sight word instruction generalization of reading skills to new and unknown words seldom or never occurs (Conners, 1992). Although acquisition of sight words is a significant achievement, the emphasis on sight word acquisition has resulted in reading programs for persons with intellectual disability that focus largely on "skill-and-drill" activities with few, if any, opportunities to listen to, read, or write text beyond the single word (Koppenhaver & Yoder, 1993). This almost exclusive emphasis on sight word recognition has meant that students with intellectual disability are often not taught strategies for decoding unknown words. Students need a working sight vocabulary, but they also need the ability to decode unknown words using phonetic analysis within the context of connected text. In sight word approach the student is directly taught each word in his/her reading vocabulary. In contrast, well developed word attack skills allow an individual to read untaught words that are composed of new combination of previously taught sound relation.

Other components of such a programme may be (a) word analysis instruction, (b) strategies for promoting response generalization and stimulus generalization of reading skills (i.e., functional use of reading skill and comprehension. Didden, Graaff, Nelemans, Vooren, Lancioni, (2006). An important advantage of word analysis over sight word instruction appears to be that generalization across (new) words may take place. A disadvantage is that word analysis training may take too long before children have acquired this skill.

A number of authors mentioned the significance of functionality in selecting words and other reading materials. Langone (1986) stated that the basis for developing reading and written expression activities for any capable intellectually disabled learner is functionality of the skill being taught. Ediger (1999) observed that the objectives of instruction need to stress relevant functional words for pupils to master.

Teaching the children with intellectual disability functional reading skills is important because acquisition of such skills may (a) enhance their daily living and self-help skills and (b) increase their participation in general educational and community setting (Lalli & Browder, 1993).

According to research on explicit vocabulary instruction, selected vocabulary should include words that are important for understanding text, as well as functionally important words or word that students will encounter often (Stahl, 1986). Explicit instruction also include the use of word's context and definition, opportunities for deep processing (finding synonyms, antonyms (opposites), making up a novel sentence with word and classifying the word with other words.

Several authors (Bos & Vaughn,1994; Myreddi & Narayan, 1998; Langone, 1986; Payne, Polloway, Smith & Payne, 1981) mentioned the Fernald method (1988) as an effective method for teaching vocabulary. This is a multi sensory or visual –auditory –kinesthetic-tactile (VAKT) approach. This approach has four stages through which students' progress as they learn to identify unknown words more effectively.

Langone (1986) mentioned the functional whole word approach which involves pairing pictures with corresponding words, using both auditory and visual modalities. The whole word approach teaches words that have immediate application to the community.

Myreddi and Narayan (1998) explained the whole word approach (sight word approach) in which the imagery level of the word to be learned is stressed. High imagery words are usually concrete and include nouns such as mango, fan house etc.

Bos and Vaughn (1994) also listed several cues and strategies the reader use to recognize unfamiliar word. These strategies can be applied in teaching children with mild intellectual disability. They are: 1. Visual configuration, 2. Picture clue, 3. Semantic clues, 4. Syntactic clues, 5. Context clues, 6. Structural analysis or morpheme analysis and 7. Phonic analysis or phonics.

Hanley-Maxwell, (1982) conducted a comparison study of vocabulary learning of moderately intellectually disabled students under direct instruction and incidental presentation. These six students were taught 10 reading vocabulary words in the presence of the group. Experimental group students were tested periodically on their own 10 words, 50 words presented to peers, and 10 uninstructed control words. They showed significant learning of their own words, with some also learning their classmates' words.

Berends and Reitsma (2007) examined whether transfer of training effects to untrained (neighbour) words can be enhanced by training with an orthographic focus as compared with emphasizing semantics. Two groups of reading disabled children (mean age=7 year 11 months) were given repeated reading training with limited exposure duration (350 ms) in which

15 target words were repeated 20 times in exercises focused on either orthography (N=26) or semantics (N=25). The children were required to either read the target words aloud or perform the exercises silently but this requirement appeared to have no effect on training results. The results show that untrained neighbour words benefited more from training target with an orthographic focus than exercises with a semantic emphasis.

Allington (1981) assessed the sensitivity to orthographic structure in English words of educable intellectually disabled children. These children were presented an item selection task. Analysis of performance indicated that educable intellectually disabled children do acquire implicit knowledge of orthographic rules and that their ability is related to the development of reading skills.

Barudin and Hourcade (1990) studied the relative effectiveness of three instructional procedures (sight word, fading, tactile-kinesthetic) in teaching students with moderate to severe intellectual disability to read a series of monosyllabic words.

In addition, the relative effectiveness of each approach in teaching students generalized reading skills when presented with novel untaught words was also studied. Results indicated all three reading approaches were superior to the control non-instructional condition in learning to read words specifically taught. However, no one experimental condition was superior to others. No significant differences were found in the acquisition of skills in reading novel untaught words.

Sella, Tenorio, Bandini and Bandini (2016) studied on generalization of vocabulary skills of children who have reading writing deficits. These researchers used games as a measure of reading writing generalization after computerized teaching of reading skills. The result shows that reading skills mastered with computerized learning to read in small steps programme generalized to new contexts (games) and new responses (writing and new matching relations).

Reading instruction for students with intellectual disability (ID) has traditionally focused on single skill instruction such as sight word reading. In a recent literature review on multi component reading intervention for students with intellectual disability by Afacan, Wilkerson, and Rupper (2018) found that students with ID who were exposed to multi component reading programmes (phonetic awareness, vocabulary and comprehension, fluency, spelling etc.) significantly improved their reading skills compared to their peers with ID who received traditional sight word instruction.

Cazzell, Browarnik, Skinner, Skinner, Cihak, Ciancio, McCurdy, Forbes (2016) evaluated the effects of computer-based flash card reading (CFR) intervention developed using Microsoft power point software on students' ability to read health related words within 3 seconds. Result support the effectiveness of CFR intervention for enhanced word reading in students with intellectual disabilities who enrolled in post secondary college education programme with average learning rates ranging from approximately one word acquired per 1.5 minutes of instruction to one word acquired per 2.5 minutes of instruction. Data collected one month after intervention procedures ceased showed that maintenance and generalization (i.e ability to read words embedded within passages) varied across students.

READING COMPREHENSION IN CHILDREN WITH INTELLECTUAL DISABILITY

Comprehension is the ultimate goal of reading process. It is constructing meaning by integrating the information provided by the author with the reader's background knowledge. It requires that the reader interact with the text to construct meaning.

Reading involves two basic processes a decoding or word recognition process and a comprehension process. Word recognition is not the primary goal of reading programme. The goal of reading is obtaining meaning from printed material. But comprehension cannot occur unless individual has the necessary skills to expand his sight vocabulary and attack words in a systematic manner. The student's difficulty in understanding abstract concepts and generalizing information often adversely affects their ability to comprehend written material. Therefore their reading programme must emphasize comprehension.

Rubin (1997) observed reading comprehension as a complex intellectual process involving a number of abilities. Two major abilities involve word meaning and verbal reasoning. Without word meaning and verbal reasoning there will be no reading comprehension.

The skilled reader uses word recognition skills and knowledge about people, places and the things to determine intended meaning of the passage. Knowledge possessed by the reader and information from text interact to produce full comprehension.

Williams (2005) stated, the rationale of teaching comprehension strategies is that readers derive more meaning from the text when they engage in intentional thinking. That is, when people run into difficulties in understanding what they have read, the application of specific strategic cognitive processes will improve their comprehension. Instruction in comprehension strategies is effective in helping students learn strategies and when the strategies are applied, better comprehension follows.

Many of the new ideas about comprehension are based on schema theory. This theory states that what the reader already know about a topic can greatly influence the reader's comprehension. This notion was originally advanced by Bartlett (1932) and later developed by Anderson (1977),

Rumelhart (1981) and others. It suggests that when readers recognize words on a print page, they think and react based on their background information (schemata). McCormic (1995) observed in order to comprehend we employ both our knowledge of language and knowledge of world. The latter is known as background information/prior knowledge.

Sweet (1993) stated, comprehension is the active construction of meaning. One must combine old and new information to be good comprehenders. The old information comes from the brain and new information is what the reader dealing with from the written text.

For children with intellectual disability, reading comprehension should centre on instruction which will allow the children to (1) understand thoughts contained in sentences, (2) comprehend meaning contained in paragraphs and (3) grasp the meaning and implications of entire selections. For some children these objectives are reasonable, for other children, intellectual limitations will decrease the possibility of satisfactory achievement of these three aims.

For teaching reading comprehension Bos and Vaughn (1994) divide comprehension into types of reasoning according to how readers have to activate their background knowledge to construct meaning. These three arbitrary categories are: (1) Textually explicit (2) Textually implicit and (3) Scriptually implicit. Rubin (1997) gave a similar explanation to the comprehension. Comprehension involves thinking. As there are various levels in the hierarchy of thinking, so are there various levels of comprehension. Higher levels of comprehension include higher levels of thinking. The four comprehension categories are: (1) literal comprehension, (2) interpretation, (3) critical thinking and (4) creative reading.

Literature on reading comprehension and children with intellectual disability conveys the fact that comprehension is difficult for this group of children. Carter (1975) noticed that of various aspects of reading, comprehension appears to be most difficult for them. Westling (1986) reported that reading is generally considered the weakest area of learning, especially reading comprehension. Comparatively students who are mildly intellectually disabled tend to do better on reading words than on understanding what they have read.

Researches conducted with persons with intellectual disability on reading comprehension are limited. The existing researches brought mixed results. Rousseau and Foshee (1981) investigated the effect of decreasing the difficulty of reading material on comprehension by 57 direct care trainees at a residential facility for person with intellectual disability confirmed that decreasing reading difficulty of printed material increases the trainee's comprehension levels.

In the study conducted by Katims (2001) on literacy assessment with 132 students with mild to moderate intellectual disability, a comprehension section was included. After each passage was read aloud by a student, the examiner asked specific questions pertaining to the passage. Questions ranged from each student's ability to recall facts of the story, to combining two or more explicitly stated facts, to connecting individual prior knowledge with the story, to evaluating and judging aspects of the story. Students demonstrated relative strengths in the areas of naming the main idea of a narrative passage and reciting facts found within the passage. Students demonstrated difficulty with terminology, cause/effect relationships, inferential comprehension questions and making conclusions. In summary, students demonstrated difficulty in higher level, more language based reading comprehension.

Bigler (1984) examined the effect of two direct teaching procedures in increasing inferential comprehension scores of intermediate age (9-12 years) midly intellectually disabled students. Inferential questions required to predict outcome and draw conclusions were asked after reading a story passage and after listening. Performance of all experimental students improved from baseline to follow-up assessment.

To promote comprehension Bos and Vaughn (1994) suggested to incorporate many of the aspects of cognitive behaviour modification and socio cultural theory of learning. He insisted that before reading activate student's background knowledge for the selected passage, during reading encourage students to self questions and monitor their comprehension as they read, and after reading use follow up activities.

Many authors (Rubin, 1997, Gunning, 1998; McCormic, 1995) mentioned about three types of reading levels. They are:- Independent reading level, Instructional reading level, frustrational reading level.

Polloway and Patton (1997) stressed the importance of teaching oral reading. Oral reading is particularly necessary in the early stages of reading programme, because it gives insight into beginning reader's knowledge of sight words and decoding skills. With most children oral reading has three major purposes-diagnosis, conveying directions or instructions and personal pleasure. For learners with special needs, oral reading has four additional purposes-articulation and vocabulary practice, memory reinforcement, rereading for better comprehension and group participation.

Oral reading can assist development of correct word pronunciation by providing the disabled reader who seldom verbalizes with a structured opportunity to speak. When reading aloud, the student takes in information both auditorily and visually, adding an additional pathway to leaning that is often necessary for memory. Rereading a passage orally after it has been read silently assists comprehension, particularly when teacher designates a purpose for each reading.

Students also need practice and guidance in the transition from oral to silent reading because silent reading is a critical skill to develop.

Polloway and Patton (1997) listed several strategies for teaching reading comprehension. They are: 1. Predection strategies, 2. Graphic strategies, 3. Fluency strategies, 4. Reciprocal teaching and 5. Questioning

Both the oral and silent reading passages must have questions based on each passage and questions must be text dependent. These are usually literal comprehension questions, interpretive questions and word meaning questions (Rubin, 1997).

Smith (1968) stress in teaching comprehension to children with intellectual disability the teacher needs to give attention to the vital role of the feedback and monitoring systems. As children read selections of various lengths, gaining meaning will depend on their remembering what has been visually and/or auditorially read. If words are being called and the child is not alert to the meaning contained in each passage, comprehension will be reduced. A central aim of the reading programme, is for each child to eventually move from over attending the process of attacking words to focusing on their meaning and content. Often it will be necessary for the teacher to act as a monitor during the reading process by stopping the child at the end of a sentence and questioning him concerning the meaning of what was just read. In more difficult cases, it will be help for the teacher to read short passages in content with the child so that feedback and memory are emphasized more dramatically. Gradually the child will develop a style which is characterized by greater attention being given to thought contained in passages.

Idol (1987) examined the effectiveness of mapping strategy in two mildly retarded high school juniors and four high school sophomores in remedial reading class. The strategy was used for thinking critically about expository text focusing on the passage's main idea, major supporting points, other view points, reader's conclusion and relevance to a contemporary situation. It is found the mapping strategy was effective in improving reading comprehension in children with mild intellectual disability as well as other students.

Polloway (1986) studied the effectiveness of corrective reading programme (a direct instruction approach) in children with intellectual disability and learning disability. The study resulted in significantly greater improvements in word recognition and comprehension than prior years for learning disabled and 41 educable intellectually disabled students (Grades, 8-12).

Fowler and Davis (1985) examined the effect of story-frame approach for improving reading comprehension in educable intellectually disabled children. In story frame approach, teachers construct a frame that becomes the focus of children's discussion and written assignment. The result showed that the story frame approach can improve educable intellectually disabled children's reading comprehension skills.

In two investigations, one with average readers (Hansen,1981) and a follow up study with poor readers (McCormic & Hill, 1984) students' comprehension was boosted when teachers used a systematic method of focusing on prediction before stories were read.

Burns, Dean, and Foley (2004) investigated the effect of teaching unknown key words as a pre teaching strategy with 20 students identified as learning disabled in basic reading skills and reading comprehension. This strategy led to improvement in reading fluency and comprehension with effect size of 0.38 and 1.76 respectively.

Recent researches on reading comprehension of children with intellectually disabled also focus on various strategies of instruction. Systematic review of literature conducted by Alnahdi (2015) related to instructional strategies to improve reading skills for students with intellectual disabilities concluded that students with intellectual disabilities are in need to receive very intense practice and instruction to improve their reading skills and it should be provided explicitly, systematically, and consistently.

In a recent study conducted by Hua, Woods-Groves, Ford and Nobles (2014) regarding reading comprehension instruction using paraphrasing strategy on expository reading comprehension of young adults with intellectual disability resulted in improvement of the above skills. Specifically they investigate the effectiveness of teaching a three step paraphrasing (RAP) i.e. (1) Read a paragraph (R) (2) Ask myself what was the main idea and two details (A) (3) Put in to my own words (P). These authors recommended further studies which focus on generalization and maintenance of the strategy.

Wood, Browder and Flynn (2015) studied about the use of self questioning strategy to comprehend social studies text for an inclusive setting and found that participants improved the number of questions generated and answered from baseline to intervention.

Lundberg and Reichenberg (2013) in their research on developing reading comprehension among students with mild intellectual disabilities found out these students were capable of constructing meaning from written text by guided social interaction. Reciprocal Teaching (RT) and Inference Teaching (IT) were two intervention conditions used. In RT students practiced four active strategies – prediction, generating questions, clarifying and summarizing – whereas IT involved practice in answering inference questions. Improvements of test results were obtained for both conditions to about the same extent indicating that both interventions were beneficial.

Shurr & Taber-Doughty (2017) investigated the use of Picture Plus Discussion (PPD) intervention on the comprehension abilities of high school students with moderate intellectual disability when expository texts were read. Effect of this intervention was measured across three different types of texts including leveled readers, stories from a local newspaper and sections from employee handbooks. Results indicate that the PDP intervention was successful in increasing student comprehension and this enable the researchers to find out text access for high school students with moderate intellectual disability.

Research studies in the areas of generalization and maintenance of reading comprehension skills in children with ID are rare. It may be because as mentioned by Kauffman and Hung (2009), generalizations are difficult with such diverse population as those with intellectual disabilities. But for these students generalization of learned skills is important. Anything taught (acquired) in the classroom or training situation need to be generalized so that the student should be able to apply the skill learnt to any appropriate situation. Similarly the student should be able to maintain the skill overtime even after training procedures are withdrawn.

PHONOLOGICAL AWARENESS IN CHILDREN WITH INTELLECTUAL DISABILITY

Phonemic awareness (phonological awareness) is the understanding that spoken words consists of sequence of sounds (Ball and Blachman, 1991). Phonic awareness is not very important to our purposes in spoken language, but it become central in learning to read. There is direct evidence that lack of phonemic awareness is major cause of word identification (Vellutino and Denckla, 1991).

Several authors highlighted the significance of phonological awareness in reading. Phonemic awareness permits students to use letter sound correspondence, to employ phonic strategies and identify unknown words more quickly (Griffith and Olson, 1992; Catts and Kamhi, 2005). It is a prerequisite to spelling and writing which also require hearing and making sounds (McCormick, 1995), is a critical variable in emergent literacy (Sulzby & Teale, 1991), and beginning reading acquisition (Juel, 1991).

Research has shown that phonemic awareness is more powerful determiner than intelligence in predicting whether students will be successful in reading. It is also a strong predictor than general knowledge proficiency (Lomax & McGee 1987). Share and Stanovich (1995) stated phonemic awareness is important for young children to become accurate readers as quickly as possible, because words must be read accurately a number of times before they can become part of child's sight vocabulary.

The most important of this evidence come from well designed experiments in which instruction in phonemic awareness has been shown to facilitate the acquisition of beginning word reading skills, particularly phonemic decoding skills (the process by which children obtain initial information about phonemes in unknown words).

In a recent analysis of results from fifty two, carefully selected experimental studies Ehri, Nunes, Willows, Schuster, Yaghoub-Zabeh & Shanahen (2001) reported a highly consistent effect of training phonemic awareness on the development of reading skills. These studies showed that the effect of training in phonemic awareness was strongest for phonemic decoding skills in reading, and less strong, but still statistically significant, for measures of reading comprehension. These findings make sense conceptually, given close theoretical links between phonemic awareness and phonemic decoding skills and the fact that several factors other than word reading accuracy, such as vocabulary knowledge, contribute to individual difference in performance of measures of reading comprehension (Catts & Kamhi, 2005).

Gillon (2002) expressed a similar idea when she wrote "measures of phonological awareness, particularly at phoneme level are powerful predictors of reading success and can predict early literacy performance more accurately than variables such as intelligence scores, vocabulary knowledge and socio economic status".

In a qualitative meta analysis of phonological awareness training studies, Bus and Van Ijzendoorn (1999) showed that training of phonological awareness improves young children's reading skills and that these gains are more consistent and robust when phonological awareness has been trained together with letter sound correspondence.

Majority of the observation mentioned above are made by authors after studying the performance of normal intelligent children. Very few studies were conducted among children with intellectual disability to know their phonological development.

Of the skills that have been identified as correlates of reading achievement in individuals without cognitive disabilities, one strong predictor is phonological awareness. Only few researchers have addressed to question of whether phonological awareness skills that are correlates of reading ability in typical capable children also correlate with reading ability in individuals with intellectual disability. Most of these studies involve children with Down Syndrome.

Bysteveldt, (2006) investigated the effectiveness of a phonological awareness intervention for 4 year-old children with Down syndrome. Their performance on measures of phonological awareness (initial phoneme identity), letter name and sound knowledge, and print concepts pre-intervention and post intervention, was compared with that of randomly selected group of age-matched pairs with typical development. The results indicated a significant treatment effect of phonological awareness and letter knowledge for children with Down syndrome. Additionally, above performance on the initial phoneme identity task was contingent on letter knowledge of particular phoneme.

There are few review on reading instruction, investigators have concluded that some children with moderate to mild intellectual disability may benefit from phonic instruction (Conners, 1992; Joseph & Seery 2004).

Saunders and Defulio (2007) conducted a study in 30 adults with mild intellectual disability to determine whether phonological awareness and rapid naming skills are correlates of single word reading. The investigators presented four tests of phonological awareness (for rhyme, first, middle and end sound categorization) two rapid naming tests (pictures and letters) and the Woodcock word identification and word attack subtests. All four phonological awareness measures and both rapid naming measures were significantly correlated with both word attack and word identification skills. The outcome is consistent with findings from typically developing children, suggesting that instruction in phonological awareness would facilitate the acquisition of word attack skills in individuals with intellectual disability.

Yopp (1988) identified two levels of phonemic awareness (1) simple phonemic awareness in which tasks such as isolation of sound, blending, segmentation are included and (2) compound phonemic awareness which consists of phonemic deletion and word to word matching tasks. Compound phonemic awareness seems to result from reading experience, but may be important for further advancement in reading (McCormick, 1995).

Several authors give guidelines to maximize the effectiveness of instruction in phonemic awareness. Bus and Van Ijzendoorn (1999) reminds to start instruction early, that is, in preschool and kindergarten before children have begun to read. At this age most children benefit from small group instruction that is relatively brief (eg., 15 minutes daily) and that includes engage in game like activities. Ehri, Nunes, Willows, Schuster, Yaghoub-Zabeh & Shanahen (2001) directs to focus on limited set of skills such as blending and segmenting and to teach these skills explicitly and systematically. Also use methods that integrate instruction in sound letter correspondence to directly link newly acquired phoneme awareness to reading and spelling (Bus & Van Ijzendoorn, 1999; Ehri, Nunes, Willows, Schuster, Yaghoub-Zabeh & Shanahen, 2001; National reading panel, 2000).

Whiteley, Smith, and Conners, (2007) Conducted a longitudinal project that identified young children at risk of literacy difficulties and asked why some of these children fail to benefit from phonologically based intervention. Reception class children were screened to identify a group at risk of literacy difficulties and a matched group of children not at risk. Profiles were compiled for each child including measures of reading, spelling, memory, rapid naming, vocabulary and phonological awareness. A daily 15 week, small group intervention was implemented with 67 at risk children. Those who had not made progress in their literacy following this intervention participated in a second, individually administered intervention. The results indicate that letter knowledge and expressive vocabulary are key factors mediating a child's ability to benefit from a phonologically based intervention.

Frederickson and Wilson (1996) evaluated a phonological awareness training programme (PAT) the results of which suggested that phonological awareness training which incorporates reading, spelling and writing can form a useful part of a literacy progaramme for children with reading disabilities. Significant improvements in reading and spelling were found in the children who had followed the PAT programme. In addition to this, phonological skills such as rhyme fluency and spoonerisms, as measured by the phonological assessment battery, also showed significant improvement.

Dessemontet, de Chambrier, Martinet, Moser, and Bayer (2017) explored the phonological awareness skills of children with intellectually disability. Specifically the study aimed at identifying strengths and weakness in phonological awareness displayed by primary school pupils with intellectual disability (7-8 years children) with an unspecified etiology in comparison to typically developing pupils (4-5 years old) matched for gender, early reading skills (letter/sound knowledge, non word reading and word reading) and expressive vocabulary. This study also aimed at exploring their evolution in phonological awareness skills across 2 years. Result shows that children with intellectual disability showed a marked weakness in rhyme detection and slight weakness in phoneme blending. Two school years later, these deficits no longer remained. Marked weakness appeared in phoneme segmentation and first/last phoneme detection. The findings suggest that children with intellectual disability displays an atypical pattern in phonological awareness that changes with age.

In their article Mihai, Friesen, Butera, Horn, Lieber and palmer (2015) suggested that development of phonological awareness of young children can be acquired by intentionally embedding phonological awareness skills in story book reading. In preschool years all children including children with delays/disabilities, get lot of opportunities to hear/read story books. Embedding phonological awareness in story book reading prepare these children for more targeted instruction in phonemic awareness and decoding that are part of early reading instruction.

Barker, Sevick, Morris and Romski (2013) examined the structure of phonological processing in 294 school aged children with mild intellectual disability and the relationship between its components, expressive and receptive language and reading skills using structural equation modeling. Phonological processing consisted of two distinct but, correlated latent abilities: phonological awareness and naming speed. Phonological awareness (which include blending words, blending non words, elision, sound matching, segmentation of words and segmentation of non words) had strong relationships with expressive and receptive language and reading skills. Naming speed (consists of rapid colour naming and rapid letter naming) had moderate relationship with these variables. Result also suggest that children with intellectual disability bring the same skills to the task of learning to read as children with typical development, highlighting the fact that phonologically based reading instruction should be considered a viable approach.

Channell, Loveall and Conners (2013) compared reading skills of youth with intellectual disabilities (ID) with those of typically developing (TD) children of similar verbal ability level. The group with ID scored lower than the TD group on word recognition and phonological decoding. The group with ID also underperformed the TD group on phonological awareness and phonological memory. The data suggest that poor word recognition in youth with ID may be due largely to poor phonological decoding which in turn may be largely to phonological awareness and poor phonological memory.

READING FLUENCY IN CHILDREN WITH INTELLECTUAL DISABILITY

Reading fluency is the smoothness with which students read. A fluent reader group words into meaningful phrases and reads with appropriate expression.

Perfetti (1985) observed that in slow word processing speed interferes with automaticity of reading and, therefore, with comprehension. Perfetti also suggests that slow word reading is debilitating because it consumes working memory and therefore prevents individual from thinking about the text while reading. Slow word reading clogs working memory with processing of word level reading so as to prevent understanding at content level. Thus both rapid reading of high frequency words and rapid decoding as a means to text understanding appear critical for typical reading development (Fuchs, Fuchs, Hosp and Jenkins, 2001).

Students with learning or reading disabilities demonstrate difficulties in the area of fluency. A common core problem is the ability to read signal words, decode words, and read phrases and sentences automatically and rapidly. Thus reading fluency is an essential skill for all students (Chard, Vaughn & Tyler, 2002).

The U.S. national research council's committee for the prevention of reading failure noted that because the ability to obtain meaning from print depends so strongly on the development of word recognition accuracy and reading fluency, the latter should be regularly assessed in classroom permitting timely and effective instructional responses when difficulty or delay is apparent (Snow, Burns, & Griffin, 1998).

Gunning (1998) stated that by one estimate, students may require thirty five or more exposures to a word before learning it, with the slowest students needing almost three times as many exposures as the brightest students. Once the students can recognize words accurately, emphasize speed so that words are recognized instantaneously and fluent reading is fostered.

Although some students can recognize most of the words in the text, they continue to sound out the words rather than rely on visual configuration of the word, context clues and memory. Consequently, their reading, whether oral or silent, become very slow. They expend so much effort on identifying the words that they frequently miss main points of the passage (Bos & Vaughn, 1994).

Fluency instruction is designed to increase both word recognition and rate of reading. According to the theory of automaticity (Samuals, 1987) fluent readers automatically process information at the visual and phonological levels, and are therefore able to focus most of their attention on the meaning codes in the text and integrate this information with their background knowledge. Researchers have found that fluency is a good predictor of comprehension (Rasinski, 1990).

Students develop reading fluency through reading and through listening and watching others read aloud. Anderson, Wilson, and Fielding, (1998) found that one of the better predictors of reading achievement was the amount of time students spent reading books out of school.

Kimmel and Segal (1998), identified the importance of reading aloud to children as a means of developing not only an enjoyment of literature and books, but also as an avenue for learning to read and building fluency. Reading aloud promotes the development of fluency in a number of ways. (1) It allows the teacher to model fluent reading, (2) reading aloud allows the students to listen to and discuss books that may be difficult for them to read. Many students with learning and behaviour problems have listening comprehension that is several years more advanced than their reading comprehension, (3) reading aloud provides background knowledge for the students reading the book themselves. Once children have listened to a book, they are more likely to select it as a book they want read.

Polloway and Patton (1987) explain the teaching techniques that help students to become more fluent readers in terms of word recognition and ultimately comprehension. They are: 1. Neurological impress method, 2. Repeated readings, 3. Choral repeated reading.

Bos and Vaughn (1994) suggested when teaching fluency, techniques for improving word identification skills and comprehension should be taught. They are: 1. Imitative reading, 2. Paired reading and 3. Wide reading.

Gunning (1998) listed many other activities for enhancing reading fluency. They include: 1. Words on wall, 2. Sight word commands, 3. Read the label, 4. Forming words, 5. Forming phrases and sentences, 6. Sorting 7. Audio visual aids - CD Rom and read alongs.

Research studies in the area of reading fluency of children with intellectual disability are rare. Studies in this area are mainly done with children with learning disabilities. Stevens, Walker, and Vaughn (2017) did a review synthesizing fluency intervention research from 2001 to 2014 and examined reading fluency and comprehension outcomes of reading fluency intervention for students with learning disability in kindergarten to 5th grade. Result showed repeated reading, multi component interventions and assisted reading with audio books produced gains in reading fluency and comprehension. Findings suggest that repeated reading remains the most effective intervention for improving reading fluency for students with learning disability.

In the same year (2017), Merimee did an investigation to find out if there is a relation between repeated reading and choral reading and the words correct minute of six high school students with intellectual disabilities. The study also examined the extent to which fluency impacts reading comprehension. The result shows that out of six participants, five demonstrated an increase of words correct per minute from baseline to treatment. Also, four of six participants improved their mean reading comprehension score during treatment.

Jones (1987) investigated the effect of a new computer assisted instructional programme designed to increase decoding fluency in reading with learning disabled students. After ten weeks of daily 15 minute practice sessions, subjects showed substantial improvement on word practiced, words never practiced, and reading speed and accuracy.

Henk, Helfeldt, & Platt (1986) reported that learning disabled students with lack of fluency in oral reading may be helped to experience a feel for fluency through any of six alternative reading techniques: (1) imitative reading, (2) repeated reading, (3) radio reading, (4) phrase reading, (5) paired reading and (6) neurological impress method.

Fuchs, Fuchs and Compton, (2004) contrasted the validity of word identification fluency and nonsense fluency with 151 at risk children studying in first grade. In word identification fluency the child is presented with a single page of 50 high frequency words. The student had one minute to read words. If a student hesitated on a item for 4 seconds, the examiner prompted him/her to proceed to the next word. In nonsense word fluency students have one minute to read consonant-vowel- consonant- pseudo words. The score is the number of sounds pronounced correctly. The study showed the superiority of word identification fluency over nonsense word fluency.

Hurst and Joliyette (2006) examined the effect of private versus public assessment on the reading fluency of middle school students with mild intellectual disabilities. An alternating treatment design was used. Both methods of timed reading appeared to be effective in improving student's reading fluency, however students preferred the public assessment.

WRITING SKILL DEVELOPMENT IN CHILDREN WITH INTELLECTUAL DISABILITY

The development of written language skills represents the summit of the language literacy. Built on and closely related to listening, speaking, and reading, writing is a critical component and an important goal within programmes of language development. Reading and writing cannot be separated each other but are complementary. Adequate emphasis should be placed upon pupils in writing. In writing students read their own written products as well as those of other learners (Ediger, 1999).

Written language subsumes the areas of handwriting, spelling and written expression and thus demands that the communication has a variety of mechanical memory, conceptual and organizational skills (Polloway & Patton, 1997). Therefore writing can present a variety of significant challenges to students with special needs who may have existing linguistic deficits in oral language and/or reading, low societal expectation for success and limited encouragement and reinforcement for appropriate usage. Writing has increasingly become a critical occupational skill. Successful performance in a variety of occupation requires the ability to write well (Graham, 1992). It is clear that writing is a critical life skill.

Written expression is the most sophisticated of the language arts. Written expression requires or subsumes several needed skills: (1) hand writing, (2) spelling, (3) vocabulary, (4) syntax, (5) sentence composition and (6) punctuation (Sedlak & Sedlak, 1985).

Educational programme for mildly and moderately intellectually disabled should focus on writing skills. It has to be developed among them in order to achieve overall rehabilitation. Written skills help an individual in daily living situations (Reddy, Malini & Kusuma, 2004).

Written language is commonly viewed as the highest and most complex form of language and communication. Because of many interacting factors such as generally sub average performance, low societal expectations for success and a concomitant low rate of positive reinforcement for writing, the children with intellectual disability often uses written language ineffectively in communicating with others. The possession of even minimal written language skill will help to open another avenue of communication and normalization of life.

Langone (1986) stated that in written expression area mildly intellectually disabled children can perform the following skills: (1) spells consonant and vowel sounds correctly both out of context and in the context of words, (2) spell a variety of phoneme-grapheme groups both out of context and in the context of words, (3) use dictionary location skills in spelling, (4) demonstrate match-to-sample manuscript writing skills (e.g. use of verbal models), (5) demonstrate match-to-sample cursive writing skills (e.g. use of models), (6) arrange words in logical order to form sentences, (7) write a name, address and other personal information, (8) fills out employment, bank and other applications, (9) write brief letters of complaint, (10) write personal letters and thank you notes, (11) list activities that needs to be accomplished, (12) record brief directions and (13) record notes concerning job description or community activities.

At initial or minimal levels, students must develop the capability to write their names and other personality identifying information. At more advanced levels they need to take notes, respond to test questions, and write letters of inquiry and complete job applications as their transition into adult life (Polloway & Patton, 1997).

Written Languages Instruction

Written language involves a very intricate integration and coordination of memory, vision, and motor skills to produce and record written symbols for later decoding by a reader. The very intricacy of this visual symbol system makes it necessary that the teacher have a firm knowledge of good methods for helping the child to gain and refine writing skills. The person who is learning to communicate through the written medium must be exposed to systematic instruction. In this area in order to grasp essential skills needed in learning to write and spell. Prior problems in listening, speaking or reading may be reflected, and perhaps magnified, in the area of writing. In order to write in a coherent, understandable manner, one must be able to think, read and comprehend in a logical way. Graves (1994) stresses that while meaning in writing is paramount, it should not result in the ignoring of handwriting.

Graham and Miller (1980) provide a review of effective instructional techniques and sequence to facilitate letter formation. The following procedure is based on the specific steps they outline for instruction. The first step is the teacher to demonstrate the formation of individual letters while students observe the specific strokes involved. Students' attention should be directed to the distinctive features of these letters and their comparison with letters previously learned. As the children begin to transcribe letters teacher provide prompting (e.g. manual guidance directional arrows), then instruction on copying (form near point and far-point). While copying and writing from memory, students should be

encouraged to engage in self instruction by verbalizing to themselves the writing procedures being followed. Finally corrective feedback from the teacher, extrinsic reinforcement, and/or self correction can be used so that the letter will be retained and increased legibility will be achieved.
As the students master the formation of additional letters, they should be encouraged to write more about events occurring in the environment.

Alston and Taylor (1987) have suggested a four-step approach to maintenance of writing skill: (1) the whole school must become involved. Teachers are to monitor, praise and instruct, (2) each class should have occasional writing session to practice handwriting. Work should be displayed to encourage and motivate the students, (3) allowance should be made for those with chronic or severe handwriting problems. These students should be instructed on the basics (e.g. grip, posture, paper position) as well as letter formation (e.g. size, shape, reversals, spacing) and 4) group lessons should be included.

Spelling represents an important area of curricular concerns for students with disabilities. Graves (1994) noted that good spelling has social status because it reflects an educated person. Further because writing is communication, spelling must be accurate enough for the reader to respond. The child with intellectual disability needs to have many functional words in his/her spelling vocabulary as possible. Functional words can be defined as words which will help the student communicate more effectively and aid the person when he is older to gain and maintain employment and help him to adjust to environmental and social demands, thus achieving some social independence (Payne, Polloway, Smith, & Payne, 1981).

A variety of instructional strategies can assist students having difficulty with spelling. The most successful word-study techniques use multi-sensory approaches, promote revisualization of words, or assist students in formulating specific rules for accurate spelling. One example of word study technique is the Fernald multi sensory approach. (Fernald 1943) It is one of the best known educational techniques for use with learners with disabilities.

Dixon, Carnine, and Kameenui, (1994) explain cognitive strategy instruction in writing. This focuses on using text structures to improve writing and features conspicuous strategies. Through modelling and think alouds, the teacher demonstrates and makes visible the writing process and the strategies used in his/her own writing. Using modeling, coaching, discussion and other techniques teacher focuses on the following features of process writing: topic selection, purpose (the kinds of questions the text might be expected to answer) identification of audience, brainstorming use of text structure, grouping ideas, using key or signal words, revising, editing and publishing. The instructional program was broken down into four phases: text analysis, modelling the writing process, guiding students, and providing opportunities for independent writing (Raphael & Englert, 1990).

Rousseau (1993) studied on the syntactic complexity in the writing of students with and without intellectual disability. Both groups were compared on nine measures of syntactic complexity in writing in three grade levels. A Multivariate Analysis of Variance revealed significant difference for group, but not for grade level or group by grade level. Students without intellectual disability scored significantly better than those with intellectual disability in all components of syntactic complexity except clause length. These results support other research in which students with intellectual disability showed significant deficits in written language.

Guzel-ozmen (2006) investigated the effectiveness of modified cognitive strategy instruction in writing (CSIW) with mildly intellectually disabled student's skill in writing problem/solution texts. Participants were from two self contained and multiage classrooms in Turky. Instruction had a positive impact on the amount of time student spent planning and writing problem/solution texts. There was also an increase in text length, elements, coherence and quality of students' composition. Those effects were maintained overtime.

Katims (2001) investigated the literacy performance of students with mild to moderate intellectual disability in elementary middle and high school. Vocabulary was one part of the investigation. The task examined the quality and quantity of each students writing/spelling behaviour. Students were given 10 minutes to write as many as words they could. The result showed that number of words correctly written accelerated by grade level, although there was almost no difference between average words spelled correctly for middle school students compared to high school students (11.1 Vs 11.9. words spelled correctly).

Joseph and Konrad (2009) conducted a review to identify effective methods of teaching writing to students with intellectual disabilities. Findings revealed that strategy instruction was investigated more frequently than other types of approaches. Strategy instruction was consistently found to be very effective for teaching writing skills to students with intellectual disabilities.

In a recent research, Zihyun and Suk-Hyang ((2019) investigated on the effect of process based approach to writing interview articles using class wide social net work site (SNS) on the writing abilities and self- esteem of middle school students with intellectual disabilities. It also aimed at investigating these effects on the attitudes of students' peers who were interviewed. The intervention improved the writing abilities of three participants along with increases of their self-esteem. The participants' peers in the inclusive classroom also showed positive changes in their attitude toward the students with intellectual disabilities.

Pennington, Flick, and Smith-Wehr (2018) examined the effects of response prompting strategies (i.e constant time delay, system of least prompts) and frames on sentence writing of three participants with moderate intellectual disability. During intervention the teacher taught two students to construct sentences using selection based software and another to generate handwritten responses across three different writing frames (i.e I want ————, I see —————, The ———— is ————). The findings suggest that the package was effective and produced variable levels of maintenance and generalized responding for all three participants.

In a recent article (Cannella-Malone, Konrad and Pennington, 2015) the authors provided teachers tools that they can use to teach written expression to school age students with intellectual disabilities. The tool was presented around the Mnemonic – ACCESS : accommodations and assistive technologies, concrete topics, critical skills, explicit instruction, systematic evaluation. Here teachers are to consider all six components of ACCESS while planning.

LITERACY RICH APPROACH

The components of literacy rich approach are: (1) small group practices, (2) story reading by teacher/adults, (3) class room library, (4) writing centre, (5) ongoing monitoring, (6) positive feedback and (7) continuous reinforcement.

Although literature on this approach for literacy instruction is not investigated including all of its components there are studies which examined the benefits of the components separately. Following is the review of available literature in this area.

Literacy – rich environment

Literacy development begins long before children begin formal instruction in elementary school. It proceeds along a continuum, with children acquiring literacy skills in a variety of ways and at different ages. Early behaviours such as reading from pictures and writing scribbles are an important part of children's literacy development.

Children need these skills to become good readers. Good readers have an understanding of how alphabet works, an awareness that reading is about meaning and sufficient fluency in reading. The most effective way to convey this is to provide children with a literacy– rich environment.

Clarke (2001) stated literacy – rich environment includes daily reading, extended discourse, (talking or writing), experimentation with reading materials, book talk (discussion of characters, actions and plot) and dramatic play. In this environment children have many opportunities to see how printed words are used for many purposes. In literacy rich environment, children learn about the world through talking and reading refining these skills along the way. Children's knowledge of language is built on their own investigative skills applied to interesting topics.

In a study (Katims, 1996) elementary age students with mild to moderate levels of intellectual disability made academically significant progress in their understanding written language, comprehension of stories read aloud by adults, word decoding and emerging reading and writing when exposed to literacy-rich environment that used direct and strategic instruction to develop skills in context.

Butler (1975) documents a natural, immersion – oriented approach to literacy development involving a young developmentally delayed child with intellectual, physical, sensory, learning and health disabilities. His book "Cushla and her books" chronicles the child's journey from passive helplessness, to a wide variety of vocal, verbal, physical, cognitive and emotional responses to literature in her home.

Through continuous exposure to a literature rich environment, Cushla eventually was able to follow a story line, understand story action, and identify main characters within stories.

Stone, Rivera, and Weiss (2018) in their article provided strategies that address three areas (creating class room library, incorporating environmental print, establishing writing activities) for beginning teachers for creating literacy rich environments to support the academic and functional needs of young students with significant developmental disabilities.

Some authors (Dennis, Lynch and Stockall, 2012) described how to plan literacy environments for diverse preschoolers. They observed that children who are immersed in literacy-rich environments learn about language, reading and writing by participating in meaningful activities such as handling books and listening stories read aloud.

Small Group Instruction

Group instruction refers to structured, data based teaching activities in which two or more students are taught simultaneously (Brown, Holvoet, Guess & Mulligan, 1980). Research indicated that group instruction has been used to teach a variety of language tasks to students with handicaps (Browder, Hines, McCarthy& Fees, 1984).

It has been reported that group instruction may facilitate incidental learning (Oliver, 1983; Orelove, 1982), produce more skill generalization and provide more control of motivational variables (Brown, Holvoet, Guess, Mulligan, 1980), result in more peer social interactions (Alberto, Jones, Sizemore & Doran, 1980), efficiently use teacher time and students learn from each other by hearing the response of peers and by sharing problem solving experiences (McCormic,1995).

Alig-cybriwsky, Wolery and Gast, (1990) and Winterling (1990) have shown that the students of various ages and disability levels can learn non target task during group instruction. Students may be prepared to function in less restrictive environments which frequently use group arrangements (Fink & Sandall, 1978).

Because one-to-one introduction is not always feasible many reading teachers work in small groups. Where more than one student has the same educational requirement grouping students is appropriate. Deciding how and when to group students is based on educational assessment, not only those judgments preceding the instruction of a programme, but also during informal daily on-going evalution of students reading progress (McCormic, 1995).

Polloway and Patton (1997) also noted the importance of small groups in reading instruction. Strategies matching individual readers to appropriate reading materials require that students be divided into small groups. Teachers must consider options that introduce change and flexibility, into grouping procedures. Interest and skill groups, as well as pupil pairs should be incorporated into programmes at regular intervals.

Ediger (1999) stated the benefits of small groups in reading instruction. Reading cooperatively in small groups can provide much enjoyment and interest in literature. Being with others is a favourite learning style for some individuals. They prefer to work together rather than working on individual basis. They receive practice in reading. Cumulative practice should make increased knowledge, skills and attitude towards reading.

The size of group is one of the first decision that the teacher need to make. The teacher when making decision on number of students include in a group should consider the following variables (Collins, Gast, Ault & Wolery, 1991): (a) the handicapping condition of the student, (b) the student's experience in group setting, (c) the student's command of appropriate group skills (i.e., ability to sit and attend appropriate social skills), (d) the type of task to be taught and (e) session length.

In a study on professionals teaching small group found three to be workable number. When there were more than three children with low entry literacy levels, it was difficult to maintain appropriate level of feedback and involvement (Hiebert, 1994). However in a study of a supplementary programme for low achieving first graders, teachers were able to work successfully with five to seven students (Taylor, Strait, & Medo, (1994). In a review of studies of successful corrective programme, Guthrie, Seifert, and Kline, (1978) found that ratio of students to teacher was no higher than four to one. Apparently as ratios grow higher, the teacher efforts are stretched too thin. Based on the research, then, three to four would seem to be the optimum number for small group instruction.

The question of how many is too many in a corrective group depends on the severity of the student's difficulties. The greater the needs, the smaller then group should be (Gunning, 1998).

Despite some positive features of group instruction McCormic (1995) suggests to take some precautions that teachers must ensure that readers in the group do not receive unequal treatment. Explanation, prompts, opportunities for response, reassurance and support should be directed to all students in a balanced manner to guarantee equitable student participation in learning endeavors. Bloom (1984) contends that teachers are frequently unaware that they supply more occasion for active engagement of some students than they do for others. Studies have shown that the readers who need most help are the ones who are often ignore (Brophy & Good, 1970).

Vaughn, Bos, and Schumm, (1997) list Various types of grouping: (1) homogeneous grouping (same ability group). It is the practice of putting students at approximately same achievement level together for instruction and (2) heterogeneous grouping (mixed ability Group). It is the practice of putting students with a range of achievement levels together for instruction. Homogeneous grouping widens the gap between high and low achievers (Slavin, 1987), it restricts friendship choices.

Although homogeneous grouping may enhance the motivation and self esteem of high achieving students, it lowers the motivation and self-esteem of low achieving students. Also this type of grouping results in social stratification.

Barr and Dreeben (1991) observed, homogeneous grouping has a detrimental effect on low achieving students. Students in low-achieving group are given less attention by the teacher, are less involved in classroom activities and are given less instructional time. They spent less time on reading and are frequently interrupted by other class members. They read fewer pages, are given more concrete assignments, and are more likely to read orally than silently, which means accurate pronunciation of printed words is likely to be stressed rather than comprehension (Allington, 1984).

Elbaum, Schumm and vaughn, (1995) surveyed 549 elementary students (grades 3, 4, and5) including 25 students with learning disability. Result revealed that students at all levels of reading ability liked mixed ability groups and mixed ability pairs most followed by whole class instruction. Students in mixed ability groups were perceived as getting more help from classmates, working more cooperatively and making more progress in reading than those in same ability groups were perceived to be desirable for nonreaders only.

Kamps, Abbot, Greenwood, Wills, Veerkamp & Kauffman, (2008) examined the effects of small group reading instruction and curriculum differences for students most at risk in kindergarten. It was the implementation of small group reading instruction as secondary and tertiary level components of three-tier model of prevention and intervention. The study consisted of 83 students who were targeted as being at risk for reading failure. Intervention consisted of evidence-based curriculum delivered in groups one to six students during 30 to 40 minutes sessions a minimum of 3 times per week over a 2 year period. Outcome data were collected for early literacy skills. Result indicated that students in the more directed explicit intervention groups generally outperformed students in the comparison groups.

Helf, Cook, and Flowers, (2009) studied the effects of two grouping conditions on students who are at risk for reading failure. The authors used a true group experimental design to compare two group conditions – 1:1 (1 tutor to 1 student) and 1:3 (1 tutor -3 students) on the reading achievement of 1st grade students who were identified as at risk. The result indicated that students made comparable progress and gains in reading when instructed in small groups of 3. Because 1:3 conditions used resources more efficiently, it may be preferable to the 1:1.

Moody, Vaughn, Hughes, and Fischer (2000) examined grouping practices and reading outcomes for students with learning disability in resource room set up. Whole class instruction was the determinant grouping format although several teachers used small group and individualized activities. No significant gains in reading comprehension were evidenced by students in this study. Results from the fluency test were also revealed inadequate student progress in reading.

Farmer, Gast, Wolery, and Winterling, (1991) conducted a study to determine if the effectiveness of the progressive time delay procedure when used in small group instruction with students with severe handicaps to teach functional community referenced word reading. This study also investigated whether these students learn other students words through observational learning. Analysis of data indicated that teaching in small group instructional arrangement was an effective way to teach these students using progressive time delay.

Whalen, Schuster and Hemmeter., (1996) investigated the use of unrelated instructional feedback when teaching in small group instruction arrangement. In this study these authors confirmed one of the benefits of small group instruction, that is, it allows students to learn from one another. Out of three students in this study, two were mildly mentally retarded. All three students learned each other's unrelated stimuli provided during instructional feedback.

Story Reading Aloud by Teachers/Adults

Ediger (1999) explained the need for reading story to students. Each day teacher should read aloud to students during story time. The books chosen should be interesting to students. Words should be pronounced clearly and accurately. For young children it is especially good to show the books illustrations. Throughout the story time students should understand an increased number of facts, concepts and generalizations. Knowledge received provides background information for more complex ideas that should be forthcoming. A love for reading by students might be a further end result when the teacher reads orally to students during story time.

Trelease (1989 a) suggested many benefits of reading aloud. They are: (1) provide positive reading role model, (2) furnishes new information, (3) demonstrate the pleasure of reading, (4) develops vocabulary, (5) provides examples of good sentences and good story grammar and (6) enable students to be exposed to a book they might not otherwise be exposed to.

McCormic (1995) elaborated the advantages of reading aloud selection of reading materials. According to her reading to student is one of the best ways to get them interested in reading. Not only does reading to students inspire desire to read on their own, it is a direct route to vocabulary development. A good principle to follow when reading aloud to students is to read materials slightly above the level they could read for themselves. Studies (eg., Leung, 1992) show that reading aloud tends to most affect words that are already slightly familiar students enlarge their understanding of these words, becoming able to use them with greater exactness.

Gunning (1998) also mentioned the relevance of reading aloud. He reminded to read aloud to students even to older ones, on a regular basis. Also set aside a time during the day for free reading, in which students may select to read anything they wish.

Rankhorn, England, Collins, Lockavitch, and Algozzine, (1998) studied the effect of failure free reading programme on students with learning disability who also have severe reading disabilities, 39 students with severe reading problems were taught word recognition and comprehension skills. The intervention was based on their principles identified in research on successful reading programmes. Key steps in the programmes included: (1) previewing the story, (2) listening to the story being read, (3) presenting content from the story, (4) reading the story and (5) reviewing the story. Improved performance in letter word identification, word attack, comprehension, and dictation was evident after intensive intervention. Discrepancies between intellectual ability and reading achievement decreased in more than half of the students.

Fuller (1991) investigated the primacy of story. This researcher applied the Ball-stick-Bird reading system to the teaching of reading to individuals with severe to moderate mental retardation. The system incorporates developmental linguists to make story reading easier for the beginning student. The first books of the series are composed primarily of nouns and their action verbs, and gradually adjectives are added. In some individuals an intellectual explosion is triggered, as the teaching system taps fundamental building block of human cognitive organization, namely a miniature story built with nouns at first progressing to nouns and verbs, constituting a fundamental unit of cognitive organization which has been termed in story engram. Every human culture talk with the engram, thinks with it, and uses it as a building block to produce bigger and bigger stories. It is the universal trade mark of human brain that it spends much of its walking life listening to, telling and thinking up stories. Two intellectually disabled individuals who experienced dramatic personality changes along with the growth in cognition through the use of this approach are profiled.

Mims, Browder, Baker, Lee, and Spooner (2009) studied the effect of shared stories on the listening comprehension level of students with significant intellectual disabilities and found that this helped to increase emerging literacy in these students. The procedure was evaluated via a multiple probe design across materials (i.e.,books). Outcomes indicate that both students of the study improved on the correct number of comprehension questions answered during all three books.

In the study conducted by Rabren, Darch, and Eaves (1999) on reading comprehension of learning disabled student it was found that a small but significant relationship between children's interest in being read aloud and later reading ability.

Classroom Library

Research indicates that a key to becoming a good reader is to have opportunities to read. Teacher's goal is to provide students with a wide choice of literature and other reading materials, with opportunities to read and discuss what is being read and with instruction in strategies that allow students to comprehend actively and think critically about what they are reading (Bos & Vaughn,1994).

Rubin (1997) states the library, properly utilized, becomes the students' storehouse of information and reservoir of endless delight.

Gunning (1998) explains how to build a classroom library. Even if school has a fine library, it is important that each class also have books close at hand. Students are far more likely to borrow books if they are readily available. The classroom library should be as extensive and diverse as the teacher can make. Because they are inexpensive and have a mature look, paperback books are recommended, especially for older students. Also include hardcover books, young pupils magazines and newspapers.

In addition to creating a physical environment that fosters wide reading, Gunning suggests to build a sense that the class is composed of a community of readers. Help students to see the many roles that reading can full fill provide enjoyment, aesthetic pleasure, raise interesting questions, help solve problems, foster personal growth, open up new horizons, stimulate the mind and imagination. Too often students see only that reading fulfils a school role. It provides them practice and help them answer questions that the teachers ask. Discuss books with students. Talk about books in the same way as discussing book with friends.

Writing Centre

Graves (1983) gives guidelines on setting a writing centre. The setting should create a working atmosphere similar to a studio, which promotes independence and in which students can easily interact. Materials and supplies for writing and the students' individual writing folder are to be stored in specific locations in the room. Students know where materials could be found so they do not have to rely on teacher to get them started, at the beginning of the writing period. The room is to be arranged so students could work together or individually. Conferencing between small groups of students, teacher and students, and student and student should be facilitated with the room arrangement.

McCormick (1995) listed the following points to arrange a learning centre/writing centre.

1. To begin select a single skill, strategy or knowledge area (eg. learning a word identification strategy, or editing stories). Develop or locate materials and media related to this area. These could include books, pens, pencils, dictionaries, games, newspapers, flannel board and so on.
2. To develop a comprehensive learning experience for the topic chosen for focus at the centre include a variety of response opportunities such as reading, manipulating, observing, writing, creating, comparing, researching, orally answering questions in a tape recorder or typing into a computer.
3. Organize materials at the table or desk maintained permanently for students use.
4. Whenever possible device ways for students to self correct.
5. Post clear and simple instructions at the writing centre so students can complete their activities independently until direct teacher assistance is available.
6. Device a system of keeping records of what students accomplish. Maintain a scheduling calendar for assigning students to the centre.

Positive Feedback

Feedback is defined as providing the student information on how well he/she performed during training (Mcguire, 1986). Providing students with frequent and clear feedback during training will reinforce this behavior and encourage them to attend future training sessions. It can be provided by teacher/trainer or by peers (Schloss, Smith, & Schloss, 1995). Teacher must monitor student responses, inform them in a positive manner to those that are correct and those that are not, and provide immediate assistance in correcting strategies that lead students to inappropriate interpretations.

Feedback to students and instituting corrective procedures necessitates formative evaluation. Formative evaluations are the specific assessment procedures a teacher undertakes periodically throughout instruction to aid in identifying immediate needs (McCormic, 1995). For feedback to have an impact on students understanding, the teacher must be a sensitive observer one who understands the reasons why the student make miscues or offers erroneous explanations of text.

Clinton and Boyce (1975) differentiate the words and phrases used by teachers into two types. They refer to affirmative reinforcers, which are characterized by words such as right and correct. Informative reinforcers would commonly be referred to as constructive feedback. When feedback used as a reinforcer, it is always prefaced with an affirmative, followed by a specific phrase statement that focuses on the accuracy or appropriateness of the behavior as in "that's it, you put the puzzle piece on the table". Verbal feedback may also be used to reinforce an attempt in or approximation. For example, "Good, try, you got two out of three right. Now do this the same way".

Swinson and Knight (2007) conducted a study in which teacher verbal behavior that was directed towards those pupils that the teacher had nominated as being especially difficult to teach. A series of lessons was observed in a secondary school. The quality and quantity of teacher verbal feedback directed to the class as a whole and to the designed pupils was recorded, as was the on-task behavior of the pupils. It was found that the designated pupils were less on-task than their peers and were more likely to "shut-out" in lessons. However they were found to behave appropriately in well run lessons, where on-task rates were high for all pupils. Teacher tended to give more attention to the designated pupils in the form of positive feedback directed toward their work, but also negative attention directed towards their behavior. A positive relationship was found between teacher's use of positive feedback and on-task rates of the designated pupils.

Haigh (2007) evaluated the effect of class quiz as assessment tool in a case study. The author made the following observation. "Commencing each class session with a class quiz, which emphasizes the previous week's work and is supported by immediate feedback, encourages students to revise their notes ahead of the session, undertake more reading and keep pace with course progression. It reduce the necessity for any spoken review of the previous week's work, provides guidance on the status of current student learning, and creates a knowledge platform upon which deeper learning may be constructed. When pitched at an accessible level, regular class quizzes are popular with students because they reinforce student engagement with the course and provide immediate positive feedback and reward.

SUMMARY

The researcher has done a comprehensive and exhaustive literature review. This work enabled the researcher to go through and furnish current theoretical and empirical knowledge about literacy development of children with intellectual disability in the following areas: reading vocabulary, reading comprehension, phonological awareness, reading fluency and writing skills. It can be seen that lot of research work has been done in the area of reading vocabulary development. However in other areas very few research studies have taken place. The review further revealed that technology assisted literacy instruction helps children with intellectual disability progress highly in literacy skills. Thus the review conducted was really beneficial to the researcher to form hypotheses, design research methodology, particularly tools and reading/writing package, select statistical tests and in analysis and interpretation of data.

Methodology

INTRODUCTION

This chapter deals with the methodology of the study. Methodology includes method adopted, research design, development of tools, standardization of tools, description of tools, population, sample and sampling techniques, data collection procedure, intervention, development of reading-writing package, research setting, scoring and processing of data and plan for data analysis.

METHOD ADOPTED

In order to accomplish the objectives of the study, the investigator selected experimental research. As Gay (1996) stated experimental research is the only type of research that can truly test hypothesis concerning cause and effect relationships. In an experimental study the researcher manipulates independent variable, controls relevant extraneous variables and observes the effect of dependent variable. Manipulation of independent variable is the one characteristic that differentiate all experimental research from other types of research (Gay, 1996).

Research Design

Among the various experimental designs, the pre test-post test-control group design was selected for the present study.

Pretest-post Test-control Design

As Gay (1996) states this is a true experimental design which involves at least two randomly formed groups, both groups are pre tested, one group receives a new or unusual treatment and both groups post tested.

Stages of the Study

There were three stages for this study. The first stage was the pre test stage in which students were tested on language development.

Second stage was the conduct of the experiment (intervention). During this stage instruction through conventional approach was given to experimental and control groups and then experimental group was given additional intervention using Literacy Rich Approach (LRA).

The third stage was the post intervention test stage. In this students were tested on their performance on language development using three tests. They are (1) parallel test (to measure acquisition level of language development), (2) post test (to measure generalization level of language development) and (3) retention test (to measure maintenance level of language development). The retention test was administered after six months of intervention.

Variables of the Study

Variables are the conditions or characteristics that the experimenter manipulates or controls. The present study involves the following independent and dependent variables.

Independent Variable

In experimentation the manipulated variable is called independent variable. It is under the direct control of the experimenter who may vary it in any direction (Sax, 1980).

In this study the independent variable (experimental variable) is instruction through Literacy Rich Approach (LRA).

Dependent Variable

Dependent variables are conditions or characteristics that appear, disappear or change as the experimenter introduces, removes or changes independent variable (Best & Kahn, 1999). Here the language development of students in vocabulary, reading comprehension, phonological awareness, reading fluency and writing skills is the dependent variables.

The detailed design of the study is presented in the following flow chart.

POPULATION

Population selected for this study was children with mild intellectual disability.

SAMPLE AND SAMPLING TECHNIQUES

The selected sample included 60 children belong to the category of mild intellectual disability. Random sampling was used in the selection of sample. Investigator collected a list of students studying in Nirmala Sadan special school.

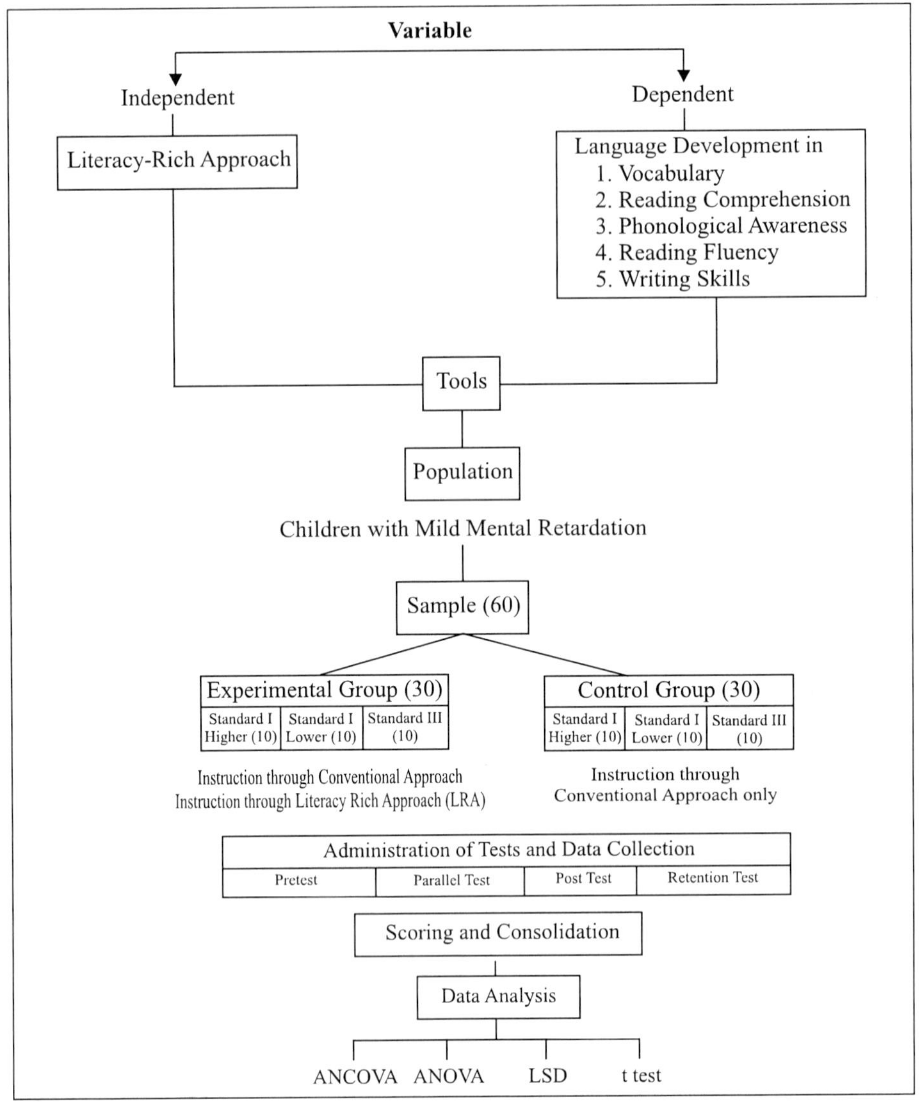

After consulting the school psychologist and class teachers, investigator randomly selected 60 children who belong to mild intellectual disability (IQ between 50 and 69). The IQ assessment of these children is done by school psychologist using Malin's Intelligence Scale for Indian Children (MISIC), which is the Indian adaptation of WISC. The criteria for inclusion in sample were: (1) mild intellectual disability, (2) age between 7-20 years and (3) ability to communicate verbally. Those who were having additional handicaps such as cerebral palsy, hearing impairment, visual impairment, and autism were excluded.

The investigator administered pretest to all 60 children. After considering the literacy performance level, 20 students were received standard III test and they were in standard III level. Out of 40 children who have taken standard I test, the 20 top scorers were in standard I higher level and the rest were in standard I lower level. Thus there were 20 students each in standard 1 higher, standard 1 lower and standard 3 levels.

Each level subjects were randomly assigned to experimental or control groups. The procedure explained by Gay (1996) was adopted for random assignment. The procedure was as follows: investigator ranked all subjects from highest to lowest based on their scores in the pretest. The first two subjects (the subjects with the highest and the next highest scores) were the first pair. No matter how far apart their scores were, one member was randomly assigned to one group and one member to the other. The next two subjects (subjects with third and fourth highest scores) were the next pair and so on. Thus after selection there were three experimental groups and three control groups and each group contain 10 children. To determine whether there were any significant difference between the experimental and control groups on pretest, the independent 't test' was employed. Result indicated that both experimental and control groups in three levels do not differ significantly in the pretest mean scores. Table 3.1 shows the mean, standard deviation and t value of the pretest scores.

Table 3.1: Mean, SD and t value of the pretest scores of the experimental and control groups at various levels

Level	Group	N	Mean	SD	t value
Standard I Higher	Experimental	10	303.90	185.72	0.83
	Control	10	277.58	167.21	
Not significant					
Standard I lower	Experimental	10	58.33	26.54	0.48
	Control	10	52.43	28.69	
Not significant					
Standard III	Experimental	10	940.08	459.67	0.38
	Control	10	867.93	385.08	
Not significant					

The investigator also used 't test' to check whether there is any significant difference between experimental and control groups regarding their IQ scores. This is shown in table 3.2. This test also shows there is no significant difference between the two groups in three levels. Later two students, one from standard I lower experimental group and one from standard III control group were excluded from the study due to continuous absence.

Table 3.2: Mean, SD and t value of the IQ scores of the experimental and control groups at various levels

Level	Group	N	Mean IQ	SD	t value
Standard I Higher	Experimental	10	60.35	4.99	-0.32
	Control	10	61.10	5.55	
Not significant					
Standard I Lower	Experimental	10	58.70	6.15	-0.18
	Control	10	59.20	6.39	
Not significant					
Standard III	Experimental	10	62.20	4.85	-0.35
	Control	10	62.80	2.44	
Not significant					

DEVELOPMENT OF TOOLS

For the collection of relevant data the investigator developed the following tools:

1. Functional Reading Assessment Test (FRAT) for standard I
2. Functional Writing Assessment Test (FWAT) for standard I
3. Functional Reading Assessment Test (FRAT) for standard III
4. Functional Writing Assessment Test (FWAT) for standard III
5. Parallel Functional Reading Assessment Test (PFRAT) for standard I
6. Parallel Functional Writing Assessment Test (PFWAT) for standard I
7. Parallel Functional Reading Assessment Test (PFRAT) for standard III
8. Parallel Functional Writing Assessment Test (PFWAT) for standard III

The investigator reviewed the following assessment tools that are presently used in India for functional assessment of children with intellectual disability.

(a) Madras Developmental Programming System (MDPS) (Jayachandran & Vimala, 1992).

(b) Grade Level Assessment Device (GLAD) (Narayan, 1997).

(c) Functional Assessment Checklist for Programming (FACP) (NIMH, 1994).

(d) Behavioral Assessment Scales for Indian Children with Mental Retardation (BASIC-MR) (Peshawaria & Venkatesan, 1992).

(e) Gray Oral Reading Tests – Diagnostic (GORT–D) (Bryant & Wiederholt, 1991).

Of these, MDPS, FACP and BASIC-MR are prepared for assessing functional skills of children with intellectual disability. Since these tests include all adaptive behavior areas, the coverage for literacy (reading and writing) is inadequate. The GORT –D is intended to measure oral reading fluency and diagnose oral reading problems.

The scale GLAD covers many items of reading and writing under English section. Therefore this test was a major reference material for the preparation of present tests. The tools for the present study has to measure the reading and writing skill development in Malayalam language, the investigator used the above scales as reference materials and developed new reading and writing tools in Malayalam language. To do this investigator also thoroughly reviewed the Malayalam textbooks from Standard I to standard 4 prepared by Government of Kerala. Another reason for reviewing these texts is that the tool has to be standardized and the standardization sample is composed of children studying in regular schools. These textbooks are in vernacular language and are presently followed in government and government-aided schools in the state.

Formation of item Pool

After undertaking an extensive review of the above mentioned scales, and Malayalam textbooks and observing classroom teaching being conducted in special schools for children with intellectual disability, items were formulated for standard I to standard 4. These items were shown to a person who is an expert in Malayalam language as well as Malayalam subject teacher. After this, initial try out of the draft test was done with two students each from standard I to standard 4 at regular school and eight children belong to mild category of intellectual disability studying in special school. After the initial try out and comments and corrections secured from regular class teachers and special education teachers, test items were modified.

Standardization of Tool

For standardization, item analysis has to be done. Item analysis is the process of establishing the suitability of an item for inclusion in the final test. In order to do the item analysis a pilot study was conducted on a random sample of 20 students each from Standard II, III, IV and V in two regular schools (Little Flower L.P.School and St.Auguestin's U.P School at Muvattupuzha). Since this study was done in the month of July (second month of the academic year in Kerala) each class's test was given to the immediate high class. For example, standard I test covers the format of standard I Malayalam text at regular school and therefore the standard I test was given to standard II students, who have completed the content during previous year. Likewise standard II, III, and IV tests were given to students in standard III, IV, and V respectively.

After completing the tests results were tabulated. As a first step in doing item analysis the 20 subjects in each class (standard 2 to standard 5) were rank ordered on the basis of total score acquired in the draft scale. The upper and lower one third of the subjects were selected as the high and low scoring groups respectively. The t values for the items of the high scoring and low scoring groups were computed. Those items showed significant difference between high and low scoring groups were retained in the final form of reading and writing test in each standard.

Preparation of Final Test

It was observed that the items found insignificant in the reading and writing test cannot be simply deleted because the children with intellectual disability in special schools still have to learn them. Many of the items have not yet introduced. Therefore, in order to choose needed items a trial test was given to few students in special school. (Standard I-10, standard II-6, standard III-10, standard IV-6). The results of the tests were tabulated. It was decided to delete the items which got the score 80% and above.

Thus the final selection was as follows: (1) All significant items from the pilot study were retained. (2) Items got below 80% score in the trial test given to children with intellectual disability were also retained. Again a few modifications were made to make even number of items in a given test.

Considering the performance of the students with intellectual disability in the trial test, it was decided to choose only standard 1 (reading and writing) and standard III (reading and writing) tests.

Standard 2 and 4 tests were not selected.

Description of Tools

Tools used for pre test, post test, and retention test:

1. Functional Reading Assessment Test (FRAT) for standard I
2. Functional Writing Assessment Test (FWAT) for standard I
3. Functional Reading Assessment Test (FRAT) for standard III.
4. Functional Writing Assessment Test (FWAT) for standard III.

Tools used for parallel test:

1. Parallel Functional Reading Assessment Test (PFRAT) for standard I
2. Parallel Functional Writing Assessment Test (PFWAT) for standard I
3. Parallel Functional Reading Assessment Test (PFRAT) for standard III
4. Parallel Functional Writing Assessment Test (PFWAT) for standard III.

The functional reading and writing tests were prepared by giving due importance to the functional needs of children with intellectual disability. It is a well known fact that these children have limitations in learning academic skills due to their intellectual deficiency. Whatever they learn should enable them to become independent in day to day activities. Therefore the content of the test (vocabulary, reading comprehension, phonological awareness, reading fluency and writing skills) were planned in such a way that mastery of these skills will allow them to function properly in home, school and community.

The description of tools is given below:

Tools used for pre test, post test, and retention test:

Functional Reading Assessment Test (FRAT) for Standard 1

The test contain following subtests: (a) alphabet test, (b) vocabulary test (c) reading comprehension test (d) phonological awareness test and (e) fluency test.

(a) Alphabet test

This test measures student's knowledge about Malayalam alphabets. Distinguishing letters is important in reading readiness programme. This test includes (i) identification of alphabets (vowels and consonants), (ii) reading alphabets (vowels and consonants) and (iii) reading alphabets (letters having signs and compound letters).

(b) Vocabulary test

Here student's general level of word knowledge is assessed. Maria (1990) stated 'reader's level of vocabulary is the best predictor of his/her ability to understand the text. This test includes (i) identification of words (simple words and words with compound letters, (ii) reading of words (simple words and words with compound letters), (iii) fill in the blanks with suitable word and (iv) matching of words. First two tests measure students' ability to look at a word and identify/name it and third and fourth tests need comprehension at word level.

(c) Reading comprehension

This test measures weather the student has the ability to understand what is read. There are four sections in this test: (i) two word sentences with questions, (ii) long sentences with questions, (iii) short paragraph with questions, and (iv) long paragraph with questions. All questions in this subtest require the student to read the sentences/paragraph independently and then answer to the questions that the examiner asks.

(d) Phonological awareness test

Studies show that tests of phonological awareness are better indicators of students who are at risk of reading performance than any other commonly assessed factors such as oral language processes (Uhry, 1993). There are five sections in this test .The first three phonological awareness tasks are identified by Yopp (1988) and fourth test is based on the sound categorization tasks used by Bradley and Bryant (1985). Details of the tests are given below.

(i) Phonemic isolation - say the first sound in a word after hearing the word pronounced.

(ii) Phonemic segmentation - say the sounds heard in a word.

(iii) Phonemic deletion - isolate a sound in a word and blend the remaining sounds. Isolation of sounds is given at initial, middle and end levels.

(iv) Sound categorization - name same first sound words, same end sound words and same middle sound words.

(v) Word segmentation - isolate the words in a sentence.

(e) Reading fluency

This test measures the student's ability to read easily, smoothly and correctly. A fluent reader smoothes letter into words and words into meaningful phrases and reads with appropriate expression (Gunnning, 1998).

There are six subsections in this test, three at word level and three at sentence level. They are: (i) two letter words, (ii) three letter words, (iii) long words, (iv) two word sentences, (v) three word sentences, and (vi) paragraph.

Here the student is asked to read each unit for one minute continuously in which the examiner records the reading sample in a tape recorder.

Functional Writing Assessment Test (FWAT) for Standard I

Writing is a tool for communication. It is both a skill as well as means of self expression. Written language involves a very intricate integration and coordination of memory, vision and motor skills to produce and record written symbols for later decoding by a reader.

This test contains the following subtests: (i) pre writing skill- copy shapes, (ii) write letters, (iii) write words, and (iv) write sentences.

(i) Pre writing skill - copy shapes

This includes coping of three basic shapes triangle, square, and rectangle.

(ii) Write letters

This test measures student's ability to print letters when dictated by tester. This includes: (i) writing vowels and consonants and (ii) write letters with signs and compound letters.

(iii) Write letters

This test measures student's ability to hear a word as a complete unit and print it. This test includes four sub sections: (i) write simple words, (ii) write long words, (iii) write words using given letters, and (iv) fill blanks with given letters to make words.

(iv) Write sentences

This test measures student's ability to combine word and make sentences. Writing comprehension is also measured. This test has four subsections: (i) copy sentences, (ii) write sentences independently when dictated by tester, (iii) write suitable word and complete sentence, and (iv) read small paragraph and write answers to questions.

Functional Reading Assessment Test (FRAT) for Standard III

This test contains four subtests: (i) vocabulary, (ii) reading comprehension, (iii) phonological awareness and (iv) reading fluency.

(i) Vocabulary

All sections of this subtest measures students' level of word knowledge. This test has 6 subsections: (i) read given words, (ii) fill up blanks with suitable word, (iii) find synonyms, (iv) make word with given letters, (v) find single word for given phrase and (vi) find odd word from a group of words.

(ii) Reading comprehension

This test measures the students' ability to make meaningful sentences with given words, oral reading with comprehension, recall sequences of events or idea, locate and/or recall answer to questions, follow simple cause and effect relationships, make questions and follow written directions.

This test has following subsections: (i) make sentences using the words given in rows and columns, (ii) read given paragraph, (iii) read story and choose correct answer for the questions, (iv) read paragraph and make questions from it, and (v) read paragraph silently and find answer to the questions.

(iii) Phonological Awareness

This includes sound categorization tasks, that is, find the same first sound words. same middle sound words and same end sound words.

(iv) Reading Fluency

It has 6 subsections. The first 5 tests are the same ones used in standard I and the last one is to read a passage from standard III text book.

Functional Writing Assessment Test (FWAT) for standard III

This test is divided in to two main sections: (a) writing words, and (b) writing sentences.

(a) Write words

This test measures the students' ability to write words using correct spelling and use words according to context. Writing comprehensions at word level is also measured.

This subtest has 6 subsections: (i) write dictated words, (ii) write singular/plural of given words, (iii) write related words, (iv) choose correct gender pair of given words, (v) write past form of given word, and (vi) write opposites of given words.

(b) Write sentences

This test measures students' ability to write sentences for functional usage. Writing comprehension at sentence level is the main area of measurement.

This test has 5 subsections: (i) use given word in a sentence, (ii) write positive sentences, (iii) write negative sentences, (iv) arrange given words and make meaningful sentences, (v) write on a given topic, and (vi) read given paragraph and write answer to questions.

Tools used for Parallel Test

The purpose of the study is to find out the effect of LRA in the generalization and maintenance of language (literacy) development of children with intellectual disability. The standardized tools measured these aspects. To meet this goal of finding out generalization and maintenance an alternative content was necessary. That is, the acquisition level literacy development has to be assured first. Therefore the investigator prepared an alternative content called parallel content for standard 1 and standard 3 and taught this using conventional approach. The investigator also prepared tools to test this parallel content. This is parallel test. These tests have the same characteristics as the standardized tests, that is, same number of subtests in each tool, same number of items in each sub test, and equal difficulty level for all items as the standardized tests. Name of the tests are: (1) Parallel Functional Reading Assessment Test (PFRAT) for standard I, (2) Parallel Functional Writing Assessment Test (PFWAT) for standard I, (3) Parallel Functional Reading Assessment Test (PFRAT) for standard III, and (4) Parallel Functional Writing Assessment Test (PFWAT) for standard III.

Evaluation of the Tests

(a) Reliability of the tests

Reliability coefficients of the above tests were calculated using split half method. The pretest scores of the sample in each standard (that is, standard I higher, standard 1 lower and standard III) were used for this. Each subtest was grouped separately into even and odd items. The reliability of the tool was established by using Guttman's split–half method followed by Spearman Brown prophecy formula. The reliability coefficients obtained for all tests were 0.99.

(b) Validity of the tests

A test is valid if it measures what it purports to measure. Content validity of the test is usually determined by examining the appropriateness of the types of items included, the completeness of items, the way in which the items assess the content (McLoughlin & Lewis, 1981). Content validity is often assessed by experts in the field. This was done in preparation stage of the test. After preparing the test it was shown to a person who is expert in Malayalam language as well as Malayalam subject teacher. When the initial try out is over, the researcher got comments and corrections from regular class teachers of respective classes (standard I and standard III) as well as special education teachers. Required modifications in the test items were made according to their comments. Hence t the test has content validity.

DATA COLLECTION PROCEDURE

The investigator contacted the special school authorities. The scope and details of the study was explained and permission was sought for collecting data from students. The permission of parents was also sought through letter. After getting permission from school authorities and parents, the investigator went to the special school and assessed each student individually.

The procedure for data collection was as follows: The researcher and the student sat in opposite seats. Printed reading/writing test was handed over to the testee and specific directions were given on how to respond to various items in the test. Specific instructions used for administration of tool at each level No time limits were imposed for completing the test items and therefore students were given ample time to respond to the questions. However, the examiner verbally encouraged the students to respond.

The data was collected in four stages: pre test, parallel test, post test, and retention test.

Pretest

The main areas of pretest were alphabet test (only for standard I higher and lower levels), vocabulary, reading comprehension, phonological awareness, reading fluency, and writing skills. The tools prepared and standardized by the investigator were used for pre testing.

Parallel Test

Investigator prepared a parallel content of the pretest (for standard I and standard III) and this was taught during intervention programme. Based on this, a test was prepared and administered and this is the parallel test. This parallel test was given after completing the intervention and this assessed student's acquisition level of language development.

Post Test

Post test was done by administering the same tool used for pre testing. It was given after completion of intervention and the next day after the parallel test. By administering the post test the investigator assessed student's ability to generalize the learned skills in unfamiliar material (response generalization). In other words the test measures how much the student is able to generalize the acquired skill.

Retention Test

Six months after the post test, all the six groups were assessed again using the same tools which were given for pretest and post test. This test is known as retention test. This test was meant to find out student's ability to maintain the learned skills overtime.

THE EXPERIMENT CONDUCTED (INTERVENTION)

This study was intended to find out the effectiveness of Literacy Rich Approach (LRA) in the generalization and maintenance of language (literacy) development of children with intellectual disability when compared to the conventional approach (existing approach).

Content

The aim of the study was to find out the generalization and maintenance skills of the sample in selected skills when used two different approaches. Therefore the investigator prepared a parallel programme which resembles the content of the pretest. This parallel content was taught to all groups using conventional approach (i.e parallel content of standard I is taught to standard I higher and lower groups and parallel content of standard III is taught to standard III group.

Instruction of Parallel Content through Conventional Approach

The existing method was used, that is, specific goals and objectives were selected. These objectives were further divided into sequential steps and these steps were taught using detailed lesson plans and appropriate teaching materials. This is the conventional approach in this study and investigator used this approach to both experimental and control groups. The reason for teaching parallel content using conventional approach to experimental group is that acquisition level of literacy skills of both groups has to be established first in order to find out generalization and retention levels. Daily evaluation, weekly evaluation, home work etc. were part of this programme. Instructional time taken for this approach was one hour per day.

Instruction through Literacy Rich Approach (LRA)

For the experimental groups the investigator planned an additional programme which is known as instruction through Literacy Rich Approach

(LRA). After each day's one hour training using conventional approach the investigator provided additional one hour training using the Literacy- Rich Approach for all treatment groups. Each group, (standard I higher, standard I lower and standard III), one by one came to the literacy rich room and got training.

The content of LRA was additional literacy activities and experiences designed by the investigator. Main activities corresponded to the activities in parallel content lesson plans. Actually they are planned generalization activities. They are planned in such a way that special educators can adopt them if the LRA found effective. Instead of expecting automatic generalization to happen, teachers can plan generalization activities along with each day's class room teaching. Investigator provided lot of literacy materials and planned various activities, in addition to the main activities, in the LRA room. Each group of students took part in the activities according to their functional literacy level All components of LRA are embedded in each day's lesson plan.

The components of Literacy Rich Approach were: (1) small group practice, (2) on going monitoring, (3) positive feed back, (4) continuous reinforcement, (5) classroom library, (6) daily story reading and (7) writing centre. Details of each component are given below.

Small Group Practice

When the experimental groups of children came to the treatment room (literacy rich room) investigator divided them into small groups. Each group contained three or four students. Depending on the specific activities of the day different types of grouping were followed. That is, either homogeneous grouping (same ability grouping) or heterogeneous grouping (mixed ability grouping).

Ongoing monitoring

When students were in the treatment room investigator monitored them closely and continuously. Through this monitoring they got correction, clarification and explanations.

Positive Feed Back

Mcguire (1986) defined feedback as providing information on how well he/she performed during training. For all treatment groups investigator gave feedback in positive terms. As Alberto and Troutman (1995) explains when feedback is given and it is prefaced with an affirmative and followed by a praise statement that focuses on the accuracy or appropriateness of the behaviour it was very effective. Investigator adopted the three forms of constructive verbal feedback explained by the above authors. Examples are given below.

Affirmative	Feedback
"Great"!	(Description of correct response) You finished your work on time"
"Good try!"	(Reinforcement of approximation) You almost got finished this time"
"Much Better"!	(Suggestion for modification) If you keep trying not to make careless mistakes, you'll finish all of them next time".

Continuous Reinforcement

Reinforcement is the contingent presentation of a desired stimulus, immediately following the response which increases the rate and/or probability of the response. Delivery of reinforcement on a continuous basis is called continuous reinforcement. In other words, each time the student produces the target response he/she immediately receives reinforcement.

As Alberto and Troutman (1995) stated the continuous schedule of reinforcement is useful in teaching new behaviours (acquisition) especially for young children and children with disabilities. In the present study investigator used this continuous delivery model in the following way. The primary reinforcers (e.g. edible reinforcers) even though it has high motivational value, were rarely used. When used, it was used with low functioning and younger students and paired with secondary reinforcers. Pairing helped to teach the student to be motivated solely by secondary reinforcers. Some of the secondary reinforcers used were social stimuli such as words of praise, opportunity to engage in preferred activities etc. Many times these preferred activities itself were opportunities that involved them in literacy works. For example, when completing a particular day's worksheet, the student can watch a C.D. Rom which they prefer very much. Here they are getting reinforcement at the same time they get lot of repeated practice in reading. Secondary reinforcers such as tokens were used regularly in this programme.

Classroom Library

In the literacy rich classroom there was a special area for classroom library. It was well furnished with books of various kinds (stories, dramas, poems, novels, picture books, story charts etc.). During the treatment session specific time is allotted in which students can select books on their choice and read. They read in small groups or before the whole class. Older students take these books to home and read the assigned portion. Next day they report on their reading content. Investigator kept registers in which the details of student's library usage were recorded. CD Library was an interesting aspect of the Library which enabled the students to watch CDs having stories. They are read along stories having visuals.

Writing Centre

Writing centre is also a specially furnished area in the literacy – rich classroom. In this area adequate paper, pen, crayons etc. with low-level black board are neatly kept. Students have the freedom to use the writing centre as they wish. Besides this there are specific times all students practice writing.

Daily Story Reading

Investigator read stories to the treatment groups everyday especially to the lower functioning students. Older students take turn in reading stories. For reading stories CD Rom, story books, story charts, magazines etc. were used.

Details of the conventional approach and Literacy – Rich Approach can be seen in the Reading – writing package prepared by the investigator. The intervention phase of this study took place for 2 months, Monday through Friday for a total of 40 school days (i. e 40 hours for control groups and 80 hours for experimental groups).

TEACHERS AND TEACHER TRAINING

To increase the external validity of the study three teachers were selected to teach in three levels (Standard I higher, Standard I lower, and Standard III) for teaching parallel content using the conventional approach. All of them were trained teachers having Diploma in Special Education (intellectual disability). Then mean age of these teachers was 45 and their average teaching experience was 18 years. These teachers taught parallel content to the experimental and control groups following the lesson plan and materials prepared by the investigator. Teachers were never given any information about the outcome of this study. They followed the same set of classroom rules for all experimental and control groups.

RESEARCH SETTING

The study was conducted in Nirmala Sadan School for Mentally Retarded Children at Muvattupuzha, Ernakulam District, Kerala. The instruction using Conventional Approach (CA) was conducted in three classrooms known as conventional classrooms. Each classroom had a seating capacity of 10 students. At a time either one experimental or control group attended the class. When they finished the next group came to the class. Teaching materials were brought to the classroom and were distributed individually.

The instruction using Literacy Rich Approach (LRA) was done by the investigator and it took place in a specially designed classroom which is known as literacy – rich classroom. The investigator designed this room with literacy –specific materials. Every day the three treatment groups came to this classroom for one hour duration. They took turns in coming here.

SCORING AND PROCESSING OF DATA

For standard I reading test a score of 1 mark is given for all correct items of alphabet test, vocabulary test, and comprehension test except comprehension of small paragraph and long paragraph. For small paragraph and long paragraph the score for correct response is 2 marks. For vocabulary and comprehension partially correct answers were considered with ¼ mark deduction for each letter error and sign error. In phonological awareness test the score for correct answer is 1 mark and in reading fluency a score of 1 mark is given for each correct sound. In standard I writing test a score of 1 mark is given for correct answers in prewriting, writing letters and writing words. In writing sentence test the score for correct item is 2 marks. As it is done in reading test, partially correct writing answers were considered with ¼ mark deduction for each letter error and sign error.

For standard III reading test a score of 1 mark is given for all correct items except for making meaningful sentences and making questions. A score of 2 marks is given for these items. The subtest oral reading carries the score of 10 marks, out of which 8 marks are given for correct reading and 2 marks for reading fluency. The scoring of phonological awareness and reading fluency tests are done exactly as that of standard I tests. For standard III writing a score of 1 mark is given for all correct items except for using given word in sentence, arrange words to make meaningful sentence, write on topic and write answer to questions. Here each correct item carried 2 marks. Deduction of marks for letter error and sign error was done as explained in standard I tests.

The data collected for each group (standard I higher, standard I lower, and standard III) were entered separately in computer. The name of the subjects in each group was arranged alphabetically and their reading writing scores were entered in the following order: pretest, parallel test, post test, and retention test.

STATISTICAL TECHNIQUES USED FOR DATA ANALYSIS

The data were analyzed based on the objectives and hypotheses by employing appropriate statistical methods using SPSS. The following statistical techniques were used for this purpose.

1. Computation of mean, standard deviation, and percentage.
2. The Student's 't test'.
3. Analysis of covariance (ANCOVA)

   Analysis of Covariance (ANCOVA) is a form of ANOVA, which is used to determine whether there is significant difference between two or more means at a selected probability level. For a study based on a pretest –post test -control group design Analysis of Covariance (ANCOVA) is a superior method for controlling for pretest differences (Gay, 1996; Shavelson,1988). ANCOVA adjust post test scores for initial pretest differences. The procedure given by Brace, Kemp, and Snelgar, (2003) is used for reporting the result of ANCOVA.

4. Repeated Measures Analysis of Variance (Repeated Measures ANOVA)
5. The test of Least Significant Difference for post hoc comparisons. The critical difference was calculated as per the procedure given by Steel and Torrie (1980).

SUMMARY

This chapter has dealt with the research methodology, which is experimental method: pre test-post test-control group design. It also describes about the setting and population. Description of the development of tools and details of conventional and Literacy Rich approaches were also presented. It also explains the description of data collection technique, data collection, intervention and data analysis.

Analysis and Interpretations

This chapter deals with analysis and interpretations of data collected using different tools.

The analysis and interpretations of the results are presented under the following heads.

- The effect of literacy rich approach in the total language development of children with intellectual disability
- Effect of literacy rich approach in the development of vocabulary.
- Effect of literacy rich approach in the development of reading comprehension.
- Effect of literacy rich approach in the development of phonological awareness.
- Effect of literacy rich approach in the development of reading fluency.
- Effect of literacy rich approach in the development of writing skills.

THE EFFECT OF LITERACY RICH APPROACH IN THE TOTAL LANGUAGE DEVELOPMENT

This section deals with the general research question itself. The result is analyzed in three levels, that is, standard I higher, standard I lower and standard III. In each level the students were given four tests – pretest, parallel test, post test and retention test. The total language development (total reading-writing score) is calculated from the scores attained by the students in the following areas – vocabulary, reading comprehension, phonological awareness, reading fluency and writing skills. Tables 4.1-4.18 show the results of the analysis.

Table 4.1: Mean values, standard deviations and percentages of total reading and writing scores in post, parallel and retention tests of standard I higher level students with intellectual disability

(Maximum possible score is 1506)

Test	Group	N	Mean	SD	Percentage
Post Test	Experimental	10	601.63	214.48	39.95
	Control	10	466.55	173.91	30.98
Parallel Test	Experimental	10	690.80	194.01	45.87
	Control	10	556.75	184.69	36.97
Retention Test	Experimental	10	569.90	231.38	37.84
	Control	10	447.38	204.38	29.71

Table 4.1 shows the means, standard deviations and percentages of total reading and writing scores of standard I higher level students in post, parallel and retention tests. The percentage of the mean score was calculated by dividing the obtained mean by the maximum possible reading-writing score. It can be seen from the table 4.1 that experimental group acquired 45.87% of total score in the parallel test, generalized 39.95% in the post test and retained 37.84% in the retention test. Likewise control group acquired 36.97% in the parallel test, generalized 30.98% in the post test and maintained 29.71% in the retention test.

Table 4.2: Summary of Analysis of Covariance (ANCOVA) of total reading and writing scores in post, parallel and retention tests of standard I higher level students with intellectual disability

Test	Source	Sum of squares	df	Mean square	F ratio
Post Test	Corrected Model	683101.03[a]	2	341550.51	61.57**
	Intercept	265060.11	1	265060.11	47.78**
	PreRdWr Total	591874.75	1	591874.75	106.69**
	Between groups	64699.14	1	64699.14	11.67**
	Within groups	94311.01	17	5547.71	
	Total	6482401.19	20		
	Corrected Total	777412.03	19		
a. R Squared = .879 (Adjusted R Squared = .864)					
Parallel Test	Corrected Model	602549.44[a]	2	301274.72	38.50**
	Intercept	577334.97	1	577334.97	73.77**
	PreRdWr Total	512702.43	1	512702.43	65.51**
	Between groups	65196.72	1	65196.72	8.33**
	Within groups	133044.04	17	7826.12	
	Total	8517498.50	20		
	Corrected Total	735593.49	19		
a. R Squared = .819 (Adjusted R Squared = .798)					

(Table Contd...)

Retention Test	Corrected Model	65792.21[a]	2	382896.11	38.98**
	Intercept	163866.00	1	163866.00	16.68**
	PreRdWr Total	690730.33	1	690730.33	70.33**
	Between groups	49536.49	1	49536.49	5.04*
	Within groups	166970.85	17	9821.82	
	Total	107005.19	20		
	Corrected Total	32763.06	19		
[a]. R Squared = .821 (Adjusted R Squared = .800)					

** Significant at 0.01 level * Significant at 0.05 level

Table 4.2 provides the summary of ANCOVA of total reading and writing score in post, parallel and retention tests of standard 1 higher level students with intellectual disability. The ANCOVA reveals that after adjusting for pretest scores, there is a significant difference in the post test mean values of experimental and control groups ($F_{1,17}$ =11.67, p <0.01). This indicates that the Literacy Rich Approach (LRA) was effective for language development of children with intellectual disability. Since the post test reveals the generalization skills, it can be concluded that students of experimental group were able to generalize the learned skills better than the control group with the help of LRA.

In the parallel test also the mean difference between both groups in total reading and writing is significant ($F_{1,17}$=8.33, p<0.01). Parallel test is based on the content taught directly in the classroom. Even though the instruction in parallel test content is same for experimental and control groups, the LRA might have helped the experimental group to gain a higher score.

The obtained F-ratio in the retention test is 5.04 which is higher than that of the table value for 1 and 17 df at 0.05 level of significance. Hence it can be concluded that the experimental group has significantly more total reading and writing scores than that of the control group. The significant difference reveals that the LRA was highly effective in the maintenance of literacy skills developed by the experimental group.

Table 4.3: Mean values, standard deviations and percentages of total reading and writing scores in post, parallel and retention tests of standard 1 lower level students with intellectual disability

(Maximum possible score is 1506)

Test	Group	N	Mean	SD	Percentage
Post-test	Experimental	9	277.83	97.03	18.45
	Control	10	170.20	60.67	11.30
Parallel Test	Experimental	9	360.56	129.56	23.94
	Control	10	233.73	91.60	15.52
Retention Test	Experimental	9	246.97	113.49	16.40
	Control	10	110.53	42.60	7.34

Table 4.3 provides the means, standard deviations and percentages of total reading and writing scores of standard I lower level students in post, parallel and retention tests. Here also it can be seen that the highest score was obtained in parallel test which measures the extent of information acquired (experimental-23.94%, control-15.52%), then post test which is a measure of the ability to generalize (experimental – 18.45%, control - 11.30%)and lowest in retention test which gives an index of the amount of the information retained (experimental-16.40%, control -7.34%).

Table 4.4: Summary of ANCOVA of total reading and writing scores in post, parallel and retention tests of standard I lower level students with intellectual disability

Test	Source	Sum of squares	df	Mean square	F ratio
	Corrected Model	109005.80[a]	2	54502.90	16.05 **
	Intercept	31784.52	1	31784.52	9.36 **
	PreRdWr Total	54129.80	1	54129.80	15.94 **
Post test	Between groups	33588.00	1	33588.00	9.89 **
	Within groups	54324.55	16	3395.29	
	Total	1092857.00	19		
	Corrected Total	163330.36	18		
a. R Squared = .667 (Adjusted R Squared = .626)					
	Corrected Model	171110.13[a]	2	85555.06	11.92 **
	Intercept	56147.92	1	56147.92	7.82 **
	PreRdWrTotal	94913.33	1	94913.33	13.22 **
Parallel Test	Between groups	43767.37	1	43767.37	6.10 *
	Within groups	114889.32	16	7180.58	
	Total	1926079.19	19		
	Corrected Total	285999.45	18		
a. R Squared = .598 (Adjusted R Squared = .548)					
	Corrected Model	152759.10[a]	2	76379.55	22.30**
	Intercept	6328.39	1	6328.39	1.85
	PreRdWrTotal	64569.31	1	64569.31	18.85**
Retention test	Between groups	57820.66	1	57820.66	16.88 **
	Within groups	54799.30	16	3424.96	
	Total	790483.88	19		
	Corrected Total	207558.40	18		
[a] R Squared = .736 (Adjusted R Squared = .703)					

** Significant at 0.01 level * Significant at 0.05 level

Table 4.4 provides the summary of ANCOVA of total reading and writing score in post, parallel and retention tests of standard 1 lower level students with intellectual disability. In the post test the obtained between groups F ratio is 9.89 (df = 1 and 16, p <0.01) and this indicates that there is significant difference between the scores of experimental and control group. As the post test shows the generalization ability of students, this result indicates the LRA significantly helped the experimental group to generalize the learned literacy skills than the control group.

A similar result was obtained in the parallel test. The difference between both groups is significant ($F_{1,16} = 6.10$ $p<0.05$). This again indicates the high influence of LRA that in spite of the same content, method and materials used for instruction, experimental group got a significantly high score in reading and writing.

In the retention test the obtained F-ratio is 16.88 which is much higher than the table value and it reveals there is significant difference ($p<0.01$) between experimental and control group in the retention scores. Here also, the effect of Literacy Rich Approach is significantly high that the experimental group maintained the reading and writing skills better than the control group.

Table 4.5: Mean values, standard deviations and percentages of total reading and writing scores in post, parallel and retention tests of standard III students with intellectual disability

(Maximum possible score is 2443)

Test	Group	N	Mean	SD	Percentage
Post-test	Experimental	10	1283.73	530.68	52.55
	Control	9	983.92	355.52	40.28
Parallel Test	Experimental	10	1381.20	553.30	56.54
	Control	9	1067.64	357.62	43.70
Retention Test	Experimental	10	1302.60	544.36	53.32
	Control	9	951.81	336.97	38.96

Table 4.5 shows the means, standard deviations and percentages of total reading and writing scores of standard III students in post, parallel and retention tests. Unlike the score of lower level students, standard III experimental group scored high in retention test than in post test.

Table 4.6: Summary of ANCOVA of total reading and writing scores in post, parallel and retention tests of standard III students with intellectual disability

Test	Source	Sum of squares	df	Mean square	F ratio
Post test	Corrected Model	3810939.50[a]	2	1905469.74	189.86**
	Intercept	81818.87	1	81818.87	8.15**
	PreRdWr Total	3385168.26	1	3385168.26	337.29**
	Between groups	79781.28	1	79781.28	7.95**
	Within groups	160582.18	16	10036.39	
	Total	28740000.00	19		
	Corrected Total	3971521.66	18		
a. R Squared =.960 (Adjusted R Squared =.955)					

(Table Contd...)

Parallel Test	Corrected Model	903355.96[a]	2	1951677.98	91.64**
	Intercept	185452.70	1	185452.70	8.71**
	PreRdWr Total	3437626.95	1	3437626.95	161.41**
	Between groups	95516.03	1	95516.03	4.49*
	Within groups	340757.42	16	21297.34	
	Total	33110000.00	19		
	Corrected Total	4244113.38	18		
a. R Squared =.920 (Adjusted R Squared =.910)					
Retention test	Corrected Model	823054.80[a]	2	1911527.40	91.24**
	Intercept	96749.27	1	96749.27	4.62
	PreRdWr Total	3240154.44	1	3240154.44	154.65**
	Between groups	159241.46	1	159241.46	7.60**
	Within groups	335226.68	16	20951.67	
	Total	28700000.00	19		
	Corrected Total	4158281.48	18		
[a]. R Squared =.919 (Adjusted R Squared = .909)					

** Significant at 0.01 level * Significant at 0.05 level

The summary of ANCOVA of total reading and writing scores in post, parallel and retention tests of standard III students with intellectual disability is presented in table 4.6. In the post test the calculated F-ratio is 7.95 and it indicates that the score difference between experimental and control group is significant at 0.01 level. Hence, it can be concluded that the exposure to the LRA was highly effective for the experimental group to generalize the acquired literacy skills better than the control group.

It is also seen from the table 4.6 that for the parallel test the acquired F ratio is 4.49. This means the difference between experimental and control group in the acquisition of literacy skills is significant at 0.05 level. This again reveals the effectiveness of LRA. Although the content, material and teaching method was exactly the same for both groups, the LRA helped the experimental group to gain high reading and writing score.

In the retention test the calculated F- ratio is 7.60 and this also indicates that significant mean difference at 0.01 level exists between experimental and control group. A close observation of mean values reveals that LRA helped experimental group to maintain the literacy skills learned.

When looking at the results of post test, parallel test and retention test of standard I higher, standard I lower and standard III students with intellectual disability it can be concluded that the Literacy Rich Approach (LRA) was highly effective in acquiring, generalizing, and maintaining language (literacy) skills. In all the above tests, the experimental group obtained high mean scores and the difference between mean scores of experimental and control group are statistically significant.

The result of the study is in agreement with the findings of earlier research (Katims, 1991) where effect of literacy rich environment found it highly promising. This also agrees with recent researches (Allor, Mathes, Roberts, Jones, & Champlin, 2010) in which treatment group of students with intellectual disability improved tremendously in skills including phonemic awareness, phonics, word recognition, comprehension and oral language when given consistent, explicit and comprehensive reading instruction across extended period of time.

Table 4.7: Mean values and standard deviations of total reading and writing scores in pre, post, parallel and retention tests of standard I higher experimental and control groups

(Maximum possible score is 1506)

Group	N	Mean	SD
Pre experimental	10	297.70	178.40
Post experimental	10	601.63	214.48
Parallel experimental	10	690.80	194.01
Retention experimental	10	569.80	231.45
Pre control	10	277.58	167.21
Post control	10	466.55	173.91
Parallel control	10	556.75	184.69
Retention control	10	447.38	204.38

Table 4.7 shows the mean values and standard deviations of total reading and writing scores of standard I higher experimental and control groups in pre, post, parallel and retention tests. From the table it can be seen that the score attainment pattern (from highest to lowest) for both groups is in the descending order of parallel – post – retention – pre tests.

Table 4.8: Summary of repeated ANOVA of total reading and writing scores in pre, post, parallel and retention tests of standard I higher experimental and control groups

Group	Source of variation	Sum of Squares	df	Mean Square	F ratio
Experimental	Between trials	861356.09	3	287118.70	100.43**
	Between subjects	1444131.06	9		
	Error	77191.02	27	2858.93	
	Total	2382678.17	39		
Control	Between trials	407372.21	3	135790.74	50.87**
	Between subjects	1134636.06	9		
	Error	72073.08	27	2669.37	
	Total	1614081.35	39		

** Significant at 0.01 level

Table 4.8 shows the F- ratio obtained for experimental group is 100.43, which is significant at 0.01 level. The F- ratio obtained for control group is 50.87, which is also significant at 0.01 level.

The Least Significant Difference (LSD) test of pair wise comparisons is required to locate the pairs in which significant difference exists. Table 4.9 and Table 4.10 illustrate this.

Table 4.9: LSD test for significance between pairs of mean scores of total reading and writing of standard I higher experimental group

Sl No.	Pairs	Mean values	Mean difference
1.	Pre experimental	297.70	303.93**
	Post experimental	601.63	
2.	Pre experimental	297.70	393.10**
	Parallel experimental	690.80	
3.	Pre experimental	297.70	272.10**
	Retention experimental	569.80	
4.	Post experimental	601.63	89.17**
	Parallel experimental	690.80	
5.	Post experimental	601.63	31.83
	Retention experimental	569.80	
6.	Parallel experimental	690.80	121.00**
	Retention experimental	569.80	

** Significant at 0.01 level

Table 4.9 shows the least significant difference test for paired comparisons of total reading and writing scores of standard I higher experimental group. It reveals that significant difference exists ($p<0.01$) in all pairs except 'post-retention' experimental pair. The significant mean difference at 0.01 level in the first three pairs, (pretest and post test, pretest and parallel test and pretest and retention test) indicate that there are observable gain of scores in post, parallel and retention tests from pretest. The significantly higher mean value of the parallel test than that of the post test reveals that the ability of students with intellectual disability to generalize the skills is significantly less than that of the acquisition skills. This result is expected as the parallel test is based on the content taught directly in the classroom and the post test is given to find out the generalization of the parallel content. A similar result was seen in the pair parallel and retention tests. The insignificance in the mean scores of post test and retention test indicates that generalization skills obtained by the experimental group has maintained in the retention test which was conducted six months after intervention.

Table 4.10: LSD test for significance between pairs of mean scores of total reading and writing of standard I higher control group

Sl. No.	Pairs	Mean values	Mean difference
1.	Pre control	277.58	188.97**
	Post control	466.55	
2.	Pre control	277.58	279.17**
	Parallel control	556.75	
3.	Pre control	277.58	169.80**
	Retention control	447.38	
4.	Post control	466.55	90.20**
	Parallel control	556.75	
5.	Post control	466.55	19.17
	Retention control	447.38	
6.	Parallel control	556.75	109.37**
	Retention control	447.38	

** Significant at 0.01 level

The least significant difference test for paired comparisons shown in table 4.10 indicates that significant mean difference at 0.01 level exists for all pairs except post-retention pair. The significant mean difference at 0.01 level in the first three pairs (pretest and post test, pre test and parallel test and pre test and retention test) with low mean score for pretest in each pair indicate that there is observable gain of scores in post, parallel and retention tests from pretest. This can be explained as in the case of experimental group that the control group also has gained acquisition, generalization and maintenance skills compared to the pretest score. In the pairs post-parallel and parallel-retention, the significantly higher mean score of the parallel test reveals that compared to the generalization and maintenance skills students with intellectual disability have significantly more acquisition skills. The insignificance in the post-retention pair indicates, after six months students had kept the post test performance in the retention test.

Table 4.11 provides the mean values and standard deviations of total reading and writing scores of standard I lower experimental and control groups in four tests. From the table it can be seen that the score attainment pattern (from highest to lowest) for both group is in the descending order of parallel – post – retention – pre tests.

Table 4.11: Mean values and standard deviations of total reading and writing scores in pre, post, parallel and retention tests of standard I lower experimental and control groups

(Maximum possible score is 1506)

Group	N	Mean	SD
Pre experimental	9	62.67	24.09
Post experimental	9	277.83	97.03
Parallel experimental	9	360.56	129.56
Retention experimental	9	246.97	113.49
Pre control	10	52.43	28.69
Post control	10	170.20	60.67
Parallel control	10	233.73	91.60
Retention control	10	110.53	42.60

Table 4.12: Summary of repeated ANOVA of total reading and writing scores in pre, post, parallel and retention tests of standard 1 lower experimental and control groups

Group	Source of variation	Sum of squares	df	Mean square	F ratio
Experimental	Between trials	426824.03	3	142274.68	34.18**
	Between subjects	217377.08	8		
	Error	99909.20	24	4162.88	
	Total	744110.31	35		
Control	Between trials	182227.56	3	60742.52	41.31**
	Between subjects	92690.76	9		
	Error	39697.46	27	1470.28	
	Total	314615.78	39		

** Significant at 0.01 level

According to the Table 4.12 the F-ratio obtained for experimental group and control group indicate significant difference ($p<0.01$) among the mean scores of four groups in both sets.

Table 4.13: LSD test for significance between pairs of mean scores of total reading and writing of standard I lower experimental group

Sl. No.	Pairs	Mean values	Mean difference
1.	Pre experimental	62.67	215.16**
	Post experimental	277.83	
2.	Pre experimental	62.67	297.89**
	Parallel experimental	360.56	
3.	Pre experimental	62.67	184.30**
	Retention experimental	246.97	
4.	Post experimental	277.83	82.73*
	Parallel experimental	360.56	
5.	Post experimental	277.83	30.86
	Retention experimental	246.97	
6.	Parallel experimental	360.56	113.59**
	Retention experimental	246.97	

** Significant at 0.01 level * Significant at 0.05 level.

The test of least significant difference for pair wise comparisons for standard I lower experimental group yielded a significant mean difference at 0.01 level in four pairs, that is, total reading writing scores in pre-post, pre-parallel, pre-retention and parallel-retention. Result of the first three pairs indicates that there is observable gain of mean scores of total reading and writing in post, parallel and retention tests from pretest score. Significant mean difference between the post-parallel ($p<0.05$) and parallel-retention ($p<0.01$) pairs and a high parallel test score in both cases indicates that generalization and maintenance scores obtained by students are not very close to the level of acquisition of skills. The insignificance of the mean difference in the post-retention pair reveals that students with intellectual disability could maintain whatever skills they generalize.

The least significant difference test for paired comparisons of total reading and writing scores of standard I lower control group shows that significant mean difference at 0.01 level exists in all pairs. The significant mean difference in the first three pairs (pre-post, pre-parallel and pre-retention) indicates that students have considerable gain of scores from pre test score. In the case of fourth and sixth pairs (post-parallel and parallel-retention), the significant difference and higher mean for parallel test indicate that in post test and retention test students did not perform as parallel test. As explained earlier it is natural that scores go down because in post test the generalization skill and in retention test, the maintenance skills are measured. The significant mean difference in the post-retention pair indicates that performance rate of the control group students was further gone down after six months compared to the post test score.

Table 4.14: LSD test for significance between pairs of mean scores of total reading and writing of standard I lower control group

Sl. No.	Pairs	Mean values	Mean difference
1.	Pre control	52.43	117.77**
	Post control	170.20	
2.	Pre control	52.43	181.30**
	Parallel control	233.73	
3.	Pre control	52.43	58.10**
	Retention control	110.53	
4.	Post control	170.20	63.53**
	Parallel control	233.73	
5.	Post control	170.20	59.67**
	Retention control	110.53	
6.	Parallel control	233.73	123.20**
	Retention control	110.53	

** Significant at 0.01 level.

Table 4.15: Mean values and standard deviations of total reading and writing scores in pre, post, parallel and retention tests of standard III experimental and control groups

(Maximum possible score is 2443)

Group	N	Mean	SD
Pre experimental	10	940.08	459.67
Post experimental	10	1283.73	530.68
Parallel experimental	10	1381.20	553.30
Retention experimental	10	1302.60	544.36
Pre control	9	790.56	315.34
Post control	9	983.92	355.52
Parallel control	9	1067.64	357.62
Retention control	9	951.81	336.97

Table 4.15 shows the mean values and standard deviations of total reading and writing scores of standard III experimental and control groups in pre, post, parallel and retention tests.

Table 4.16: Summary of repeated ANOVA of total reading and writing scores in pre, post, parallel and retention tests of standard III experimental and control groups

Group	Source of variation	Sum of squares	df	Mean square	F ratio
	Between trials	1150336.41	3	383455.47	
Experimental	Between subjects	9639618.29	9		47.31**
	Error	218856.28	27	8105.79	
	Total	11008810.98	39		
	Between trials	363652.09	3	121217.36	
Control	Between subjects	3613625.06	8		23.34**
	Error	124636.65	24	5193.19	
	Total	4101913.80	35		

** Significant at 0.01 level

As given in the table 4.16 the F-ratios obtained for experimental group (47.31) and control group (23.34) reveal significant difference (P<0.01) among the mean scores of four groups in both sets.

Table 4.17: LSD test for significance between pairs of mean scores of total reading and writing of standard III experimental group

Sl. No.	Pairs	Mean values	Mean difference
1.	Pre experimental	940.08	343.65**
	Post experimental	1283.73	
2.	Pre experimental	940.08	441.12**
	Parallel experimental	1381.20	
3.	Pre experimental	940.08	362.52**
	Retention experimental	1302.60	
4.	Post experimental	1283.73	97.47*
	Parallel experimental	1381.20	
5.	Post experimental	1283.73	18.87
	Retention experimental	1302.60	
6.	Parallel experimental	1381.20	78.60
	Retention experimental	1302.60	

** Significant at 0.01 level * Significant at 0.05 level

The table 4.17 shows that there are significant differences at 0.01 level in the first three pairs, that is, pre-post, pre-parallel, and pre-retention. This result indicates that there is observable gain of mean scores of total reading and writing in post, parallel and retention tests from pretest score. The significant difference in the post-parallel pair (p<0.05) and the higher mean score for parallel test reveals that post test score is significantly lower compared to that of parallel test. The insignificance of the mean difference in the post-retention pair reveals that group of students were able to retain the post test scores after six months. The insignificance in the mean score difference of the last pair (parallel-retention) indicates that there is no significant difference between the extent of language skills acquired and maintained. A possible explanation for this result is that the exposure to LRA might have enabled the students to generalize the skills that they have acquired.

Table 4.18: LSD test for significance between pairs of mean scores of total reading and writing of standard III control group

Sl. No.	Pairs	Mean values	Mean difference
1.	Pre control	790.56	193.36**
	Post control	983.92	
2.	Pre control	790.56	277.08**
	Parallel control	1067.64	
3.	Pre control	790.56	161.25**
	Retention control	951.81	
4.	Post control	983.92	83.72*
	Parallel control	1067.64	
5.	Post control	983.92	32.11
	Retention control	951.81	
6.	Parallel control	1067.64	115.83**
	Retention control	951.81	

** Significant at 0.01 level * Significant at 0.05 level.

The least significant difference test for paired comparisons yielded significant mean difference at 0.01 level in the pre-post, pre-parallel and pre-retention pairs. This indicates there is significant gain of scores in post, parallel and retention tests compared to the pre test. Significance in the post-parallel, and parallel-retention scores with high mean score for parallel test reveal that the children in the control group were unable to generalize and maintain as much as they acquired. The insignificance in the post-retention pair reveals that there is no significant difference in the amount of language skills generalized and maintained.

The results of repeated ANOVA of standard 1 higher, standard 1 lower and standard III students highlight the following points: (1) Even though the mean score difference in total reading and writing exists between experimental and control groups (as illustrated in tables 4.1-4.6), there was significant increase in the scores of experimental and control groups in post, parallel and retention tests compared to pre test score. This indicates that if systematic instruction takes place students will progress in literacy skills. (2) The students with intellectual disability in all the experimental and control groups generalized only significantly less amount of skills they learned. (3) Except in standard I lower control group, in all the other five experimental and control groups the students were able to maintain whatever skills they generalized, whereas standard I lower control group students were able to maintain only significantly less language skills than they could generalize. (4) Except in standard III experimental group, the students in all the other five groups were able to maintain only significantly less amount of the skills they acquired. Only the standard III experimental group students were able to maintain whatever skills they learned.

EFFECT OF LITERACY RICH APPROACH IN THE DEVELOPMENT OF VOCABULARY

This section deals with the analysis of effect of literacy rich approach in the vocabulary development of children with intellectual disability. The total vocabulary score is calculated from scores of sub skills in vocabulary at each level. The sub skills in standard I are: identify words, read words, select suitable word and match words. Sub skills in standard III are : read words, fill in the blanks with suitable words, find synonyms, make word with letters, find single word for given phrase and find odd words.

The details of the analysis are presented from Tables 4.19 to 4.36.

Table 4.19: Mean values, standard deviations and percentages of vocabulary scores in post, parallel and retention tests of standard 1 higher level students with intellectual disability

(Maximum possible score is 52)

Test	Group	N	Mean	SD	Percentage
Post-test	Experimental	10	48.40	4.01	93.08
	Control	10	39.63	11.77	76.21
Parallel Test	Experimental	10	47.18	5.76	90.73
	Control	10	46.43	9.13	89.29
Retention Test	Experimental	10	48.50	4.84	93.27
	Control	10	40.40	12.90	77.69

Table 4.19 provides the mean values, Standard deviation and percentages of total vocabulary scores in post, parallel and retention tests of standard I higher level students with intellectual disability. It can be clearly seen from the table that the mean score of vocabulary of the experimental group increased from parallel test to post test and again increased to retention test. For the control group the highest mean score is parallel test and next highest is in retention test and lowest score is in post test.

Table 4.20: Summary of ANCOVA of vocabulary scores in post, parallel and retention tests of standard I higher level students with intellectual disability

Test	Source	Sum of squares	df	Mean square	F ratio
	Corrected Model	1116.17[a]	2	558.08	14.39**
	Intercept	2377.57	1	2377.57	61.30**
	PreVocTotal	731.17	1	731.17	18.85**
Post test	Between groups	383.92	1	383.92	9.90**
	Within groups	659.39	17	38.79	
	Total	40517.56	20		
	Corrected Total	1775.56	19		
a. R Squared =.629 (Adjusted R Squared =.585)					
	Corrected Model	418.42[a]	2	209.21	5.62**
	Intercept	3552.62	1	3552.62	95.35**
	PreVocTotal	415.61	1	415.61	11.16**
Parallel Test	Between groups	2.74	1	2.74	0.07
	Within groups	633.40	17	37.26	
	Total	44856.63	20		
	Corrected Total	1051.83	19		
a. R Squared =.398 (Adjusted R Squared =. 327)					
	Corrected Model	881.13[a]	2	440.56	6.49**
	Intercept	2783.56	1	2783.56	40.98**
	PreVocTotal	553.08	1	553.08	8.14**
Retention test	Between groups	327.18	1	327.18	4.82*
	Within groups	1154.57	17	67.92	
	Total	41551.75	20		
	Corrected Total	2035.70	19		
a. R Squared =. 433 (Adjusted R Squared =. 366)					

** Significant at 0.01 level * Significant at 0.05 level

In the post test the obtained F-ratio for the between groups is 9.90. This indicates that the mean difference between experimental and control group is significant ($p<0.01$). It can therefore be concluded that LRA was effective in generalizing the vocabulary skills of children with intellectual disability.

In the parallel test the obtained F-ratio (0.07) for the between groups is not significant either at 0.01 level or at 0.05 level. This means that the mean difference between experimental and control group is not significant. Compared to the maximum possible score (52) both group got high score and therefore it can be concluded that the common teaching sessions using conventional approach was effective.

In the retention test the F- ratio obtained is 4.82 which indicated mean difference between experimental and control group is significant at 0.05 level. From this result it is clear that LRA was highly effective for the experimental group in the maintenance of vocabulary skills.

Table 4.21: Mean values, standard deviations and percentages of vocabulary scores in post, parallel and retention tests of standard I lower level students with intellectual disability

(Maximum possible score is 52)

Test	Group	N	Mean	SD	Percentage
Post Test	Experimental	9	35.11	11.07	67.52
	Control	10	19.45	10.65	37.40
Parallel Test	Experimental	9	36.48	11.92	70.15
	Control	10	23.25	13.35	44.71
Retention Test	Experimental	9	36.86	9.96	70.88
	Control	10	15.28	4.66	29.38

From the table 4.21 it can be seen that in the retention test experimental group got a better score than parallel and post tests. Control group's score kept the usual pattern as high parallel test score, followed by post test score and lower retention test score.

Table 4.22: Summary of ANCOVA of vocabulary scores in post, parallel, and retention tests of standard I lower level students with intellectual disability

Test	Source	Sum of squares	df	Mean square	F ratio
Post test	Corrected Model	1641.32[a]	2	820.66	8.63**
	Intercept	2227.54	1	2227.54	23.42**
	PreVocTotal	479.51	1	479.51	5.04*
	Between groups	509.16	1	509.16	5.35*
	Within groups	1521.86	16	95.17	
	Total	16879.50	19		
	Corrected Total	3163.17	18		
a. R Squared = .519 (Adjusted R Squared = .459)					
Parallel Test	Corrected Model	1342.89[a]	2	671.45	5.39*
	Intercept	2780.43	1	2780.43	22.32**
	PreVocTotal	514.77	1	514.77	4.13
	Between groups	302.06	1	302.06	2.43
	Within groups	1993.04	16	124.57	
	Total	19885.44	19		
	Corrected Total	3335.93	18		
a. R Squared = .403 (Adjusted R Squared = .328					

(Table Contd...)

Retention test	Corrected Model	2356.51[a]	2	1178.26	22.42**
	Intercept	2741.70	1	2741.70	52.17**
	PreVocTotal	149.33	1	149.33	2.84
	Between groups	1462.68	1	1462.68	27.83**
	Within groups	840.86	16	52.55	
	Total	15552.13	19		
	Corrected Total	3197.38	18		
a. R Squared = .737 (Adjusted R Squared = .704					

Significant at 0.01 level Significant at 0.05 level

In the post test the obtained F ratio for the between groups is 5.35 and it reveals that the mean difference between experimental and control groups is significant ($p<0.05$). Hence it can be concluded that the LRA was effective in enabling the experimental group to generalize significantly more vocabulary skills than that of the control group.

F-ratio in the parallel test reveals that no significant difference exists between both groups. As it was explained earlier parallel test is based on the content directly taught in the classroom, both groups got scores without significant difference.

In the retention test the obtained F-ratio (27.83) for the between groups is much higher than that of the table value. Therefore it can be concluded that statistically significant difference exists between the mean scores of experimental and control groups at 0.01 level. The highly significant difference indicates that the LRA was highly effective in the maintenance of vocabulary skills developed by experimental group than that of control group.

Table 4.23: Mean values, standard deviations and percentage of vocabulary scores in post, parallel and retention tests of standard III students with intellectual disability

(Maximum possible score is 42)

Test	Group	N	Mean	SD	Percentage
Post Test	Experimental	10	36.43	4.34	86.74
	Control	9	31.44	5.00	74.85
Parallel Test	Experimental	10	38.83	2.93	92.45
	Control	9	35.94	5.30	85.57
Retention Test	Experimental	10	35.03	4.68	83.40
	Control	9	27.64	6.12	65.81

The mean values, standard deviation and percentages of total vocabulary scores in post, parallel and retention tests of standard III students are shown in table 4.23.

Table 4.24: Summary of ANCOVA of vocabulary scores in parallel, post and retention tests of standard III students with intellectual disability

Test	Source	Sum of squares	df	Mean square	F ratio
Post Test	Corrected Model	328.54[a]	2	164.27	16.56 **
	Intercept	1090.86	1	1090.86	109.99**
	PreVocTotal	211.04	1	211.04	21.28**
	Between groups	80.16	1	80.16	8.08**
	Within groups	158.69	16	9.92	
	Total	22536.31	19		
	Corrected Total	487.23	18		
a. R Squared =.674 (Adjusted R Squared =.634)					
Parallel Test	Corrected Model	154.34[a]	2	77.17	6.61**
	Intercept	1713.36	1	1713.36	146.64**
	PreVoc Total	115.03	1	115.03	9.85**
	Between groups	23.91	1	23.91	2.05
	Within groups	186.95	16	11.68	
	Total	27003.81	19		
	Corrected Total	341.28	18		
a. R Squared =.452 (Adjusted R Squared =.384)					
Retention test	Corrected Model	618.44[a]	2	309.22	36.07 **
	Intercept	636.06	1	636.06	74.19 **
	PreVoc Total	360.02	1	360.02	41.99 **
	Between groups	184.86	1	184.86	21.56**
	Within groups	137.17	16	8.57	
	Total	19639.86	19		
	Corrected Total	755.61	18		
a. R Squared =.818 (Adjusted R Squared =.796)					

** Significant at 0.01 level

As per the table 4.24, the obtained F-ratio for the between groups in the post test is 8.08 and it is significant at 0.01 level. This indicates that there is significant mean difference between experimental and control groups in vocabulary scores. The LRA was highly effective for the experimental group to generalize the learned skills.

In the parallel test as usual the obtained F-ratio (2.05) is not significant either at 0.01 level or at 0.05 level. This means no significant difference exists between the mean scores of both groups.

In the retention test, there is difference in the mean scores of both groups and it is statistically significant at 0.01 level. The highly significant F-ratio (21.56) can be explained as the influence of LRA for experimental group to get a high score in the maintenance of vocabulary skills.

The results indicate that for all three levels of children (standard I higher, standard I lower and standard III) significant mean difference in vocabulary development was found between experimental and control groups in post test and retention test. In parallel test no significant mean difference exists.

From the above tests the following observations can be made. While teaching children with intellectual disability the existing conventional approach may be adequate during acquisition stage. Children may learn the content if systematic instruction is provided. But the aim of special education is to enable the children to generalize and maintain the learned skills. For generalization and maintenance existing conventional approach is not enough. Students need stimulating, creative and innovative approach. The LRA with wide verity of activities and experiences used in this study enabled experimental group of students to generalize and maintain vocabulary skills better than control group.

Table 4.25: Mean values and standard deviations of vocabulary scores in pre, post, parallel and retention tests of standard I higher experimental and control groups

(Maximum possible score is 52)

Group	N	Mean	SD
Pre experimental	10	30.35	12.37
Post experimental	10	48.40	4.01
Parallel experimental	10	47.17	5.76
Retention experimental	10	48.50	4.84
Pre control	10	30.33	13.48
Post control	10	39.63	11.77
Parallel control	10	46.43	9.13
Retention control	10	40.40	12.90

Table 4.25 shows the mean values and standard deviations of total vocabulary scores of standard I higher experimental and control groups in pre, post, parallel and retention tests. The score attainment pattern for the experimental group is in the descending order of retention- post- parallel-pre tests and that of the control group is in the descending order of parallel-retention –post- pre tests.

Table 4.26: Summary of repeated ANOVA of vocabulary scores in pre, post, parallel and retention tests of standard I higher experimental and control groups

Group	Source of variation	Sum of Squares	df	Mean square	F ratio
Experimental	Between trials	2353.93	3	784.64	24.91**
	Between subjects	1181.44	9		
	Error	850.62	27	31.50	
	Total	4385.99	39		
Control	Between trials	1325.87	3	441.96	13.23**
	Between subjects	4227.05	9		
	Error	901.65	27	33.39	
	Total	6454.57	39		

** Significant at 0.01 level

Table 4.26 provides the summary of repeated ANOVA of total vocabulary scores of standard I higher experimental and control groups. The F ratio of both groups reveals that there is significant difference ($p<0.01$) between the mean scores of different groups in both sets.

Table 4.27: LSD test for significance between pairs of mean scores of vocabulary of standard I higher experimental group

Sl No.	Pairs	Mean values	Mean difference
1.	Pre experimental	30.35	18.05**
	Post experimental	48.40	
2.	Pre experimental	30.35	16.82**
	Parallel experimental	47.17	
3.	Pre experimental	30.35	18.15**
	Retention experimental	48.50	
4.	Post experimental	48.40	1.23
	Parallel experimental	47.17	
5.	Post Experimental	48.40	0.10
	Retention experimental	48.50	
6.	Parallel experimental	47.17	1.33
	Retention experimental	48.50	

** Significant at 0.01 level

The LSD test yielded significant mean difference at 0.01 level in the first three pairs (pre-post, pre-parallel and pre-retention) with higher mean values in post, parallel and retention tests respectively. This result indicates that in all the three occasions the students improved significantly from their pretest performance. The insignificance in the next three pairs (post-parallel, post-retention and parallel-retention) shows that students generalized and maintained the learned vocabulary skills well enough that they got similar scores as parallel test scores. The effect of Literacy Rich Approach is very convincingly evident here.

Table 4.28: LSD test for significance between pairs of mean scores of vocabulary of standard I higher control group

Sl. No.	Pairs	Mean values	Mean difference
1.	Pre Control	30.33	9.30**
	Post Control	39.63	
2.	Pre Control	30.33	16.10**
	Parallel Control	46.43	
3.	Pre Control	30.33	10.07**
	Retention Control	40.40	
4.	Post Control	39.63	6.80*
	Parallel Control	46.43	
5.	Post Control	39.63	0.77
	Retention Control	40.40	
6.	Parallel Control	46.43	6.03*
	Retention Control	40.40	

** Significant at 0.01 level * Significant at 0.05 level

The LSD test yielded significant mean difference at 0.01 level between the first three pairs (pre-post, pre-parallel, pre-retention) with high mean score for post, parallel and retention tests respectively. This shows the students' improvement in vocabulary skills compared to pretest score. The significant mean difference in the post- parallel and parallel-retention pairs shows that in post and retention tests experiment group was not able to reach up to the parallel test score. The insignificance in the post-retention pair indicates that students were able to maintain their post test scores after six months.

Table 4.29: Mean values and standard deviations of vocabulary scores in pre, post, parallel and retention tests of standard I lower experimental and control groups

(Maximum possible score is 52)

Group	N	Mean	SD
Pre experimental	9	9.19	4.44
Post experimental	9	35.11	11.07
Parallel experimental	9	36.47	11.91
Retention experimental	9	36.86	9.96
Pre control	10	5.10	5.43
Post control	10	19.45	10.65
Parallel control	10	23.25	12.35
Retention control	10	15.28	4.66

The mean values and standard deviations of vocabulary scores of std I lower level experimental and control groups in pre, post, parallel and retention tests are shown in table 4.29.

Table 4.30 Summary of repeated ANOVA of vocabulary scores in pre, post, parallel and retention tests of standard I lower experimental and control groups

Group	Source of variation	Sum of squares	df	Mean square	F ratio
	Between trials	4919.09	3	1639.70	
Experimental	Between subjects	1797.41	8		30.94**
	Error	1272.02	24	53.00	
	Total	7988.52	35		
	Between trials	1835.87	3	611.96	
Control	Between subjects	1846.25	9		16.42**
	Error	1006.31	27	37.27	
	Total	4688.43	39		

** Significant at 0.01 level

Table 4.30 provides the summary of repeated ANOVA of vocabulary scores of standard I lower experimental and control groups in pre, post, parallel and retention tests. The F ratios show there are significant differences ($p<0.01$) in the mean scores of various groups of both sets.

Table 4.31: LSD test for significance between pairs of mean scores of vocabulary of standard I lower experimental group

Sl. No.	Pairs	Mean values	Mean difference
1	Pre experimental	9.19	25.92**
	Post experimental	35.11	
2	Pre experimental	9.19	27.28**
	Parallel experimental	36.47	
3.	Pre experimental	9.19	27.67**
	Retention experimental	36.86	
4.	Post experimental	35.11	1.36
	Parallel experimental	36.47	
5.	Post Experimental	35.11	1.75
	Retention experimental	36.86	
6.	Parallel experimental	36.47	0.39
	Retention experimental	36.86	

** Significant at 0.01 level

Table 4.31 shows that in the first three pairs there are significant differences ($p<0.01$) in the mean scores with higher mean score for post, parallel and retention tests respectively. This can be explained as students have significant score gains in post, parallel and retention tests compared to pretest score. Students learned, generalized and maintained vocabulary skills. There are no significant mean difference in the pairs post-parallel, post- retention and parallel-retention tests which indicates that scores of post test and retention test are similar to parallel test scores and post and retention test scores are close.

Table 4.32: LSD test for significance between pairs of mean scores of vocabulary of standard I lower control group

Sl. No.	Pairs	Mean values	Mean difference
1.	Pre Control	5.10	14.35**
	Post Control	19.45	
2.	Pre Control	5.10	18.15**
	Parallel Control	23.25	
3.	Pre Control	5.10	10.18**
	Retention Control	15.28	
4.	Post Control	19.45	3.80
	Parallel Control	23.25	
5.	Post Control	19.45	4.17
	Retention Control	15.28	
6.	Parallel Control	23.25	7.97**
	Retention Control	15.28	

** Significant at 0.01 level

Table 4.32 shows the least significant difference test of pair wise comparison of vocabulary scores of standard I lower control group. The significant mean difference between the first three pairs with high mean score for post, parallel and retention tests respectively indicate that the students have significant gain of scores in post, parallel and retention test scores compared to pretest scores. The insignificance in the mean difference in post-parallel and post-retention pairs shows that these scores are very close. The significant difference at 0.01 level in parallel- retention pair and higher mean score in parallel test indicates that students' retention test score is lower than parallel test score.

Table 4.33: Mean values and standard deviations of vocabulary scores in pre, post, parallel and retention tests of standard III experimental and control groups

(Maximum possible score is 42)

Group	N	Mean	SD
Pre experimental	10	21.53	10.74
Post experimental	10	36.43	4.34
Parallel experimental	10	38.83	2.93
Retention experimental	10	35.03	4.68
Pre control	9	22.17	6.59
Post control	9	31.44	5.00
Parallel control	9	35.94	5.30
Retention control	9	27.64	6.12

Table 4.33 shows the mean values and standard deviations of vocabulary scores of standard 3 experimental and control groups in pre, post, parallel and retention tests. Both groups follow the general score pattern, that is, highest for parallel test followed by post test, retention test and pretest scores respectively.

Table 4.34: Summary of repeated ANOVA of vocabulary scores in pre, post, parallel and retention tests of standard III experimental and control groups

Group	Source of variation	Sum of squares	df	Mean square	F ratio
Experimental	Between trials	1814.28	3	604.76	23.54**
	Between subjects	788.49	9		
	Error	693.76	27	25.70	
	Total	3296.53	39		
Control	Between trials	921.52	3	307.17	41.91**
	Between subjects	896.81	8		
	Error	175.90	24	7.33	
	Total	1994.23	35		

** Significant at 0.01 level

The summary of repeated ANOVA of standard III experimental and control groups are shown in table 4.34. The F- ratio of both experimental and control groups are significant at 0.01 level. Hence it can be concluded that there are significant differences among the mean values of vocabulary scores of different stages of measurement for both experimental and control groups.

Table 4.35: LSD test for significance between pairs of mean scores of vocabulary of standard III experimental group

Sl. No.	Pairs	Mean values	Mean difference
1.	Pre experimental	21.53	14.90**
	Post experimental	36.43	
2.	Pre experimental	21.53	17.30**
	Parallel experimental	38.83	
3.	Pre experimental	21.53	13.50**
	Retention experimental	35.03	
4.	Post experimental	36.43	2.40
	Parallel experimental	38.83	
5.	Post Experimental	36.43	1.40
	Retention experimental	35.03	
6.	Parallel experimental	38.83	3.80
	Retention experimental	35.03	

** Significant at 0.01 level

Table 4.35 provides a similar result of standard I higher and lower experimental groups, as the standard III experimental group also yielded significant mean difference in vocabulary scores of first three pairs (pre-post, pre-parallel and pre-retention). This result reveals that compared to pretest score experimental group had significant gain of scores in post, parallel and retention tests. They learned, generalized and maintained significantly more vocabulary skills than that of the pretest level. The insignificance of mean score between the pairs, post-parallel and parallel-retention with high mean score of parallel test, indicate that students' post test and retention scores are very close to the parallel test score. Another point to note is that the students maintained their post test score after six months of intervention.

The result of the least significant difference test of pair wise comparison of vocabulary scores of standard III control group is shown in table 4.36. From the table it can be seen that there are significant differences ($p<0.01$) in the mean scores of all pairs. Significant mean score difference in the first three pairs indicate that significant score gains in post, parallel, and retention tests compared to pretest scores. Similarly, significant mean score differences ($p <0.01$) were found in last three pairs indicating the post (generalization) and retention (maintenance) scores are significantly lower than parallel test score (acquisition). Their maintenance skills (retention) are lower than generalization (post test) skills.

Table 4.36: LSD test for significance between pairs of mean scores of vocabulary of standard III control group

Sl.No.	Pairs	Mean values	Mean difference
1.	Pre Control	22.17	9.27**
	Post Control	31.44	
2.	Pre Control	22.17	13.77**
	Parallel Control	35.94	
3.	Pre Control	22.17	5.47**
	Retention Control	27.64	
4.	Post Control	31.44	4.50**
	Parallel Control	35.94	
5.	Post Control	31.44	3.80**
	Retention Control	27.64	
6.	Parallel Control	35.94	8.30**
	Retention Control	27.64	

** Significant at 0.01 level

The results of repeated ANOVA and least significant difference test of vocabulary scores of standard I higher, standard I lower and standard III students indicate that:

1. Both experimental and control group gained significantly high vocabulary scores in post parallel and retention tests compared to pretest scores. This marked improvement in vocabulary scores can be attributed to the systematic instruction took place in this study.
2. The post, parallel and retention test scores are close (without significant mean difference) for experimental group of standard I higher, standard I lower and standard III. This is the effect of LRA that kept generalization and maintenance scores close to parallel test score.

   Post test and retention test scores are significantly lower than parallel test score for control groups of standard I higher and standard III students. This means students failed to apply the skills when new material is presented (post test) and maintain the skills when the test is given in a later time (retention test). Control group of standard I lower students obtained low score in parallel test and they kept a similar score in post test.
3. Post-retention scores are close (without significant mean difference) for experimental groups of standard I higher, standard I lower and standard III students. These students were able to maintain their post test score in the retention test with help of LRA. For control groups, the closeness in post-retention scores is found in standard I higher and standard I lower while for standard III there is significant difference in the mean score. Their maintenance score went down compared to generalization score.

EFFECT OF LITERACY RICH APPROACH IN THE DEVELOPMENT OF READING COMPREHENSION

This section includes the analysis of the effectiveness of Literacy Rich Approach in the development of reading comprehension in children with intellectual disability. The total reading comprehension score is calculated from the scores of it's sub skills in standard I and standard III. Sub skills in standard I are: (1) Read two word sentences and answer to questions, (2) Read long sentences and answer to questions, (3) Read small paragraph and answer to questions, (4) Read long paragraph and answer to questions.

Sub skills in standard III are : (1) Make sentences using given words in rows and columns, (2) Read paragraph, (3) Read story and choose correct answer to questions, (4) Read paragraph and make questions, and (5) Read paragraph silently and say answer to questions.

The details of analysis are presented from Tables 4.37-4.54.

Table 4.37: Mean values, standard deviations and percentages of reading comprehension scores in post, parallel and retention tests of standard I higher level students with intellectual disability

(Maximum possible score is 28)

Test	Group	N	Mean	SD	Percentage
Post Test	Experimental	10	22.68	7.46	81.00
	Control	10	14.95	9.73	53.39
Parallel Test	Experimental	10	27.03	1.43	96.54
	Control	10	21.73	8.67	77.61
Retention Test	Experimental	10	24.48	5.01	87.43
	Control	10	12.43	10.26	44.39

From the table 4.37 it can be seen that experimental group gained higher mean score in parallel test followed by retention test and post test. Control group is in the usual pattern – parallel, post and retention.

Table 4.38: Summary of ANCOVA of reading comprehension scores in post, parallel and retention tests of standard I higher level students with intellectual disability

Test	Source	Sum of squares	df	Mean square	F ratio
Post Test	Corrected Model	740.25[a]	2	370.13	6.91**
	Intercept	2101.25	1	2101.25	39.20**
	PreRcTotal	441.88	1	441.88	8.24**
	Between groups	370.13	1	370.13	6.91*
	Within groups	911.23	17	53.60	
	Total	8729.69	20		
	Corrected Total	1651.48	19		
a. R Squared =.448 (Adjusted R Squared =.383)					

(Table Contd…)

Parallel Test	Corrected Model Intercept PreRcTotal Between groups Within groups Total Corrected Total	279.67[a] 4918.03 139.22 167.55 556.02 12718.50 835.69	2 1 1 1 17 20 19	139.83 4918.03 139.22 167.55 32.71	4.28* 150.37** 4.26 5.12*
a. R Squared =.335 (Adjusted R Squared =.256)					
Retention test	Corrected Model Intercept PreRcTotal Between groups Within groups Total Corrected Total	1104.92[a] 2093.61 378.91 824.40 802.16 8715.13 1907.08	2 1 1 1 17 20 19	552.46 2093.61 378.91 824.40 47.19	11.71** 44.37** 8.03** 17.47**
a. R Squared =.579(Adjusted R Squared =.530)					

** Significant at 0.01 level * Significant at 0.05 level

The Summary of ANCOVA of total reading comprehension score in post, parallel and retention test of standard I higher level students is shown in table 4.38. In the post test the obtained F-ratio for the between groups is 6.91. This shows there is significant difference between the mean scores of experimental and control group at 0.05 level. This result reveals that the LRA was effective that the experimental group generalized the learned reading comprehension skills better than control group.

The F-ratio obtained in the parallel test is 5.12 which is significant at 0.05 level. This result also reveals the effect of LRA. In spite of the same content and method used for both groups experimental group acquired significantly high score in reading comprehension with the help of LRA.

The results of the retention test shows the mean difference between both groups is highly significant (F= 17.47 $p<0.01$) which again indicates the effectiveness of LRA that enabled the experimental group to gain high score of reading comprehension even after six months.

Table 4.39: Mean values, standard deviations and percentages of reading comprehension scores in post, parallel and retention tests of standard I lower level students with intellectual disability

(Maximum possible score is 28)

Test	Group	N	Mean	SD	Percentage
Post Test	Experimental	9	2.50	3.26	8.93
	Control	10	0.60	0.52	2.14
Parallel Test	Experimental	9	7.14	3.61	25.50
	Control	10	3.00	3.30	10.71
Retention Test	Experimental	9	3.89	4.65	13.89
	Control	10	0.30	0.48	1.07

Table 4.39 shows the mean values, standard deviation and percentages of reading comprehension scores of standard I Lower level students in post, parallel and retention tests.

Table 4.40: Summary of ANCOVA OF reading comprehension scores in post, parallel and retention tests of standard 1 lower level students with intellectual disability

Test	Source	Sum of squares	df	Mean square	F ratio
Post Test	Corrected Model	17.10[a]	1	17.10	3.33
	Intercept	45.52	1	45.52	8.85**
	PreRcTotal	0.00	0	0.00	
	Between groups	17.10	1	17.10	3.33
	Within groups	87.40	17	5.14	
	Total	147.25	19		
	Corrected Total	104.50	18		
a. R Squared =.164 (Adjusted R Squared =.114)					
Parallel Test	Corrected Model	81.14[a]	1	81.14	6.81*
	Intercept	486.93	1	486.93	40.88**
	PreRcTotal	0.00	0	0.00	
	Between groups	81.14	1	81.14	6.81*
	Within groups	202.51	17	11.91	
	Total	751.19	19		
	Corrected Total	283.66	18		
a. R Squared =.286 (Adjusted R Squared =.244)					
Retention test	Corrected Model	61.01[a]	1	61.01	5.93*
	Intercept	83.12	1	83.12	8.08**
	PreRcTotal	0.00	0	0.00	
	Between groups	61.01	1	61.01	5.93*
	Within groups	174.99	17	10.30	
	Total	312.00	19		
	Corrected Total	236.00	18		
a. R Squared =.259 (Adjusted R Squared =.215)					

** Significant at 0.05 level

Table 4.40 provides the summary of ANCOVA of total reading comprehension score in post, parallel and retention test of Standard I lower level students. In the post test the obtained F ratio (3.33) is not significant either at 0.01 level or at 0.05 level. This indicates the insignificance of mean scores between experimental and control groups. From this it can be concluded that even though there is mean score difference between both groups, LRA was not that much effective to get statistically significant difference in the ability for generalizing the learned skills.

In the parallel test the obtained F ratio is 6.81 and it is significant at 0.05 level. This significant mean difference reveals the effectiveness of LRA which enabled experimental group to obtain a higher reading comprehension score.

The obtained F-ratio in the retention test is also significant at 0.05 level. This significance in the difference of mean scores between experimental and control groups again indicate the effectiveness of LRA. With this approach students of experimental group maintained the literacy skills better than control group.

Table 4.41: Mean values, standard deviations and percentage of reading comprehension scores in post, parallel and retention tests of standard III students with intellectual disability

(Maximum possible score is 46)

Test	Group	N	Mean	SD	Percentage
Post Test	Experimental	10	38.18	10.32	83.00
	Control	9	33.22	4.98	72.21
Parallel Test	Experimental	10	41.28	5.51	89.74
	Control	9	39.03	4.64	84.85
Retention Test	Experimental	10	36.38	10.30	79.09
	Control	9	22.19	9.82	48.24

Table 4.41 gives the mean values, standard deviations and percentages of reading comprehension scores of standard III students in post, parallel and retention tests. It can be seen from the table that both group attained high percentage in parallel and post test. In retention test experimental group got high score while score of control group decreased.

Table 4.42: Summary of ANCOVA of reading comprehension scores in post, parallel and retention tests of standard III students with intellectual disability

Test	Source	Sum of squares	df	Mean square	F ratio
Post test	Corrected Model	560.72[a]	2	280.36	6.29**
	Intercept	4763.52	1	4763.52	106.95**
	PreRcTotal	44.52	1	444.52	9.98**
	Between groups	65.35	1	65.35	1.47
	Within groups	712.67	16	44.54	
	Total	25663.94	19		
	Corrected Total	1273.38	18		
a. R Squared =.440 (Adjusted R Squared =.370)					
Parallel Test	Corrected Model	176.40[a]	2	88.20	4.81*
	Intercept	7580.69	1	7580.69	413.60**
	PreRcTotal	152.48	1	152.48	8.32**
	Between groups	11.04	1	11.04	0.60
	Within groups	293.26	16	18.33	
	Total	31190.50	19		
	Corrected Total	469.66	18		
a. R Squared =.376 (Adjusted R Squared =. 298)					

(Table Contd...)

	Corrected Model	1623.97[a]	2	811.99	12.32**
	Intercept	2446.37	1	2446.37	37.11**
	PreRcTotal	671.45	1	671.45	10.19**
Retention test	Between groups	751.56	1	751.56	11.40**
	Within groups	1054.68	16	65.92	
	Total	19390.88	19		
	Corrected Total	2678.65	18		
a. R Squared =.606 (Adjusted R Squared =. 557)					

** Significant at 0.01 level.

Table 4.42 shows the summary of ANCOVA of total reading comprehension scores in post, parallel and retention test of standard III students. Even though the mean score is high for experimental group in post and parallel tests, this mean difference between both groups is not statistically significant. This means for the reading comprehension skills of standard III students, LRA did not influence the experimental group to gain a significant difference in the mean score. A close observation of the mean values reveal that both, experimental and control groups have high scores in post test and parallel test. That is both groups gained similarly from the intervention. This may be the reason for the lack of significant difference between the two groups. However, the ANCOVA prove a significantly higher performance of the experimental group than that of the control group in case of retention test. This better performance can be attributed to the effectiveness of LRA.

When analyzing the results of reading comprehension of standard I higher, standard I lower and standard III students, the following conclusions can be drawn. Applications of LRA was highly effective with standard I higher students because this approach enabled them to gain high reading comprehension score during acquisition stage, generalization stage and maintenance stage. For standard I lower level it was effective for acquiring the skills (parallel test) and maintaining the skills (retention test). For standard III students, effectiveness of LRA was clearly seen in maintaining the skills.

Findings of this study can be considered as very important in the area of special education. Many researchers (Westling, 1986; Katims, 2001) reported that reading comprehension as the weakest area of learning for children with intellectual disability. Since reading with meaning is the ultimate aim of reading instruction, this study will motivate educators to find creative activities to increase reading comprehension level of children with intellectual disability.

Table 4.43: Mean values and standard deviations of reading comprehension scores in pre, post, parallel and retention tests of standard I higher experimental and control groups

(Maximum possible score is 28)

Group	N	Mean	SD
Pre experimental	10	6.00	6.33
Post experimental	10	22.68	7.46
Parallel Experimental	10	27.03	1.43
Retention Experimental	10	24.48	5.09
Pre control	10	7.35	8.10
Post control	10	14.95	9.73
Parallel Control	10	21.73	8.67
Retention control	10	12.43	10.26

Table 4.43 shows the mean values and standard deviations of total reading comprehension scores of standard I higher experimental and control group in pre, post, parallel and retention tests. The score attainment pattern (from highest to lowest) for experimental group is parallel – retention – post – pre tests. For control group it is in the descending order of parallel – post – retention – pre tests.

Table 4.44: Summary of repeated ANOVA of reading comprehension scores in pre, post, parallel and retention tests of standard I higher experimental and control groups

Group	Source of variation	Sum of squares	df	Mean square	F ratio
	Between trials	2725.24	3	908.41	
Experimental	Between subjects	550.78	9		43.61**
	Error	562.46	27	20.83	
	Total	3838.48	39		
	Between trials	1072.31	3	357.44	
Control	Between subjects	2262.09	9		11.98**
	Error	805.60	27	29.84	
	Total	4140.00	39		

** Significant at 0.01 level

Table 4.44 shows the summary of repeated ANOVA of total reading comprehension scores in pre, post, parallel and retention tests of standard I higher experimental and control groups. The F-ratio obtained for experimental group is 43.61 and for control group is 11.98. Both values are significant at 0.01 level which indicates the presence of significant mean differences among various groups in both sets.

Table 4.45: LSD test for significance between pairs of mean scores of reading comprehension of standard I higher experimental group

Sl. No.	Pairs	Mean values	Mean difference
1.	Pre experimental	6.00	16.68**
	Post experimental	22.68	
2.	Pre experimental	6.00	21.03**
	Parallel experimental	27.03	
3.	Pre experimental	6.00	18.48**
	Retention experimental	24.48	
4.	Post experimental	22.68	4.35*
	Parallel experimental	27.03	
5.	Post Experimental	22.68	1.80
	Retention experimental	24.48	
6.	Parallel experimental	27.03	2.55
	Retention experimental	24.48	

** Significant at 0.01 level *Significant at 0.05 level

As shown in table 4.45 least significant difference test of pair wise comparisons of reading comprehension scores of standard I higher experimental group yielded significant difference at 0.01 level between the mean scores of first three pairs (pre-post, pre-parallel, and pre-retention) with higher mean values in post, parallel and retention tests respectively. Significant difference in the first three pairs (pre-post, pre-parallel and pre-retention) reveals that students learned, generalized, and maintained the reading comprehension skills. Significance in the post-parallel pair reveals students' generalization rate is lower than the content they learned directly in the classroom. The insignificance in the post- retention and parallel-retention ($p>0.05$) pairs indicates students were able to keep up their post test results after six months and also their retention score is close to parallel test score.

In the table 4.46 the test of least significant difference for paired comparisons for standard I higher control group yielded significant difference at 0.01 level between reading comprehension scores of the pre-post, pre-parallel and at 0.05 level between pre-retention with high mean values for post, parallel and retention tests respectively. This reveals the significant gain of scores in post, parallel and retention tests compared to the pre test. The significance in the mean score of post – parallel and parallel-retention indicates post test score and retention test score are farther than that of parallel test and thus generalization skills and maintenance skills in comprehension are low. The insignificance in post – retention pair means students maintained their post test score in the retention test that was conducted after 6 months.

Table 4.46: LSD test for significance between pairs of mean scores of reading comprehension of standard I higher control group

Sl. No.	Pairs	Mean values	Mean difference
1.	Pre control	7.35	7.60**
	Post control	14.95	
2.	Pre control	7.35	14.38**
	Parallel control	21.73	
3.	Pre control	7.35	5.08*
	Retention control	12.43	
4.	Post control	14.95	6.78**
	Parallel control	21.73	
5.	Post control	14.95	2.52
	Retention control	12.43	
6.	Parallel control	21.73	9.30**
	Retention control	12.43	

** Significant at 0.01 level *Significant at 0.05 level

Table 4.47: Mean values and standard deviations of reading comprehension scores in pre, post, parallel and retention tests of standard I lower experimental and control groups

(Maximum possible score is 28)

Group	N	Mean	SD
Pre experimental	9	0.00	0.00
Post experimental	9	2.50	3.26
Parallel Experimental	9	7.14	3.61
Retention Experimental	9	3.89	4.65
Pre control	10	0.00	0.00
Post control	10	0.60	0.52
Parallel Control	10	3.00	3.30
Retention control	10	0.30	0.48

Table 4.47 shows the mean values and standard deviations of reading comprehension scores of standard I lower level students in pre, post, parallel and retention tests. The pattern of score attained (from highest to lowest) for experimental group is parallel – retention – post- pre tests and for control group is parallel- post – retention- pre tests.

Table 4.48: Summary of repeated ANOVA of reading comprehension scores in pre, post, parallel and retention tests of standard I lower experimental and control groups

Group	Source of variation	Sum of squares	df	Mean square	F ratio
Experimental	Between trials	239.28	3	79.76	13.20**
	Between subjects	217.42	8		
	Error	144.98	24	6.04	
	Total	601.68	35		
Control	Between trials	56.48	3	18.83	7.18**
	Between subjects	31.73	9		
	Error	70.78	27	2.62	
	Total	158.99	39		

** Significant at 0.01 level

Table 4.48 shows summary of repeated ANOVA in which the F- ratio obtained for experimental group and control group are significant at 0.01 level. That is, there exists significant difference in mean reading comprehension scores of both the groups measured at various stages.

Table 4.49: LSD test for significance between pairs of mean scores of reading comprehension of standard I lower experimental group

Sl. No.	Pairs	Mean values	Mean difference
1.	Pre experimental	0.00	2.50*
	Post experimental	2.50	
2.	Pre experimental	0.00	7.14**
	Parallel experimental	7.14	
3.	Pre experimental	0.00	3.89**
	Retention experimental	3.89	
4.	Post experimental	2.50	4.64**
	Parallel experimental	7.14	
5.	Post Experimental	2.50	1.39
	Retention experimental	3.89	
6.	Parallel experimental	7.14	3.25**
	Retention experimental	3.89	

** Significant at 0.01 level *Significant at 0.05level

In the table 4.49, the test of least significant difference for paired comparisons for std I lower experimental group yielded significant difference at 0.01 level between reading comprehension scores of the following pairs – pre-parallel, pre-retention, post-parallel and parallel-retention. The first two pairs indicate in parallel and retention tests there is significant gain of scores compared to pre test. The post and retention test scores are not very close to parallel test score. The significant mean difference at 0.05 level of pre-post pair also indicate the gain of scores. The insignificance of post-retention pair shows after six months the experimental group gained a score that is close to post test.

Table 4.50: LSD test for significance between pairs of mean scores of reading comprehension of standard I lower control group

Sl. No.	Pairs	Mean values	Mean difference
1.	Pre control	0.00	0.60
	Post control	0.60	
2.	Pre control	0.00	3.00**
	Parallel control	3.00	
3.	Pre control	0.00	0.30
	Retention control	0.30	
4.	Post control	0.60	2.40**
	Parallel control	3.00	
5.	Post control	0.60	0.30
	Retention control	0.30	
6.	Parallel control	3.00	2.70**
	Retention control	0.30	

** Significant at 0.01 level

The test of least significant difference for paired comparisons for standard I lower control group yielded significant difference at 0.01 level between reading comprehension scores of the following pairs – pre-parallel, post-parallel and parallel-retention.

In the pre-parallel pair, the significance in the mean difference indicate students improved from pre test; post- parallel significant mean difference and higher mean score in parallel test reveals post test score is significantly lower than parallel test score; significance in parallel – retention pair and lower mean score in retention test reveals that maintenance score is much lower than acquisition score. The insignificance between the pairs – pre-post, pre-retention indicates there isn't much gain of scores in post test and retention test compared to pre test. Similarly the insignificance between post-retention pair indicates both scores are very close.

Table 4.51 shows the mean values and standard deviations of reading comprehension scores of standard III students in pre, post, parallel and retention tests. The pattern of score attainment (from highest – lowest) for experimental and control group is parallel - post –retention-pre-test scores.

Table 4.51: Mean values and standard deviations of reading comprehension scores in pre, post, parallel and retention tests of standard III experimental and control groups

(Maximum possible score is 46)

Group	N	Mean	SD
Pre experimental	10	17.68	14.23
Post experimental	10	38.18	10.32
Parallel Experimental	10	41.28	5.51
Retention Experimental	10	36.38	10.30
Pre control	9	14.94	7.444
Post control	9	33.22	4.98
Parallel Control	9	39.03	4.64
Retention control	9	22.19	9.82

Table 4.52: Summary of repeated ANOVA of reading comprehension scores in pre, post, parallel and retention tests of standard III experimental and control groups

Group	Source of variation	Sum of squares	df	Mean square	F ratio
Experimental	Between trials	3409.40	3	1136.47	24.24**
	Between subjects	2743.94	9		
	Error	1265.91	27	46.88	
	Total	7419.25	39		
Control	Between trials	3161.98	3	1053.99	69.24**
	Between subjects	1219.22	8		
	Error	365.33	24	15.22	
	Total	4746.53	35		

** Significant at 0.01 level

Table 4.52 presents summary of repeated ANOVA of standard III experimental and control groups in pre, post parallel and retention tests. The F- ratio obtained for experimental group and control group are significant at 0.01 level which indicates significant mean difference between various levels of reading comprehension scores in both the groups.

Table 4.53: LSD test for significance between pairs of mean scores of reading comprehension of standard III experimental group

Sl.No.	Pairs	Mean values	Mean difference
1.	Pre experimental	17.68	20.50**
	Post experimental	38.18	
2.	Pre experimental	17.68	23.60**
	Parallel experimental	41.28	
3.	Pre experimental	17.68	18.70**
	Retention experimental	36.38	
4.	Post experimental	38.18	3.10
	Parallel experimental	41.28	
5.	Post Experimental	38.18	1.80
	Retention experimental	36.38	
6.	Parallel experimental	41.28	4.90
	Retention experimental	36.38	

** Significant at 0.01 level

Table 4.53 shows that the test of least significant difference for paired comparisons of standard III experimental group yielded significant difference at 0.01 level between mean reading comprehension scores of the following pairs - pre-post, pre-parallel and pre-retention with higher mean score in post, parallel and retention tests respectively. This result indicates there is significant gain of scores in post, parallel and retention tests compared to pre test score. The insignificance in the mean score between the pairs – post-parallel and parallel-retention indicates post test (generalization) and retention test (maintenance) scores are close to parallel test score. The insignificance of post-retention reveals that students were able to keep up their reading comprehension abilities even after 6 months.

Table 4.54: LSD test for significance between pairs of mean scores of reading comprehension of standard III control group

Sl. No.	Pairs	Mean values	Mean difference
1.	Pre control	14.94	18.28**
	Post control	33.22	
2.	Pre control	14.94	24.09**
	Parallel control	39.03	
3.	Pre control	14.94	7.25**
	Retention control	22.19	
4.	Post control	33.22	5.81**
	Parallel control	39.03	
5.	Post control	33.22	11.03**
	Retention control	22.19	
6.	Parallel control	39.03	16.84**
	Retention control	22.19	

** Significant at 0.01 level

Table 4.54 shows the result of the least significance difference test of pair wise comparisons of reading comprehension scores of standard III control group. This test yielded significant difference at 0.01 level in all pairs. In the first three pairs – pre-post, pre-parallel and pre-retention, the students' gain of mean scores is significantly high compared to pre test score. The significance in the next two pairs – post-parallel, and post-retention, indicates the post test (generalization) and retention test (maintenance) scores are significantly lower than parallel test (based on content learned in the classroom) and post-test scores respectively. Result of parallel-retention pair reveals that the scores are significantly far apart, that is, the students of the control group were able to maintain only significantly less amount of the reading comprehension skills acquired from the class.

The results of the repeated ANOVA tests and the least significant difference test of pair wise comparisons of standard I higher, standard I lower and standard III students in reading comprehension development can be summarized as:

1. For experimental group of standard I higher, standard I lower and standard III, there are significant gain of scores in post, parallel and retention tests than that of the pretest score. For control group this gain can be seen in standard I higher and standard III, while for standard I lower it is seen in parallel test only. This gain of scores is the result of systematic instruction occurred in this study.
2. The similar parallel-post test score (acquisition and generalization) is seen in experimental group of standard III only. For other groups there is significant mean difference.
3. The similar parallel-retention tests (acquisition and maintenance) score is found in experimental groups of standard I higher and standard III. There is significant mean difference for other groups. This is the effect of LRA that experimental group kept these scores close to each other.
4. In case of post-retention comparison (generalization and maintenance) similar scores were obtained for all the pairs except the standard III control. For standard III control there is significant difference between these scores, with high mean score in post test which indicates decrease of maintenance scores.

EFFECT OF LITERACY RICH APPROACH IN THE DEVELOPMENT OF PHONOLOGICAL AWARENESS

This section deals with the analysis of effectiveness of Literacy Rich Approach in the development of phonological awareness in children with intellectual disability. The total phonological awareness score is calculated from the scores of sub skills in this section at standard I and standard III levels. Sub skills in standard I are: phoneme isolation, phoneme segmentation, phoneme deletion, phoneme categorization and word segmentation. In standard III phoneme categorization is the only skill. The details of the analysis are presented from tables 4.55-4.72.

Table 4.55: Mean values, standard deviations and percentages of phonological awareness scores in post, parallel and retention tests of standard I higher level students with intellectual disability

(Maximum possible score is 50)

Test	Group	N	Mean	SD	Percentage
Post Test	Experimental	10	44.10	6.40	88.20
	Control	10	38.40	7.41	76.80
Parallel Test	Experimental	10	41.80	8.90	83.60
	Control	10	43.20	4.83	86.40
Retention Test	Experimental	10	36.10	10.27	72.20
	Control	10	31.00	13.26	62.00

Table 4.55 shows the mean values, standard deviations and percentages of phonological awareness scores of standard I higher level students with intellectual disability in post, parallel and retention tests.

Table 4.56: Summary of ANCOVA of phonological awareness scores in post, parallel and retention tests of standard I higher level students with intellectual disability

Test	Source	Sum of squares	df	Mean	F ratio
Post test	Corrected Model	484.13[a]	2	229.07	6.86 **
	Intercept	6022.33	1	6022.33	180.37**
	PrePhTotal	295.68	1	295.68	8.86 **
	Between groups	135.09	1	135.09	4.05
	Within groups	567.62	17	33.39	
	Total	35057.00	20		
	Corrected Total	1025.75	19		
a. R Squared = .447(Adjusted R Squared = .382)					
Parallel Test	Corrected Model	469.91[a]	2	234.96	8.63 **
	Intercept	5886.67	1	5886.67	216.10 **
	PrePhTotal	460.11	1	460.11	16.89 **
	Between groups	20.18	1	20.18	0.74
	Within groups	463.09	17	27.24	
	Total	37058.00	20		
	Corrected Total	933.00	19		
a. R Squared = .504 (Adjusted R Squared= .445)					

(Table Contd...)

Retention Test	Corrected Model	1230.06[a]	2	615.03	7.31**
	Intercept	2164.23	1	2164.23	25.71**
	PrePhTotal	1100.01	1	1100.01	13.07**
	Between groups	85.84	1	85.84	1.02
	Within groups	1430.89	17	84.17	
	Total	25173.00	20		
	Corrected Total	2660.95	19		
a. R Squared = .462 (Adjusted R Squared= .399)					

Table 4.56 shows the summary of ANCOVA of phonological awareness in post, parallel and retention test of standard I higher level students. Even though experiment group got mean score higher than control group in post, parallel and retention tests, no statistically significant difference is found between the mean scores of these tests.

Table 4.57: Mean values, standard deviations and percentages of phonological awareness scores in post, parallel and retention tests of standard I lower level students with intellectual disability

(Maximum possible score is 50)

Test	Group	N	Mean	SD	Percentage
Post Test	Experimental	9	26.56	4.53	53.12
	Control	10	24.00	7.83	48.00
Parallel Test	Experimental	9	23.33	5.39	46.66
	Control	10	25.00	7.07	50.00
Retention Test	Experimental	9	26.33	8.72	52.66
	Control	10	19.10	7.39	38.20

Table 4.57 shows the means, standard deviations and percentages of phonological awareness scores of standard I lower level students in post, parallel and retention tests.

Table 4.58: Summary of ANCOVA of phonological awareness scores in post, parallel and retention tests of standard I lower level students with intellectual disability

Test	Source	Sum of squares	df	Mean	F ratio
Post test	Corrected Model	64.61[a]	2	32.31	0.76
	Intercept	6981.19	1	6981.19	163.65**
	PrePhTotal	33.68	1	33.68	0.79
	Between groups	43.53	1	43.53	1.02
	Within groups	682.55	16	42.66	
	Total	12823.00	19		
	Corrected Total	747.16	18		
a. R Squared = .086 (Adjusted R Squared = .028)					

(Table Contd...)

Parallel Test	Corrected Model	113.97[a]	2	56.98	1.57
	Intercept	5949.98	1	5949.98	163.80**
	PrePhTotal	100.80	1	100.80	2.78
	Between groups	2.48	1	2.48	0.07
	Within groups	581.20	16	36.33	
	Total	11832.00	19		
	Corrected Total	695.16	18		
a. R Squared = .164Adjusted R Squared= .059)					
Retention Test	Corrected Model	504.69[a]	2	252.34	4.80*
	Intercept	4689.74	1	4689.74	81.11**
	PrePhTotal	256.85	1	256.85	4.88*
	Between groups	345.78	1	345.78	6.57*
	Within goups	842.05	16	52.63	
	Total	10988.00	19		
	Corrected Total	1346.74	18		
a. R Squared = .375Adjusted R Squared= .297)					

* Significant at 0.05 level

Table 4.58 shows that there is no significant mean difference between the experimental and control groups in post test and parallel test. Whereas, the between groups F-ratio is significant at 0.05 level for the retention test. That is, there is significant difference between the experimental group and control group in the retention test scores. This indicates the effectiveness of LRA by which students of experimental group maintained the score after six months.

Table 4.59: Mean values, standard deviations and percentages of phonological awareness scores in post, parallel and retention tests of standard III students with intellectual disability

(Maximum possible score is 14)

Test	Group	N	Mean	SD	Percentage
Post Test	Experimental	10	13.20	1.14	94.29
	Control	9	12.44	2.13	88.85
Parallel Test	Experimental	10	13.20	1.03	94.29
	Control	9	11.67	2.74	83.36
RetentionTest	Experimental	10	14.00	0.00	100.00
	Control	9	12.44	3.09	88.86

Table 4.59 provides mean values, standard deviations and percentages of phonological awareness in post, parallel and retention test of standard III students. For this group of students there was only one item- phoneme categorization. Both groups of children acquired scores with high percentage. In all tests experimental group gained higher mean score than control group.

Table 4.60: Summary of ANCOVA of phonological awareness scores in post, parallel and retention tests of standard III students with intellectual disability

Test	Source	Sum of squares	df	Means square	F ratio
	Corrected Model	12.21[a]	2	6.12	2.55
	Intercept	291.37	1	291.37	121.67**
	PrePhTotal	9.51	1	9.51	3.97
Post Test	Between groups	1.46	1	1.46	0.61
	Within groups	38.32	16	2.40	
	Total	3184.00	19		
	Corrected Total	50.53	18		
a. R Squared = .242 (Adjusted R Squared = -.147)					
	Corrected Model	20.45[a]	2	14.72	4.59*
	Intercept	235.56	1	235.56	73.48**
	PrePhTotal	18.31	1	18.31	5.71*
Parallel Test	Between groups	7.40	1	7.40	2.31
	Within groups	51.29	16	3.21	
	Total	3037.00	19		
	Corrected Total	80.74	18		
a. R Squared = .365 (Adjusted R Squared = -.285)					
	Corrected Model	18.71[a]	2	9.36	2.17
	Intercept	326.06	1	326.06	75.64**
	PrePhTotal	7.25	1	7.25	1.68
Retention Test	Between groups	8.91	1	8.91	2.07
	Within groups	68.98	16	4.31	
	Total	34 30.00	19		
	Corrected Total	87.68	18		
a. R Squared = .213 (Adjusted R Squared = -.115)					

Table 4.60 shows that the mean score differences in all three tests were insignificant. A possible explanation for this result is that phoneme categorization task seems very simple for standard III children. Both groups acquired high scores in three tests. The usual conventional approach is adequate for the instruction of this skill.

While comparing the results of phonological awareness scores of standard I higher, standard I lower and standard III students it can be seen that there is not much variation between scores. Majority of students (both experimental and control) have developed high level of phonological awareness skills and they generalized it and maintained it. The conventional approach is enough for developing phonological awareness among students with intellectual disability.

Table 4.61: Mean values and standard deviations of phonological awareness scores in pre, post, parallel and retention tests of standard I higher experimental and control groups

(Maximum possible score is 50)

Group	N	Mean	SD
Pre experimental	10	16.80	11.28
Post experimental	10	44.10	6.40
Parallel Experimental	10	41.80	8.90
Retention Experimental	10	36.10	10.27
Pre control	10	15.60	8.28
Post control	10	38.40	7.41
Parallel Control	10	43.20	4.83
Retention control	10	31.00	13.26

Table 4:61 shows the mean values and standard deviations of phonological awareness scores of standard I higher experimental and control groups. The pattern of score attainment (from highest to the lowest) for experimental group is post- parallel- retention- and pre test scores. For control group it is parallel-post-retention and pre tests.

Table 4.62: Summary of repeated ANOVA of phonological awareness scores in pre, post, parallel and retention tests of standard I higher experimental and control groups

Group	Source of variation	Sum of squares	df	Mean square	F ratio
	Between trials	4611.40	3	1537.13	
Experimental	Between subjects	2184.90	9		41.83**
	Error	992.10	27	36.74	
	Total	7788.40	39		
	Between trials	4363.50	3	1454.50	
Control	Between subjects	1816.40	9		36.16**
	Error	1086.00	27	40.22	
	Total	7265.9	39		

** Significant at 0.01 level

Table 4.62 shows that the F-ratio obtained for both groups are significant at 0.01 level.

Table 4.63: LSD test for significance between pairs of mean scores of phonological awareness of standard I higher experimental group

Sl. No.	Pairs	Mean values	Mean difference
1.	Pre experimental	16.80	27.30**
	Post experimental	44.10	
2.	Pre experimental	16.80	25.00**
	Parallel experimental	41.80	
3.	Pre experimental	16.80	19.30**
	Retention experimental	36.10	
4.	Post experimental	44.10	2.30
	Parallel experimental	41.80	
5.	Post Experimental	44.10	8.00**
	Retention experimental	36.10	
6.	Parallel experimental	41.80	5.70*
	Retention experimental	36.10	

** Significant at 0.01 level * Significant at 0.05 level

As shown in the above table (4.63) the test of least significant difference for paired comparisons of standard I higher experimental group yielded significant difference at 0.01 level between phonological awareness scores of following pairs, pre-post, pre-parallel and pre retention. In all these pairs the significant difference with higher mean in post, parallel and retention tests respectively indicates that there is a significant gain of scores compared to pretest score. The insignificance of post-parallel pair indicates the closeness of post test scores to parallel tests, that is, students generalized the learned skills well. The significance in the mean score of the post-retention ($p<0.01$) and higher mean score in post test reveals that maintenance score was significantly lower than generalization score. The significance in the mean score of parallel-retention pair ($p<0.05$) and higher mean score in parallel test reveals that maintenance score was significantly lower than parallel test scores.

Table 4.64 shows that as in the case of experimental group here also in the first three pairs there is significant mean score difference, indicating gain of scores from pre test scores. Other findings are: parallel and post test scores are closer as no significant difference between mean scores was found. Post and retention scores are far apart that significance is found in their mean scores, and in parallel and retention scores significant mean difference was found which means that students were able to maintain only significantly less amount of the learned materials.

Table 4.64 LSD test for significance between pairs of mean scores of phonological awareness of standard I higher control group

Sl. No.	Pairs	Mean values	Mean difference
1.	Pre control	15.60	22.80**
	Post control	38.40	
2.	Pre control	15.60	27.60**
	Parallel control	43.20	
3.	Pre control	15.60	15.40**
	Retention control	31.00	
4.	Post control	38.40	4.80
	Parallel control	43.20	
5.	Post control	38.40	7.40*
	Retention control	31.00	
6.	Parallel control	43.20	12.20**
	Retention control	31.00	

** Significant at 0.01 level * Significant at 0.05 level

Table 4.65: Mean values and standard deviations of phonological awareness scores in pre, post, parallel and retention tests of standard I lower experimental and control groups

(Maximum possible score is 50)

Group	N	Mean	SD
Pre experimental	9	2.11	2.09
Post experimental	9	26.56	4.53
Parallel Experimental	9	23.33	5.39
Retention Experimental	9	26.33	8.72
Pre control	10	3.60	4.99
Post control	10	24.00	7.83
Parallel Control	10	25.00	7.07
Retention control	10	19.10	7.39

Table 4.65 shows the mean values and standard deviations of phonological awareness scores of standard I lower level experimental and control groups in pre, post, parallel and retention tests.

Table 4.66 shows that the F-ratios obtained for the experimental and control groups are 64.57 and 49.36 respectively and they are significant at 0.01 level. Hence, it can be concluded that the total phonological awareness scores of the standard I lower experimental and control group students at various levels of measurement differ significantly.

Table 4.66: Summary of repeated ANOVA of phonological awareness scores in pre, post, parallel and retention tests of standard I lower experimental and control groups

Group	Source of variation	Sum of squares	df	Mean square	F ratio
Experimental	Between trials	3721.64	3	1240.55	64.57**
	Between subjects	578.00	8		
	Error	461.11	24	19.21	
	Total	4760.75	35		
Control	Between trials	2935.48	3	978.49	49.36**
	Between subjects	1182.03	9		
	Error	535.28	27	19.83	
	Total	4652.79	39		

** Significant at 0.01 level

Table 4.67 LSD test for significance between pairs of mean scores of phonological awareness of standard I lower experimental group

Sl. No.	Pairs	Mean values	Mean difference
1.	Pre experimental	2.11	24.45**
	Post experimental	26.56	
2.	Pre experimental	2.11	21.22**
	Parallel experimental	23.33	
3.	Pre experimental	2.11	24.22**
	Retention experimental	26.33	
4.	Post experimental	26.56	3.23
	Parallel experimental	23.33	
5.	Post Experimental	26.56	0.23
	Retention experimental	26.33	
6.	Parallel experimental	23.33	3.00
	Retention experimental	26.33	

** Significant at 0.01 level

Table 4.67 shows the result of least significant difference test for paired comparisons of standard I lower experimental group. This yielded significant mean difference of phonological awareness scores in the following pairs- pre- post, pre- parallel and pre- retention which indicates the gain of scores from pre test scores. Other pairs have insignificant mean scores and it indicates that post, parallel and retention scores are not different. In other words the learned skills were generalized and maintained by experimental group of children with out much difference.

Table 4.68: LSD test for significance between pairs of mean scores of phonological awareness of standard I lower control group

Sl. No.	Pairs	Mean values	Mean difference
1.	Pre control	3.60	20.40**
	Post control	24.00	
2.	Pre control	3.60	21.40**
	Parallel control	25.00	
3.	Pre control	3.60	15.50**
	Retention control	19.10	
4.	Post control	24.00	1.00
	Parallel control	25.00	
5.	Post control	24.00	4.90*
	Retention control	19.10	
6.	Parallel control	25.00	5.90**
	Retention control	19.10	

** Significant at 0.01 level * Significant at 0.05 level

Table 4.68 shows the result of least significant difference test for pair wise comparisons of phonological awareness scores of standard I control group. Here all pairs except post-parallel have significant mean difference. The result in the first three pairs indicates that as usual the students gained significantly higher scores than the pre test scores. Insignificance in the post-parallel pair indicates that scores are very close that students generalized almost all acquired skills. Significance in the post-retention and parallel-retention pair with low mean score in retention test reveals that students were unable to maintain as much as they generalized and also were unable to maintain as much as they acquired.

Table 4.69: Mean values and standard deviations of phonological awareness scores in pre, post, parallel and retention tests of standard III experimental and control groups

(Maximum possible score is 14)

Group	N	Mean	SD
Pre experimental	10	8.40	3.24
Post experimental	10	13.20	1.14
Parallel Experimental	10	13.20	1.02
Retention Experimental	10	14.00	0.00
Pre control	9	7.56	3.21
Post control	9	12.44	2.13
Parallel Control	9	11.67	2.74
Retention control	9	12.44	3.09

Table 4.69 shows the mean values and standard deviations of phonological awareness scores of standard III experimental and control groups in pre, post, parallel and retention tests.

Table 4.70: Summary of repeated ANOVA of phonological awareness scores in pre, post, parallel and retention tests of standard III experimental and control groups

Group	Source of variation	Sum of squares	df	Mean square	F ratio
Experimental	Between trials	196.80	3	65.60	23.71**
	Between subjects	40.90	9		
	Error	74.70	27	2.77	
	Total	312.40	39		
Control	Between trials	148.31	3	49.44	13.57**
	Between subjects	167.22	8		
	Error	87.44	24	3.64	
	Total	402.97	36		

** Significant at 0.01 level

The result of the repeated ANOVA of phonological awareness scores of standard III experimental and control groups as shown in table 4.70 reveals that the F- ratio obtained for both groups are significant at 0.01 level.

Table 4.71: LSD test for significance between pairs of mean scores of phonological awareness of standard III experimental group

Sl. No.	Pairs	Mean values	Mean difference
1.	Pre experimental	8.40	4.80**
	Post experimental	13.20	
2.	Pre experimental	8.40	4.80**
	Parallel experimental	13.20	
3.	Pre experimental	8.40	5.60**
	Retention experimental	14.00	
4.	Post experimental	13.20	0.00
	Parallel experimental	13.20	
5.	Post Experimental	13.20	0.80
	Retention experimental	14.00	
6.	Parallel experimental	13.20	0.80
	Retention experimental	14.00	

** Significant at 0.01 level

Table 4.71 shows the result of the test of least significant difference for paired comparisons of standard III experimental groups. The test yielded significant mean difference at 0.01 level between the pairs pre-post, pre-parallel, and pre-retention. This indicates that the experimental group of students have scored significantly high in the post, parallel and retention tests than the pre test. No significant differences are obtained for the other three pairs compared, which means that the students were able to maintain as much as they acquired and generalized.

Table 4.72: LSD test for significance between pairs of mean scores of phonological awareness of standard III control group

Sl. No.	Pairs	Mean values	Mean difference
1.	Pre control	7.56	4.88**
	Post control	12.44	
2.	Pre control	7.56	4.11**
	Parallel control	11.67	
3.	Pre control	7.56	4.88**
	Retention control	12.44	
4.	Post control	12.44	0.77
	Parallel control	11.67	
5.	Post control	12.44	0.00
	Retention control	12.44	
6.	Parallel control	11.67	0.77
	Retention control	12.44	

** Significant at 0.01 level

Table 4.72 indicates significant mean difference between the following pairs: pre-post, pre-parallel and pre-retention. No significant mean difference was found between other pairs. The result can be explained as in the case of previous findings (Table 4.71): (1) there are significant gain of phonological awareness scores in the post test, parallel test and retention test compared to the score of pretest, (2) post test and retention test scores are close to parallel test score, and (3) post test score and retention test score are also very similar.

The repeated ANOVA results with least significant difference test for pair wise comparisons of phonological awareness scores of standard I higher, standard I lower and standard III students indicate the following:

1. Both experimental and control groups of standard I higher, standard I lower and standard III gained significantly more phonological awareness scores in post, parallel and retention tests compared to pretest score.

2. The closeness of parallel-post test scores is seen in both experimental and control groups of standard I higher, standard I lower and standard III.
3. The closeness of parallel-retention tests scores exists in experimental groups of standard I lower and standard III and control group of standard III.
4. The closeness of post-retention score is found in experimental groups of standard I lower and standard III and control group of standard III. Other groups differ significantly in their mean scores.

EFFECT OF LITERACY RICH APPROACH IN THE DEVELOPMENT OF READING FLUENCY

This section deals with the analysis of the effect of Literacy Rich Approach in the development of reading fluency in children with intellectual disability. The reading fluency score is calculated from the scores of sub skills in reading fluency in standard I and standard III. The sub skills in both levels include: two letter words, three letter words, long words, two word sentences, three word sentences, and paragraph.

The details of the analysis are presented from Tables 4.73-4.90.

Table 4.73: Mean values, standard deviations and percentages of reading fluency scores in post, parallel and retention tests of standard I higher level students with intellectual disability

(Maximum possible score is 1221)

Test	Group	N	Mean	SD	Percentage
Post Test	Experimental	10	367.40	197.20	30.09
	Control	10	278.30	136.17	22.79
Parallel Test	Experimental	10	447.80	179.94	36.67
	Control	10	322.80	150.90	26.44
Retention Test	Experimental	10	333.60	216.14	27.32
	Control	10	262.25	158.12	21.48

Table 4.73 shows the mean values, standard deviations and percentages of reading fluency scores in post, parallel and retention tests of standard I higher level students. In all tests experimental group got higher mean scores than control group.

Table 4.74 shows the summary of ANCOVA of total reading fluency scores in post, parallel and retention tests of standard I higher level students. The between groups F-ratio obtained for the post test (3.69) and retention test (0.83) are not significant either at 0.01 level or at 0.05 level which means there is no significant mean difference between experimental control groups. In other words the LRA did not significantly influence the experimental group in generalizing and maintaining learned fluency skills than that of the control group.

Table 4.74: Summary of ANCOVA of reading fluency scores in post, parallel and retention tests of standard I higher level students with intellectual disability

Test	Source	Sum of squares	df	Means square	F ratio
Post Test	Corrected Model	492062.25[a]	2	246031.13	68.84**
	Intercept	152096.63	1	152096.63	40.08**
	PrePhTotal	452368.20	1	452368.20	119.21**
	Between groups	13982.80	1	13982.80	3.69
	Within groups	64508.30	17	3794.61	
	Total	2641213.00	20		
	Corrected Total	556570.55	19		
a. R Squared = .884 (Adjusted R Squared = -.870)					
Parallel Test	Corrected Model	473112.77[a]	2	236556.39	39.66**
	Intercept	360631.89	1	360631.89	60.47**
	PrePhTotal	394987.77	1	394987.77	66.23**
	Between groups	41281.44	1	41281.44	6.92*
	Within groups	101391.43	17	5964.20	
	Total	3543626.00	20		
	Corrected Total	574504.20	19		
a. R Squared = .824 (Adjusted R Squared = -.803)					
RetentionTest	Corrected Model	570875.84[a]	2	285437.92	48.73**
	Intercept	72444.96	1	72444.96	12.37**
	PrePhTotal	545883.39	1	545883.39	93.19**
	Between groups	4837.81	1	4837.81	0.83
	Within groups	99579.92	17	5857.64	
	Total	2449517.00	20		
	Corrected Total	670455.75	19		
a. R Squared = .851(Adjusted R Squared = -.834)					

* Significant at 0.05 level

In the parallel test the between groups F-ratio is 6.92 and it is significant ($p<0.05$). This indicates that LRA was effective in the development of significantly higher fluency skills by the experimental group. It can be concluded that even though parallel test is based on the instructional content directly taught in the classroom, experimental group might have applied the LRA based abilities in the fluency test and acquired high score.

Table 4.75: Mean values, standard deviations and percentages of reading fluency scores in post, parallel and retention tests of standard I lower level students with intellectual disability

(Maximum possible score is 1221)

Test	Group	N	Mean	SD	Percentage
Post Test	Experimental	9	125.22	78.33	10.26
	Control	10	64.30	44.63	5.27
Parallel Test	Experimental	9	202.22	94.69	16.56
	Control	10	114.20	63.62	9.35
Retention Test	Experimental	9	89.44	95.46	7.33
	Control	10	29.00	24.52	2.38

Table 4.75 gives the mean values, standard deviations and percentages of reading fluency score in post, parallel and retention tests of standard I lower level students. It is clear from the table that experimental group gained higher mean scores than control group in all three tests.

Table 4.76: Summary of ANCOVA of reading fluency scores in post, parallel and retention tests of standard I lower level students with intellectual disability

Test	Source	Sum of squares	df	Means square	F ratio
Post Test	Corrected Model	32275.86[a]	2	16137.93	4.94*
	Intercept	41686.02	1	31686.02	12.75**
	PreFlTotal	14694.99	1	14694.99	4.50*
	Between groups	19208.63	1	19208.63	5.88*
	Within groups	52310.66	16	3269.42	
	Total	249476.00	19		
	Corrected Total	84586.53	18		
a. R Squared = .382 (Adjusted R Squared = -.304)					
Parallel Test	Corrected Model	49957.75[a]	2	24978.88	4.21*
	Intercept	162301.40	1	162301.40	27.37**
	PreFlTotal	13257.12	1	13257.12	2.24
	Between groups	38883.90	1	38883.90	6.56*
	Within groups	94890.04	16	5930.63	
	Total	606608.00	19		
	Corrected Total	144847.79	18		
a. R Squared = .345 (Adjusted R Squared = -.263)					
Retention Test	Corrected Model	47028.60[a]	2	23514.30	7.74**
	Intercept	3474.22	1	3474.22	1.14
	PreFlTotal	29722.40	1	29722.40	9.79**
	Between groups	19645.80	1	19645.80	6.47*
	Within groups	48591.82	16	3036.99	
	Total	158727.00	19		
	Corrected Total	95620.42	18		
a. R Squared = .492(Adjusted R Squared = -.428)					

* Significant at 0.05 level

Table 4.76 provides the summary of ANCOVA of total reading fluency scores in post, parallel and retention tests of standard I lower level students. In the post test the obtained F-ratio is 5.88. This means that there is significant mean difference between two groups at 0.05 level. This result indicates LRA was effective in generalizing learned reading fluency skills that experimental group got higher mean score than control group.

In the parallel test the obtained F ratio is 6.56. This again means that there is significant mean difference ($p<0.05$) between two groups. In spite of the same content and method used with both groups, experimental group developed reading fluency skills better than control groups.

In the retention the F ratio obtained is 6.47 which indicate a significant mean difference between both groups ($p<0.05$). This result also shows the effectiveness of LRA to maintain the learned reading fluency skills. The influence of LRA was carried on in the performance of experimental group that they gained significantly high score even after 6 months.

Table 4.77: Mean values, standard deviations and percentages of reading fluency scores in post, parallel and retention tests of standard III students with intellectual disability

(Maximum possible score is 2251)

Test	Group	N	Mean	SD	Percentage
Post Test	Experimental	10	1127.10	515.75	50.07
	Control	9	846.56	333.89	37.61
Parallel Test	Experimental	10	1213.10	539.49	53.89
	Control	9	910.89	340.46	40.47
Retention Test	Experimental	10	1148.60	533.61	51.03
	Control	9	835.00	303.45	37.09

The mean values, standard deviations and percentages of total reading fluency scores in post, parallel and retention tests of standard III students is given in table 4.77. From the test it can be seen that experimental group gained higher mean score than control group in all three tests.

Table 4.78 shows the summary of ANCOVA of total reading fluency scores in post, parallel and retention tests of standard III students. In the post test, the calculated between group F-ratio is 5.77. This means a significant mean difference ($p<0.05$) exists between experimental and control group. It can be concluded that the effect of LRA was high enough that experimental group gained a better generalization score than control group.

Table 4.78: Summary of ANCOVA of reading fluency scores in post, parallel and retention test of standard III students with intellectual disability

Test	Source	Sum of squares	df	Means square	F ratio
Post Test	Corrected Model	3482671.20[a]	2	1741335.60	158.30**
	Intercept	22032.74	1	22032.74	2.00
	PreFlTotal	3109857.17	1	3109857.17	282.71**
	Between groups	63511.86	16	63511.86	5.77*
	Within groups	176001.95	19	11000.12	
	Total	22440000.00	18		
	Corrected Total	3658673.16			
a. R Squared = .952 (Adjusted R Squared = .946)					
Parallel Test	Corrected Model	3615603.00[a]	2	1807801.50	79.51**
	Intercept	69431.58	1	69431.58	3.05
	PreFlTotal	3182979.84	1	3182.979.84	139.99**
	Between groups	86553.44	16	86553.44	3.81
	Within groups	363789.94	19	22736.87	
	Total	25730000.00	18		
	Corrected Total	3979392.95			
a. R Squared = .909 (Adjusted R Squared = .897)					
RetentionTest	Corrected Model	3429539.04[a]	2	1714769.52	81.75**
	Intercept	38243.27	1	38243.27	1.82
	PreFlTotal	2963694.49	1	2963694.49	141.29**
	Between groups	109428.23	16	109428.23	5.22*
	Within groups	335617.91	19	20976.12	
	Total	22770000.00	18		
	Corrected Total	3765156.95			
a. R Squared = .911 (Adjusted R Squared = .900)					

* Significant at 0.05 level

In the parallel test, although the experimental group obtained high mean score than control group, the mean difference is not statistically significant. In the retention test the mean difference between both groups is significant at 0.05 level. Therefore it can conclude that LRA did influence experimental group in maintaining reading fluency skills significantly more than that of the control group.

While analyzing the scores of reading fluency attained by standard I higher, standard I lower and standard III students in post, parallel and retention tests, the following points can be highlighted: Reading fluency test measures the speed and accuracy in reading. This actually is generalization of word, sentence and passage level reading. As the result shows significant mean difference in parallel test (standard I higher and lower), in post test (standard I lower and standard III) and in retention test (standard I lower and standard III), it can be concluded that even though LRA was not 100% effective, it was partially effective in developing, generalizing and maintaining reading fluency skills in children with intellectual disability.

Table 4.79: Mean values and standard deviations of reading fluency scores in pre, post, parallel and retention tests of standard I higher experimental and control groups

(Maximum possible score is 1221)

Group	N	Mean	SD
Pre experimental	10	174.70	148.98
Post experimental	10	367.40	197.20
Parallel Experimental	10	447.80	179.94
Retention Experimental	10	333.60	216.14
Pre control	10	143.80	123.13
Post control	10	278.30	136.17
Parallel Control	10	322.80	150.91
Retention control	10	262.90	158.12

Table 4.79 shows the mean values and standard deviations of total reading fluency scores of standard I higher level experimental and control group students in the pre, post, parallel and retention tests. The score attainment pattern from highest to lowest for both experimental and control group is parallel, post, retention and pre- test scores.

Table 4.80: Summary of repeated ANOVA of reading fluency scores in pre, post, parallel and retention tests of standard I higher experimental and control groups

Group	Source of variation	Sum of squares	df	Mean square	F ratio
Experimental	Between trials	394035.86	3	131345.29	51.31**
	Between subjects	4379130.63	9		
	Error	69120.88	27	2560.03	
	Total	4842287.37	39		
Control	Between trials	175303.70	3	58434.57	31.58**
	Between subjects	683331.90	9		
	Error	49960.30	27	1850.38	
	Total	908595.90	39		

** Significant at 0.01 level

Table 4.80 presents the summary of repeated ANOVA of reading fluency scores of standard I higher experimental and control groups in pre, post, parallel and retention tests. The obtained F-ratio for both groups are significant at 0.05 level which indicates that there is significant difference in the mean reading fluency scores at various levels of measurement for the both groups.

Table 4.81: LSD test for significance between pairs of mean scores of reading fluency of standard I higher experimental group

Sl. No.	Pairs	Mean values	Mean difference
1.	Pre experimental	174.70	192.70**
	Post experimental	367.40	
2.	Pre experimental	174.70	273.10**
	Parallel experimental	447.80	
3.	Pre experimental	174.70	158.90**
	Retention experimental	333.60	
4.	Post experimental	367.40	80.40**
	Parallel experimental	447.80	
5.	Post Experimental	367.40	33.80
	Retention experimental	333.60	
6.	Parallel experimental	447.80	114.20**
	Retention experimental	333.60	

** Significant at 0.01 level

In table 4.81 significant mean difference at 0.01 level can be seen in five pairs in pre-post, pre-parallel, pre-retention, post- parallel and parallel-retention pairs. The significant mean difference between first three pairs and higher mean scores in post, parallel and retention tests respectively indicate the gain of scores from pre test score. Students learned, generalized and maintained the reading fluency skills significantly more from the level measurement of the pre-test. The significance in post- parallel and parallel-retention pairs indicate that their generalization and retention scores are not as high as parallel test score. The insignificance in the mean score between post-retention pair indicates that students maintained their post test score in the retention test which was conducted after six months of intervention.

The result of the least significant difference test of pair wise comparisons of standard I higher control group in reading fluency skills is seen in table 4.82. Significant mean difference exists between all pairs except post-retention pair. The significant mean difference (at 0.01 level) between pre-post, pre-parallel and pre-retention pairs indicate that students gained scores highly compared to pretest scores. The significant difference at 0.05 level between post-parallel pair and at 0.01 level between parallel-retention pair indicate that students' generalization and maintenance scores are lower than parallel score. The insignificance in the post-retention pair indicates that students maintained their post test score after 6 months.

Table 4.82: LSD test for significance between pairs of mean scores of reading fluency of standard I higher control group

Sl. No.	Pairs	Mean values	Mean difference
1.	Pre control	143.80	134.50**
	Post control	278.30	
2.	Pre control	143.80	179.00**
	Parallel control	322.80	
3.	Pre control	143.80	119.10**
	Retention control	262.90	
4.	Post control	278.30	44.50*
	Parallel control	322.80	
5.	Post control	278.30	15.40
	Retention control	262.90	
6.	Parallel control	322.80	59.90**
	Retention control	262.90	

** Significant at 0.01 level * Significant at 0.05 level

Table 4.83: Mean values and standard deviations of reading fluency scores in pre, post, parallel and retention tests of standard I lower experimental and control groups

(Maximum possible score is 1221)

Group	N	Mean	SD
Pre experimental	9	12.11	11.04
Post experimental	9	125.22	78.33
Parallel experimental	9	202.22	94.69
Retention experimental	9	89.44	95.46
Pre control	10	13.40	15.09
Post control	10	64.30	44.63
Parallel control	10	114.20	63.62
Retention control	10	29.00	25.52

Table 4.83 shows the mean values and standard deviations of reading fluency scores of standard I lower experimental and control groups in post, parallel and retention tests. The score attainment pattern from highest to lowest for both experimental and control groups are parallel –post-retention-pre test scores.

Table 4.84: Summary of repeated ANOVA of reading fluency scores in pre, post, parallel and retention tests of standard 1 lower experimental and control groups

Group	Source of variation	Sum of squares	df	Mean square	F ratio
Experimental	Between trials	168400.53	3	56133.51	16.14**
	Between subjects	111224.00	9		
	Error	83458.22	24	3477.43	
	Total	363082.75	35		
Control	Between trials	59974.88	3	19991.63	19.80**
	Between subjects	34552.23	9		
	Error	27257.88	27	1009.55	
	Total	121784.99	39		

** Significant at 0.01 level

The summary of repeated ANOVA of reading fluency score of standard I lower experimental and control groups in pre, post, parallel and retention tests are shown in table 4.84. The F ratio obtained for both groups are significant at 0.01 level which indicate that there is significant mean difference between various groups in both sets.

Table 4.85: LSD test for significance between pairs of mean scores of reading fluency of standard 1 lower experimental group

Sl. No.	Pairs	Mean values	Mean difference
1.	Pre experimental	12.11	113.11**
	Post experimental	125.22	
2.	Pre experimental	12.11	190.11**
	Parallel experimental	202.22	
3.	Pre experimental	12.11	77.33*
	Retention experimental	89.44	
4.	Post experimental	125.22	77.00*
	Parallel experimental	202.22	
5.	Post Experimental	125.22	35.78
	Retention experimental	89.44	
6.	Parallel experimental	202.22	112.78**
	Retention experimental	89.44	

** Significant at 0.01 level * Significant at 0.05 level

The least significant difference test of pair wise comparisons of standard I lower experimental group in reading fluency skills is presented in table 4.85. Significant mean difference is found between all pairs except post-retention. The significant difference in the pairs pre-post, pre- parallel, pre retention indicates that there is significant gain in the mean scores of post, parallel, and retention tests when compared with pre test score. In post-parallel pair there is significant difference at 0.05 level and parallel–retention pair there is significant difference at 0.01 level. Both results indicate that students' generalization score and retention score are significantly lower than that of the parallel test score. The insignificant in post-retention pair shows the students that could not maintain the reading fluency skills as much as they generalized.

Table 4.86: LSD test for significance between pairs of mean scores of reading fluency of standard 1 lower control group

Sl No.	Pairs	Mean values	Mean difference
1.	Pre control	13.40	50.90**
	Post control	64.30	
2.	Pre control	13.40	100.80**
	Parallel control	114.20	
3.	Pre control	13.40	15.60
	Retention control	29.00	
4.	Post control	64.30	49.90**
	Parallel control	114.20	
5.	Post control	64.30	35.30*
	Retention control	29.00	
6.	Parallel control	114.20	85.20**
	Retention control	29.00	

** Significant at 0.01 level * Significant at 0.05 level

In the above table (4.86) the test of least significant difference of pair wise comparisons of standard I lower control group in reading fluency of post, parallel and retention tests yielded difference in all pairs except pre-retention pair. The significant difference in pre-post and pre-parallel pair indicates that there is significant gain of scores in post test and parallel test. That is compared to pre test level, the reading fluency and the ability to generalize has increased. The insignificance in pre-retention pair indicates that there is no significant difference between the level of reading fluency at the pretest level and at the retention test level. The significance in post-parallel and parallel-retention (at 0.01 level) indicates the generalization and maintenance scores are significantly lower than parallel test score likewise there is significant difference in post-retention score.

Table 4.87: Mean values and standard deviations of reading fluency scores in pre, post, parallel and retention tests of standard III experimental and control groups

(Maximum possible score is 2251)

Group	N	Mean	SD
Pre experimental	10	851.20	429.72
Post experimental	10	1127.10	515.75
Parallel experimental	10	1213.10	539.49
Retention experimental	10	1148.60	533.61
Pre control	9	810.78	287.61
Post control	9	846.56	333.88
Parallel control	9	910.89	340.46
Retention control	9	835.00	303.45

Table 4.87 shows mean values and standard deviations of reading fluency scores of standard 3 experimental and control groups in pre, post, parallel and retention tests. The score attainment pattern of experimental group is in the descending order of parallel-retention-post- pre tests and for control group is parallel-post-retention and pre tests.

Table 4.88: Summary of repeated ANOVA of reading fluency scores in pre, post, parallel and retention tests of standard III experimental and control groups

Group	Source of variation	Sum of squares	df	Mean square	F ratio
Experimental	Between trials	768894.20	3	256298.07	27.27**
	Between subjects	8984307.50	9		
	Error	253806.30	27	9400.23	
	Total	10007008.00	39		
Control	Between trials	188870.97	3	62956.99	12.42**
	Between subjects	3095948.89	8		
	Error	121623.78	24	5067.66	
	Total	3406443.64	35		

** Significant at 0.01 level

Table 4.88 shows the summary of repeated ANOVA of reading fluency scores of standard III experimental and control groups in pre, post, parallel and retention tests. The obtained F ratio for both groups is significant at 0.01 level which indicates that, significant mean difference between various groups exists in both sets.

Table 4.89: LSD test for significance between pairs of mean scores of reading fluency of standard III experimental group

Sl No.	Pairs	Mean values	Mean difference
1.	Pre experimental	851.20	275.90**
	Post experimental	1127.10	
2.	Pre experimental	851.20	361.90**
	Parallel experimental	1213.10	
3.	Pre experimental	851.20	297.40**
	Retention experimental	1148.60	
4.	Post experimental	1127.10	86.00
	Parallel experimental	1213.10	
5.	Post Experimental	1127.10	21.50
	Retention experimental	1148.60	
6.	Parallel experimental	1213.10	64.50
	Retention experimental	1148.60	

** Significant at 0.01 level

Table 4.89 shows that the mean scores between the pairs pre-post, pre-parallel and pre-retention are significant at 0.01 level. This indicates that the students' scores in post, parallel and retention test are significantly high compared to pre test scores. Students learned generalized and retained reading fluency skills. The insignificance in the mean scores of the pairs post-parallel, and parallel-retention indicate that the generalization (post test) and maintenance (retention) scores are as high as parallel test scores. The insignificance in post-retention pair indicates students maintained the post test scores after 6 months.

Table 4.90: LSD test for significance between pairs of mean scores of reading fluency of standard III control group

Sl. No.	Pairs	Mean values	Mean difference
1.	Pre control	710.78	135.78**
	Post control	846.56	
2.	Pre control	710.78	200.11**
	Parallel control	910.89	
3.	Pre control	710.78	124.22**
	Retention control	835.00	
4.	Post control	846.56	64.33
	Parallel control	910.89	
5.	Post control	846.56	11.56
	Retention control	835.00	
6.	Parallel control	910.89	75.89*
	Retention control	835.00	

** Significant at 0.01 level * Significant at 0.05 level

Table 4.90 shows that there is significant mean difference in the pairs pre-post pre–parallel, pre- retention and parallel-retention which indicates significant gain of scores from pre test score. The insignificance in post-parallel ,and post-retention pairs indicate that control group has gained generalization scores close to parallel test score and also their generalization and maintenance scores are close .

The repeated ANOVA results with least significant difference test of pair wise comparisons of reading fluency scores of standard I higher, standard I lower and standard III students can be summarized as follows:

1. Both experimental and control groups of children (except standard I lower control in retention test) gained high reading fluency scores in post, parallel and retention tests compared to pretest score (with significant mean difference at 0.01 level). This gain of scores is the result of systematic instruction given in this study.
2. The closeness of parallel-post test score (similar score in the acquisition and generalization levels) is found in standard III students (experimental and control). For other groups there are significant mean differences.
3. The closeness of parallel-retention tests (similar maintenance score as acquisition score, that is, without significant mean difference) exists only with standard III experimental students. Other groups have significant mean differences.
4. The similarity of post-retention score (similar maintenance score as generalization score, that is, without significant mean difference) is found in experimental groups of standard I higher, standard I lower and standard III as well as in control groups of standard I higher and standard III.

EFFECT OF LITERACY RICH APPROACH IN THE DEVELOPMENT OF WRITING SKILLS

This section deals with the effect of Literacy Rich Approach in the development of writing skills in children with intellectual disability. The total writing skill development is calculated from the scores attained by students in the following areas: word level writing and sentence level writing.

Word level writing for standard I includes: write dictated simple words, write dictated long words, make words with given letters, and fill blanks with given letters. For standard III skills included in word level writing are: write dictated words, write singular/plural, write related words, write gender, write past form of word, and write opposites.

Sentence level writing for standard 1 includes: copy sentences, write dictated sentences, sentence completion, and read paragraph and write answer to questions. For standard III skills included in sentence level writing are: use given word in a sentence, write positive answers, write negative answers, arrange words to make meaningful sentences, write on given topic, and read paragraph and write answer to questions.

The details of analysis are presented from Tables 4.91-4.108.

Table 4.91: Mean values, standard deviations and percentages of writing scores in post, parallel and retention tests of standard 1 higher level students with intellectual disability

(Maximum possible score is 99)

Test	Group	N	Mean	SD	Percentage
Post Test	Experimental	10	67.15	8.63	67.83
	Control	10	49.23	14.87	49.73
Parallel Test	Experimental	10	78.30	13.05	79.10
	Control	10	75.90	18.57	76.67
RetentionTest	Experimental	10	74.00	8.38	74.75
	Control	10	54.08	17.75	54.63

The mean values, standard deviations and percentages of writing scores of standard I higher level students in post, parallel and retention tests is presented in table 4.91. From the table it can be seen that in the three tests experimental group obtained high mean scores than control group. Both groups got high mean scores in parallel test followed by retention test and lowest score in the post test.

Table 4.92: Summary of ANCOVA of writing scores in post, parallel and retention tests of standard I higher level students with intellectual disability

Test	Source	Sum of squares	df	Mean square	F ratio
Post test	Corrected Model	3032.57[a]	2	1516.29	20.91**
	Intercept	2460.12	1	2460.12	33.92**
	PreWrTotal	1426.05	1	1426.05	19.66**
	Between groups	2375.69	1	2375.69	32.75**
	Within groups	1233.04	17	72.53	
	Total	71981.31	20		
	Corrected Total	4265.61	19		
a. R Squared =.711 (Adjusted R Squared=.677)					
Parallel Test	Corrected Model	3436.93[a]	2	1718.47	23.76**
	Intercept	3345.38	1	3345.38	46.25**
	PreWrTotal	3408.13	1	3408.13	47.12**
	Between groups	433.77	1	433.77	6.00*
	Within groups	1229.62	17	72.33	
	Total	123554.75	20		
	Corrected Total	4666.55	19		
a. R Squared =.737 (Adjusted R Squared=.706)					

(Table Contd...)

Retention test	Corrected Model	4183.53[a]	2	2091.77	28.05**
	Intercept	2455.38	1	2455.38	32.93**
	PreWrTotal	2198.51	1	2198.51	29.48**
	Between groups	3079.88	1	3079.88	41.30**
	Within groups	1267.75	17	74.57	
	Total	87467.31	20		
	Corrected Total	5451.28	19		

[a.] R Squared =.767 (Adjusted R Squared=.740)

** Significant at 0.01 level * Significant at 0.05 level

The summary of ANCOVA of writing scores of standard I higher level students in post, parallel and retention tests is shown in table 4.92. In the post test the obtained between groups F-ratio (32.75) is much higher than that of the table value. This indicates that there is significant difference ($p<0.01$) between the mean scores of both groups. In other words LRA was highly effective that experimental group acquired significantly high generalization score in writing than control group.

In the parallel test the obtained F-ratio is 6.00 which is significant ($p<0.05$) and indicates that in spite of the common parallel content and instructional method used, experimental group gained high score in writing with the help of LRA than control group.

The calculated F-ratio in the retention test (41.30) is also higher than the table value which shows significantly high mean difference between experimental and control groups. This reveals that LRA was highly effective in the maintenance of writing skills developed by experimental group than that of control group.

Table 4.93: Mean values, standard deviations and percentages of writing scores in post, parallel and retention tests of standard I lower level students with intellectual disability

(Maximum possible score is 99)

Test	Group	N	Mean	SD	Percentage
Post Test	Experimental	9	42.78	11.40	43.21
	Control	10	30.78	8.45	31.10
Parallel Test	Experimental	9	53.50	21.36	54.04
	Control	10	40.78	11.96	41.19
Retention Test	Experimental	9	43.44	8.14	43.88
	Control	10	20.15	6.86	20.35

Table 4.93 shows the mean values, standard deviations and percentages of writing scores of standard I lower level students in post, parallel and retention tests. In all the three tests experimental group gained high mean scores than control group.

Table 4.94: Summary of ANCOVA of writing scores in post, parallel and retention tests of standard I lower level students with intellectual disability

Test	Source	Sum of squares	df	Mean square	F ratio
Post test	Corrected Model	1008.15[a]	2	504.07	5.95**
	Intercept	1403.52	1	1403.52	16.56**
	PreWrTotal	325.73	1	325.73	3.84
	Between groups	621.21	1	621.21	7.33*
	Within groups	1356.39	16	84.77	
	Total	27622.56	19		
	Corrected Total	2364.53	18		
a. R Squared = .426 (Adjusted R Squared = .355)					
Parallel Test	Corrected Model	2058.54[a]	2	1029.27	4.52*
	Intercept	1294.28	1	1294.28	5.68*
	PreWrTotal	1291.53	1	1291.53	5.67*
	Between groups	642.95	1	642.96	2.82
	Within groups	3645.78	16	227.86	
	Total	47323.56	19		
	Corrected Total	5704.32	18		
a. R Squared = .361 (Adjusted R Squared = .281)					
Retention test	Corrected Model	3056.44[a]	2	1528.22	52.23**
	Intercept	693.39	1	693.39	23.70**
	PreWrTotal	486.09	1	486.09	16.61**
	Between groups	2420.25	1	2420.25	82.72**
	Within groups	468.16	16	29.26	
	Total	22001.25	19		
	Corrected Total	3524.61	18		
a. R Squared = .867 (Adjusted R Squared = .851)					

** Significant at 0.01 level * Significant at 0.05 level

The summary of ANCOVA of writing score of standard I lower level students in post, parallel and retention tests are presented in table 4.94. In the post test the obtained F-ratio is 7.33 and this means there is significant difference ($p<0.05$) between the mean scores of experimental and control groups. This indicates the effectiveness of LRA that experimental group obtained high generalization score than control group.

In the parallel test even though there is difference between mean scores of both groups it not statistically significant either at 0.01 level or at 0.05 level. Thus it can be concluded that the effect of LRA was not found in the results. However, in the retention test the value of F-ratio (82.72) revealed that the mean difference between both groups is highly significant. In other words, with the help of LRA experimental group was able to maintain the learned writing skills even six months after intervention.

Table 4.95: Mean values, standard deviations and percentages of writing scores in post, parallel and retention tests of standard III students with intellectual disability

(Maximum possible score is 90)

Test	Group	N	Mean	SD	Percentage
Post Test	Experimental	10	68.83	14.48	76.48
	Control	9	60.25	15.59	66.94
Parallel Test	Experimental	10	74.80	14.31	83.11
	Control	9	70.11	14.93	77.95
Retention Test	Experimental	10	68.70	15.91	76.33
	Control	9	54.75	21.41	60.83

Table 4.95 provides the mean values, standard deviations and percentages of writing scores of standard III students in post, parallel and retention tests. In all three tests experimental group gained high mean score than control group.

Table 4.96: Summary of ANCOVA of writing scores in post, parallel and retention tests of standard III students with intellectual disability

Test	Source	Sum of squares	df	Mean square	F ratio
Post test	Corrected Model	3542.40 [a]	2	1771.20	44.32**
	Intercept	7489.63	1	7489.63	187.41**
	PreWrTotal	3194.09	1	3194.09	79.93**
	Between groups	158.33	1	158.33	3.96
	Within Groups	639.41	16	39.96	
	Total	83872.88	19		
	Corrected Total	4181.81	18		
a. R Squared =.847 (adjusted R Squared =.828)					
Parallel Test	Corrected Model	2533.35[a]	2	1266.67	16.92**
	Intercept	12001.98	1	12001.98	160.31**
	PreWrTotal	2429.21	1	2429.21	32.45**
	Between groups	24.37	1	24.37	0.33
	Within Groups	1197.91	16	74.87	
	Total	103817.63	19		
	Corrected Total	3731.26	18		
a. R Squared =.679 (adjusted R Squared =.639)					
Retention test	Corrected Model	5265.66 [a]	2	2632.83	26.31**
	Intercept	5241.51	1	5241.51	52.38**
	PreWrTotal	4343.86	1	4343.86	43.41**
	Between groups	539.30	1	539.30	5.39*
	Within Groups	1601.11	16	100.07	
	Total	80119.94	19		
	Corrected Total	6866.78	18		
a. R Squared =.767 (adjusted R Squared =.738)					

* Significant at 0.05 level

Table 4.96 shows the summary of ANCOVA of writing scores of standard III students in post, parallel and retention tests. The obtained F-ratio (3.96) in post test is less than that of the table value at 0.05 level. This means the mean difference between both groups is not statistically significant. Similarly in the parallel test the F-ratio calculated is very low (0.33). Here also no significant mean difference exists. From the results of above two tests it can be concluded that the LRA was not effective in writing skill development and it's generalization.

The F-ratio obtained in retention test is 5.39 and it is significant ($p<0.05$). This indicates the mean difference between two groups. Here the effect of LRA is evident in the maintenance of writing skills developed by experimental group than that of control group.

From the analysis of results of the writing skills of standard I higher, standard I lower and standard III the following points can be highlighted: The effects of LRA in writing skill development is clearly seen in standard I higher level students in acquisition (parallel test), generalization (post test) and maintenance (retention test) stages. With the standard I lower level, this effect can be seen in generalization and maintenance stages. In the case of standard III students in post and parallel tests no LRA effect was found. However, as shown in retention test, experimental group maintained the writing skills better than control group and thus influence of LRA was clearly expressed.

Table 4.97: Mean values and standard deviations of writing scores in pre, post, parallel and retention tests of standard1 higher level experimental and control groups

(Maximum possible score is 99)

Group	N	Mean	SD
Pre experimental	10	34.85	10.86
Post experimental	10	67.15	8.63
Parallel experimental	10	78.30	13.05
Retention experimental	10	73.90	8.50
Pre control	10	42.30	16.73
Post control	10	49.23	14.87
Parallel control	10	75.90	18.57
Retention control	10	54.08	17.75

Table 4.97 shows the mean values and standard deviations of writing scores of standard I higher experimental and control groups in pre, post, parallel and retention tests.

Table 4.98 Summary of repeated ANOVA of writing scores in pre, post, parallel and retention tests of standard1 higher experimental and control groups

Group	Source of variation	Sum of squares	df	Mean square	F ratio
	Between trials	11613.35	3	3871.12	
Experimental	Between subjects	2917.87	9		104.72**
	Error	998.06	27	36.97	
	Total	15529.28	39		
	Between trials	6317.44	3	2105.81	
Control	Between subjects	9436.97	9		56.31**
	Error	1009.72	27	37.40	
	Total	16764.13	39		

** Significant at 0.01 level

The summary of ANOVA of writing score of standard I higher experimental and control groups in pre, post parallel and retention tests are shown in table 4.98. The F ratio obtained for experimental groups is 104.72 and for control group is 56.31. Both values are significant at 0.01 level.

Table 4.99: LSD test for significance between pairs of mean scores of writing skills of standard I higher experimental group

Sl. No.	Pairs	Mean values	Mean difference
1.	Pre experimental	34.85	32.30**
	Post experimental	67.15	
2.	Pre experimental	34.85	43.45**
	Parallel experimental	78.30	
3.	Pre experimental	34.85	39.05**
	Retention experimental	73.90	
4.	Post experimental	67.15	11.15**
	Parallel experimental	78.30	
5.	Post Experimental	67.15	6.75*
	Retention experimental	73.90	
6.	Parallel experimental	78.30	4.40
	Retention experimental	73.90	

** Significant at 0.01 level * Significant at 0.05 level

The result of LSD test (Table 4.99) shows significant mean difference between all pairs except parallel-retention pair. The significance of mean difference (p<0.01) between the pairs pre-post, pre-parallel and pre-retention and higher mean scores in post, parallel and retention tests respectively indicate improvement of students from the pre test scores.

The significant mean difference of post-parallel pair with higher mean in parallel test reveals that post test performance (generalization) is lower than parallel test score. The significant mean difference ($p<0.05$) in the post-retention pair and higher retention mean score indicates that the students of experimental group were able to retain more writing skills than they generalized. The insignificance in the parallel-retention pair denotes students' retention score is almost close to parallel test score.

Table 4.100: LSD test for significance between pairs of mean scores of writing skills of standard I higher control group

Sl. No.	Pairs	Mean values	Mean difference
1.	Pre control	42.30	6.93*
	Post control	49.23	
2.	Pre control	42.30	33.60**
	Parallel control	75.90	
3.	Pre control	42.30	11.78**
	Retention control	54.08	
4.	Post control	49.23	26.67**
	Parallel control	75.90	
5.	Post control	49.23	4.85
	Retention control	54.08	
6.	Parallel control	75.90	21.82**
	Retention control	54.08	

** Significant at 0.01 level * Significant at 0.05 level

The table 4.100 shows significant mean difference of the pairs pre-post ($p<0.05$), pre-parallel and pre-retention ($p<0.01$) which reveals that there is gain of score in post, parallel and retention tests compared to pretest scores. The significance in the pairs post- parallel and parallel – retention tests with high mean score in parallel test reveals that the post test (generalization) and retention (maintenance) scores are much lower than parallel test score. Insignificance in the post -retention pair indicates that post test and retention test scores are very close.

Table 4.101 shows the mean values and standard deviations of writing scores of standard I lower experimental and control groups in pre, post, parallel and retention tests. The pattern of score attainment for experimental group is in the descending order of parallel-retention-post-pre test scores and for control group is parallel-post-retention-pre test scores.

Table 4.101: Mean values and standard deviations of writing scores in pre, post, parallel and retention tests of standard I lower level experimental and control groups

(Maximum possible score is 99)

Group	N	Mean	SD
Pre experimental	9	16.36	5.83
Post experimental	9	42.78	11.40
Parallel experimental	9	53.50	21.36
Retention experimental	9	43.44	8.14
Pre control	10	15.63	6.34
Post control	10	30.78	8.45
Parallel control	10	40.78	11.96
Retention control	10	20.15	6.86

Table 4.102: Summary of repeated ANOVA of writing scores in pre, post, parallel and retention tests of standard I lower experimental and control groups

Group	Source of variation	Sum of squares	df	Mean square	F ratio
	Between trials	6811.13	3	2270.38	
Experimental	Between subjects	3471.22	9		29.98**
	Error	2019.82	24	84.16	
	Total	12302.17	35		
	Between trials	3802.01	3	1267.34	
Control	Between subjects	1510.38	9		28.38**
	Error	1205.92	27	44.66	
	Total	6518.31	39		

** Significant at 0.01 level

Table 4.102 shows the summary of repeated ANOVA of writing scores in pre, post, parallel and retention tests of standard I lower experimental and control groups. The F-ratio obtained for experimental and control groups are 29.98 and 28.38 respectively. Both values are significant at 0.01 level.

As shown in the table 4.103 the least significant difference test for paired comparison yielded significant difference of mean scores at 0.01 level between the writing scores of pre-post, pre-parallel and pre-retention pairs. This result indicates that students of experimental group gained higher scores compared to pre test scores. The significant mean difference of post-parallel pair indicates that the students were unable to generalize to the extent that they acquired. The insignificance in post –retention pair reveals that the students were successfully maintained whatever writing skills they have generalized. However, the significance in the parallel-retention pair reveals that the students were not able to maintain the skills to the extent that they acquired.

Table 4.103: LSD test for significance between pairs of mean scores of writing of standard I lower experimental group

Sl. No.	Pairs	Mean values	Mean difference
1.	Pre experimental	16.36	26.42**
	Post experimental	42.78	
2.	Pre experimental	16.36	37.14**
	Parallel experimental	53.50	
3.	Pre experimental	16.36	27.08**
	Retention experimental	43.44	
4.	Post experimental	42.78	10.72*
	Parallel experimental	53.50	
5.	Post Experimental	42.78	0.66
	Retention experimental	43.44	
6.	Parallel experimental	53.50	10.06*
	Retention experimental	43.44	

** Significant at 0.01 level * Significant at 0.05 level

Table 4.104: LSD test for significance between pairs of mean scores of writing of standard I lower control group

Sl. No.	Pairs	Mean values	Mean difference
1.	Pre control	15.63	15.15**
	Post control	30.78	
2.	Pre control	15.63	25.15**
	Parallel control	40.78	
3.	Pre control	15.63	4.52
	Retention control	20.15	
4.	Post control	30.78	10.00**
	Parallel control	40.78	
5.	Post control	30.78	10.63**
	Retention control	20.15	
6.	Parallel control	40.78	20.63**
	Retention control	20.15	

** Significant at 0.01 level

Table 4.104 shows that the LSD test yielded significant difference of mean scores at 0.01 level for all pairs except pre-retention. The significance in the pairs pre-post and pre-parallel indicates the gain of scores from pre test score. The insignificance in the pre-retention pair means that students' maintenance score of writing is very low (near to pre test score). The significance in post-parallel and parallel-retention pairs indicates post and retention scores are lower compared to parallel test score. The significance in post-retention test score indicates these two scores are far apart and students did not maintain the post test score in the retention test.

Table 4.105: Mean values and standard deviations of writing scores in pre, post, parallel and retention tests of standard III experimental and control groups

(Maximum possible score is 90)

Group	N	Mean	SD
Pre experimental	10	39.50	23.23
Post experimental	10	68.83	14.28
Parallel experimental	10	74.80	14.31
Retention experimental	10	68.70	15.90
Pre control	9	35.11	20.04
Post control	9	60.25	15.59
Parallel control	9	70.11	14.93
Retention control	9	54.75	21.41

Table 4.105 shows the mean values and standard deviations of writing scores of standard 3 experimental and control groups in pre, post, parallel and retention tests. The score attainment pattern of both group is in the descending order of parallel-post-retention and pretest score.

Table 4.106: Summary of repeated ANOVA of writing scores in pre, post, parallel and retention tests of standard III experimental and control groups

Group	Source of variation	Sum of squares	df	Mean square	F ratio
Experimental	Between trials	7579.03	3	2526.34	53.34**
	Between subjects	9611.41	9		
	Error	1255.17	27	46.49	
	Total	18445.61	39		
Control	Between trials	5863.74	3	1954.58	37.41**
	Between subjects	9356.48	9		
	Error	1253.80	24	52.24	
	Total	16474.02	35		

** Significant at 0.01 level

Table 4.106 shows the summary of repeated ANOVA of writing score of standard III experimental and control groups in pre, post, parallel and retention tests. The F- ratio obtained for both groups is significant at 0.01 level.

Table 4.107: LSD test for significance between pairs of mean scores of writing skills of standard III experimental group

Sl. No.	Pairs	Mean values	Mean difference
1.	Pre experimental	39.50	29.33**
	Post experimental	68.83	
2.	Pre experimental	39.50	35.30**
	Parallel experimental	74.80	
3.	Pre experimental	39.50	29.20**
	Retention experimental	68.70	
4.	Post experimental	68.83	5.97
	Parallel experimental	74.80	
5.	Post Experimental	68.83	0.13
	Retention experimental	68.70	
6.	Parallel experimental	74.80	6.10
	Retention experimental	68.70	

** Significant at 0.01 level

Table 4.107 shows the result of multiple comparison of standard III experimental group using the test LSD test and this yielded significant difference at 0.01 level between the mean scores of writing skills of the pairs pre-post, pre-parallel and pre-retention. This result indicates students gained high scores in post, parallel and retention test compared to pretest scores. The insignificance in the pairs post-parallel and parallel-retention indicates that the post test and retention test scores are similar or close to that of the parallel test. That is, students' generalization and maintenance skills are as similar as the content they learned in the classroom. The insignificance in the post – retention pair indicates students maintained their post test score after 6 months of intervention.

Table 4.108: LSD test for significance between pairs of mean scores of writing skills of standard III control group

Sl. No.	Pairs	Mean values	Mean difference
1.	Pre control	35.11	25.14**
	Post control	60.25	
2.	Pre control	35.11	35.00**
	Parallel control	70.11	
3.	Pre control	35.11	9.64**
	Retention control	54.75	
4.	Post control	60.25	9.86**
	Parallel control	70.11	
5.	Post control	60.25	5.50
	Retention control	54.75	
6.	Parallel control	70.11	15.36**
	Retention control	54.75	

** Significant at 0.01 level

Table 4.108 shows the test of least significant difference for pair wise comparison of writing scores in standard III control group. This yielded significant difference in the mean scores at 0.01 level between all pairs except post-retention. The significance in pre-post, pre-parallel and pre retention pairs indicate that students gained high scores in post, parallel and retention tests compared to pretest score. The significance in post-parallel and parallel- retention pairs with high mean score in parallel test indicates their post test (generalization) and retention test (maintenance) scores are lower compared to parallel test score. The insignificance in the post-retention pair indicates that students maintained their post test score in the retention test which is conducted after 6 months of intervention.

The repeated ANOVA results with least significant difference test of pair wise comparisons of writing scores of standard I higher, standard i lower and standard III students can be summarized as follows:

1. Both experimental and control groups of children (except standard I lower control in retention test) obtained high writing scores in post, parallel and retention tests compared to pretest score (with significant mean difference at 0.01 level). This gain of scores is the result of systematic instruction given in this study.
2. The closeness of parallel-post test score (similar generalization score as acquisition score, that is, without significant mean difference) exists in standard III experimental group only. Other groups have significant mean difference.
3. The closeness of parallel-retention tests (similar maintenance score as acquisition score, that is, without significant mean difference) is found with experimental groups of standard I higher and standard III. Other groups have significant mean difference. This may be due to the influence of LRA.
4. The closeness of post-retention score (similar maintenance score as generalization score, that is, without significant mean difference) exists in experimental groups of standard I lower and standard III and control groups of standard I higher and standard III.

Summary, Conclusions and Suggestions

STUDY IN BRIEF

The present study has been designed to find out effect of Literacy Rich Approach (LRA) in the language development of children with intellectual disability. The study explores the effect of LRA in development of reading vocabulary, reading comprehension, phonological awareness, reading fluency, and writing skills. The objectives, hypotheses, methodology followed and major findings are given below.

OBJECTIVES

1. To find out the effect of literacy – rich approach in the vocabulary development of children with intellectual disability.
2. To compare the vocabulary scores of children with intellectual disability of the control and experimental groups in pre, post, parallel, and retention tests.
3. To find out the effect of literacy – rich approach in developing reading comprehension in children with intellectual disability.
4. To compare the reading comprehension scores of children with intellectual disability of the control and experimental groups in pre, post, parallel, and retention tests.
5. To find out the effect of literacy – rich approach in the phonological awareness of children with intellectual disability.
6. To compare the phonological awareness scores of children with intellectual disability of the control and experimental groups in pre, post, parallel, and retention tests.
7. To find out the effect of literacy – rich approach in developing reading fluency in children with intellectual disability.

8. To compare the reading fluency scores of children with intellectual disability of the control and experimental groups in pre, post, parallel, and retention tests.
9. To find out the effect of literacy – rich approach in the development of writing skills of children with intellectual disability
10. To compare the writing Skill scores of children with intellectual disability of the control and experimental groups in pre, post, parallel, and retention tests.

HYPOTHESES

The following major research hypotheses are stated:

1. There will be significant difference between the experimental and control groups in vocabulary development.
2. There will be significant difference among the vocabulary scores of children with intellectual disability of the control and experimental groups in pre, post, parallel and retention tests.
3. There will be significant difference between the experimental and control groups in developing reading comprehension.
4. There will be significant difference among the reading comprehension scores of children with intellectual disability of the control and experimental groups in pre, post, parallel and retention tests.
5. There will be significant difference between the experimental and control groups in developing phonological awareness.
6. There will be significant difference among the phonological awareness scores of children with intellectual disability of the control and experimental groups in pre, post, parallel and retention tests.
7. There will be significant difference between the experimental and control groups in developing reading fluency.
8. There will be significant difference among the reading fluency scores of children with intellectual disability of the control and experimental groups in pre, post, parallel and retention tests.
9. There will be significant difference between the experimental and control groups in the developing writing skills.
10. There will be significant difference among the writing scores of children with intellectual disability of the control and experimental groups in pre, post, parallel and retention tests.

METHODOLOGY IN BRIEF

Experimental design (pre-test -post-test –control-design) is used for this study. The sample of the study consisted of 60 children with mild intellectual disability who belong to the age group 7-20 (30 experimental and 30 controls) and were studying in the special school. Random sampling method was used to select sample and to assign them to experimental or control groups. There were three levels – standard 1 higher, standard 1 lower and standard III – and in each level 10 students were assigned to experimental group and 10 students to control group. Later two students, one from standard I lower experimental group and one from standard III control group were excluded from the study due to continuous absence.

The study was done in three stages. In the first stage students were pre tested in language development. Tools used for this purpose were: (1) Functional Reading Assessment Test (FRAT) for standard I, (2) Functional Writing Assessment Test (FWAT) for standard I, (3) Functional Reading Assessment Test (FRAT) for standard III and (4) Functional Writing Assessment Test (FWAT) for standard III

Second stage was the conduct of the experiment (intervention). During this stage instruction through conventional approach was given to experimental and control groups and in addition to that instruction through Literacy Rich Approach (LRA) was given to experimental group.

The third stage was the post intervention test stage. In this students were tested on their performance on language development using three tests. They are (1) parallel test (to measure acquisition level of language development), (2) post test (to measure generalization level of language development) and (3) retention test (to measure maintenance level of language development). The retention test was administered after six months of intervention. The tests used for parallel test are (1) Parallel Functional Reading Assessment Test (PFRAT) for standard I (2) Parallel Functional Writing Assessment Test (PFWAT) for standard I, (3) Parallel Functional Reading Assessment Test (PFRAT) for standard III, and (4) Parallel Functional Writing Assessment Test (PFWAT) for standard III.

The test used for pre testing is used for post and retention tests.

A reading writing package was developed by the investigator for standard I and III which includes all the components of Literacy Rich Approach (LRA),that is, (1) small group practice, (2) classroom library, (3) daily story reading, (4) writing center, (5) on-going monitoring (6) positive feedback and (7) continuous reinforcement.

The effectiveness of the programme was judged by analyzing difference between (1) pretest and post test mean scores, (2) pretest and parallel test mean scores, (3) pretest and retention test mean scores, and (4) mean scores of experimental and control groups at various levels. The data collected were analyzed on the basis of objectives and hypotheses by employing the following statistical techniques using SPSS.

1. Computation of mean, standard deviation, and percentage.

2. The Student's t test.
3. Analysis of covariance (ANCOVA)
4. Repeated Measures one way Analysis of Variance (Repeated ANOVA)
5. The test of Least Significant Difference for post hoc comparisons.

MAJOR FINDINGS

Major findings that have emerged from this study are given under following heads.

Effect of LRA in the language (total reading and writing scores) development of children with intellectual disability

1. For standard 1 higher level ANCOVA results showed that LRA was highly effective in the development of total reading and writing skills as significant mean difference exists between experimental and control groups in post test ($F_{1,17}$ = 11.67, p <0.01), parallel test ($F_{1,17}$ = 8.33, p<0.01) and retention test ($F_{1,17}$ =5.04, p <0.05).
2. In the case of standard 1 lower level as per the ANCOVA, LRA was highly effective in the development of total reading and writing skills as significant mean difference exists between experimental and control groups in post test ($F_{1,16}$ = 9.89, p <0.01), parallel test ($F_{1,16}$ = 6.10, p<0.05) and retention test ($F_{1,16}$ = 16.88, p <0.01).
3. The calculated ANCOVA results for standard III in post test ($F_{1,16}$ = 7.95, p <0.01), and parallel test ($F_{1,16}$ = 4.49, p<0.05) and retention test ($F_{1,16}$ = 7.60, p<0.01) indicates significant mean difference exists between experimental and control groups in the above tests and thus LRA was highly effective in the development of total reading and writing skills.

Significance of mean difference in various pairs of experimental and control groups in total reading and writing scores

1. For standard 1 higher level the repeated ANOVA and post hoc test of least significant difference for pair wise comparisons for experimental and control groups shows significant mean difference between the following pairs – reading and writing scores of pre-post tests (p<0.01) with high mean score in post test, pre-parallel tests (p<0.01) with high mean score in parallel test, pre-retention tests (p<0.01) with high mean score in retention test, post-parallel tests (p<0.01) with high mean score in parallel test and parallel-retention tests (p<0.01) with high mean score in parallel test.
2. For standard 1 lower level the repeated ANOVA and post hoc test of least significant difference for pair wise comparisons for experimental and control groups shows significant mean difference between the following pairs – reading and writing scores of pre-post tests (p<0.01) with high mean score in post test, pre-parallel tests (p<0.01) with high

mean score in parallel test, pre-retention tests ($p<0.01$) with high mean score in retention test, post-parallel tests ($p<0.05$) with high mean score in parallel test and parallel-retention tests ($p<0.01$) with high mean score in parallel test.

3. For standard III the repeated ANOVA and post hoc test of least significant difference for pair wise comparisons for experimental and control groups shows significant mean difference between the following pairs – reading and writing scores of pre-post tests ($p<0.01$) with high mean score in post test, pre-parallel tests ($p<0.01$) with high mean score in parallel test, and pre-retention tests ($p<0.01$) with high mean score in retention test. In post-parallel tests experimental group has significant mean difference ($p<0.05$) with high mean score in parallel test.

Effect of LRA in the vocabulary development of children with intellectual disability

1. LRA was effective for development of vocabulary skills for standard 1 higher level as per the revealed ANCOVA results that significant mean difference exists between experimental and control groups in post test ($F_{1,17} = 9.90$, $p <0.01$), and retention test ($F_{1,17} = 4.82$, $p <0.05$). There is no significant mean difference exists between the two groups in the parallel test ($F_{1,17} =0.07$ $p>0.05$).
2. For standard 1 lower level ANCOVA results showed that LRA was effective in the development of vocabulary skills as significant mean difference exists between experimental and control groups in post test ($F_{1,16} = 5.35$, $p <0.05$), and retention test ($F_{1,16} = 27.83$, $p <0.01$). There is no significant mean difference exists between experimental and control group in parallel test ($F_{1,16} =2.43$, $p>0.05$).
3. A similar ANCOVA result was found for standard III that LRA was effective in the development of vocabulary skills as significant mean difference exists between experimental and control groups in post test ($F_{1,16} = 8.08$, $p <0.01$), and retention test ($F_{1,16} = 21.56$, $p<0.01$). Here also no significant mean difference exists between experimental and control groups in parallel test ($F_{1,16} =2.05$ $p> 0.05$).

Significance of mean difference in various pairs of experimental and control groups in vocabulary scores

1. For standard 1 higher level the repeated ANOVA and post hoc test of least significant difference for pair wise comparisons for experimental and control groups shows significant mean difference between the following pairs – vocabulary scores of pre-post tests ($p<0.01$) with high mean score in post test, pre-parallel tests ($p<0.01$) with high mean score in parallel test, and pre-retention tests ($p<0.01$) with high mean

score in retention test. Control group got significant mean difference in post-parallel tests ($p<0.05$) with high mean score in parallel test and parallel-retention tests $p<0.05$) with high mean score in parallel test.

2. For standard 1 lower level the repeated ANOVA and post hoc test of least significant difference for pair wise comparisons for standard 1 lower experimental and control groups shows significant mean difference between the following pairs – vocabulary scores of pre-post tests ($p<0.01$) with high mean score in post test, pre-parallel tests ($p<0.01$) with high mean score in parallel test, and pre-retention tests ($p<0.01$) with high mean score in retention test. Control group got significant mean difference in parallel-retention tests ($p<0.01$) with high mean score in parallel test.
3. For standard III the repeated ANOVA and post hoc test of least significant difference for pair wise comparisons for standard III experimental and control groups shows significant mean difference exists between the following pairs – vocabulary scores of pre-post tests ($p<0.01$) with high mean score in post test, pre-parallel tests ($p<0.01$) with high mean score in parallel test, and pre-retention tests ($p<0.01$) with high mean score in retention test. Control group got significant mean difference in post-parallel tests, post- retention tests and parallel-retention tests ($p<0.01$) with high mean score in parallel, post, parallel tests respectively.

Effect of LRA in the development of reading comprehension in children with intellectual disability

1. The result of ANCOVA for standard I higher level shows LRA was highly effective in the development of reading comprehension skills that significant mean difference exists between experimental and control groups in post test ($F_{1,17} = 6.91$, $p <0.05$), parallel test ($F_{1,17} =5.12$, $P<0.05$) and retention test ($F_{1,17} =17.47$ $p <0.01$).
2. Standard I lower level shows the significant mean difference in the reading comprehension skills between experimental and control groups in parallel test ($F_{1,16} = 6.81$, $p <0.05$), and retention test ($F_{1,16} = 5.93$, $p <0.05$) as it is expressed by ANCOVA and thus LRA was effective. No such difference was found in post test ($F_{1,16} = 3.33$, $p >0.05$).
3. In the case of standard III students the effectiveness of LRA in the development of reading comprehension skills is seen only in the retention test with a significant mean difference between experimental and control groups as shown in the ANCOVA results ($F_{1,16} = 11.40$, $p <0.01$). No significant difference was found in post test ($F_{1,16} =1.47$, $p>0.05$) and parallel test ($F_{1,16} =0.60$, $p>0.05$).

Significance of mean difference in various pairs of experimental and control groups in reading comprehension scores

1. For standard 1 higher level the repeated ANOVA and post hoc test of least significant difference for pair wise comparisons for standard I higher experimental and control groups shows significant mean difference between the following pairs – reading comprehension scores of pre-post tests ($p<0.01$) with high mean score in post test, pre-parallel tests ($p<0.01$) with high mean score in parallel test, pre-retention tests ($p<0.01$ for experimental and $p<0.05$ for control) with high mean score in retention test and post-parallel tests ($p<0.05$ for experimental and $p<0.01$ for control) with high mean difference in parallel test. Control group got significant mean difference in parallel-retention tests ($p<0.01$) with high mean score in parallel test.
2. For standard 1 lower level the repeated ANOVA and post hoc test of least significant difference for pair wise comparisons for standard 1 lower experimental group shows significant mean difference between the following pairs – reading comprehension scores of pre-post tests ($p<0.05$) with high mean score in post test, pre-parallel tests ($p<0.01$) with high mean score in parallel test, and pre-retention tests ($p<0.01$) with high mean score in retention test and parallel-retention tests ($p<0.01$) with high mean value for parallel test.

   The repeated ANOVA and post hoc test of least significant difference for pair wise comparisons for standard 1 lower control group shows significant mean difference between the following pairs – reading comprehension scores of pre-parallel tests, post-parallel tests and parallel-retention tests ($p<0.01$) with high mean score in parallel test.
3. For standard III the repeated ANOVA and post hoc test of least significant difference for pair wise comparisons for experimental and control groups show significant mean difference between the following pairs – reading and writing scores of pre-post tests ($p<0.01$) with high mean score in post test, pre-parallel tests ($p<0.01$) with high mean score in parallel test, and pre-retention tests ($p<0.01$) with high mean score in retention test. Control group got significant mean difference in post-parallel tests, post- retention tests and parallel-retention tests ($p<0.01$) with high mean score in parallel, post, parallel tests respectively.

Effect of LRA in the development of phonological awareness in children with intellectual disability

For standard 1 higher level the ANCOVA test did not prove any significant effect of LRA for the experimental group in the development of phonological awareness as it was shown in post test ($F_{1,17}=4.05$, $p>0.05$), parallel test ($F_{1,17}=0.04$, $p>0.05$), and retention test ($F_{1,17}=1.02$, $p>0.05$).

For standard 1 lower level the ANCOVA provided significant gain for the experimental group in the retention test ($F_{1,16}$= 6.57,$p<0.05$) and thus LRA was effective in the maintenance of phonological awareness. No significant difference was found in post test ($F_{1,16}$ =1.02, $p>0.05$) and parallel test ($F_{1,16}$ =0.07 $p>0.05$).

For standard III the ANCOVA test did not yield any significant effect of LRA for the experimental group as it was shown in the post test ($F_{1,16}$ =0.61, $p>0.05$), parallel test ($F_{1,16}$ =2.31,$p>0.05$), and retention test ($F_{1,16}$ =2.07, $p>0.05$).

Significance of mean difference in various pairs of experimental and control groups in phonological awareness scores

1. For standard 1 higher level the repeated ANOVA and post hoc test of least significant difference for pair wise comparisons of experimental and control groups show significant mean difference between the following pairs – phonological awareness scores of pre-post tests ($p<0.01$) with high mean score in post test, pre-parallel tests ($p<0.01$) with high mean score in parallel test, pre-retention tests ($p<0.01$ for experimental and $p<0.05$ for control) with high mean score in retention test.
2. For standard 1 lower level the repeated ANOVA and post hoc test of least significant difference for pair wise comparisons for experimental and control groups show significant mean difference between the following pairs – phonological awareness scores of pre-post tests ($p<0.01$) with high mean score in post test, pre-parallel tests ($p<0.01$) with high mean score in parallel test, pre-retention tests ($p<0.01$) with high mean score in retention test.

For standard III the repeated ANOVA and post hoc test of least significant difference for pair wise comparisons for experimental and control groups show significant mean difference between the following pairs – phonological awareness scores of pre-post tests ($p<0.01$) with high mean score in post test, pre-parallel tests ($p<0.01$) with high mean score in parallel test, pre-retention tests ($p<0.01$) with high mean score in retention test.

Effect of LRA in the development of reading fluency in children with intellectual disability

1. In the reading fluency the effect of LRA is shown for standard I higher level in parallel test ($F_{1,17}$ = 6.92, $p <0.05$) as it was expressed by ANCOVA results of experimental and control groups. No significant mean difference is found in post ($F_{1,17}$ = 3.69, $p> 0.05$) and retention test ($F_{1,17}$ = 0.83, $p>0.05$).
2. In the case of standard 1 lower level the ANCOVA results show that LRA was effective in the development of reading fluency skills as significant mean difference exists between experimental and control

groups in post test ($F_{1,16}$ = 5.88, $p<0.05$), parallel test ($F_{1,16}$ = 6.56, $p <0.05$), and retention test ($F_{1,16}$ = 6.47, $p <0.05$).

3. For standard III the effectiveness of LRA in reading fluency skills was shown in the ANCOVA results as significant mean difference exists between experimental and control groups in post test ($F_{1,16}$ = 5.77, $p<0.05$), and retention test ($F_{1,16}$ = 5.22, $p <0.05$). No significant mean difference was found in parallel test ($F_{1,16}$ =3.81, $p>0.05$).

Significance of mean difference in various pairs of experimental and control groups in reading fluency scores

For standard 1 higher level the repeated ANOVA and post hoc test of least significant difference for pair wise comparisons for experimental and control groups show significant mean difference between the following pairs – reading fluency scores of pre-post tests ($p<0.01$) with high mean score in post test, pre-parallel tests ($p<0.01$) with high mean score in parallel test, pre-retention tests ($p<0.01$) with high mean score in retention test.

For standard 1 lower the repeated ANOVA and post hoc test of least significant difference for pair wise comparisons for experimental and control groups show significant mean difference between the following pairs – reading fluency scores of pre-post tests ($p<0.01$) with high mean score in post test, pre-parallel tests ($p<0.01$) with high mean score in parallel test. In pre-retention tests significant mean score difference exist for experimental group only ($p<0.01$) with high mean score in retention test.

For standard III the repeated ANOVA and post hoc test of least significant difference for pair wise comparisons for experimental and control groups show significant mean difference between the following pairs – reading fluency scores of pre-post tests ($p<0.01$) with high mean score in post test, pre-parallel tests ($p<0.01$) with high mean score in parallel test, pre-retention tests ($p<0.01$) with high mean score in retention test. For control group there is significant mean difference for parallel-retention pair with high mean score in parallel test.

Effect of LRA in the development of writing skills in children with intellectual disability

1. The results of ANCOVA revealed that in total writing skills significant mean difference exists between experimental and control groups in the post test ($F_{1,17}$ = 32.75, $p<0.01$), parallel test ($F_{1,17}$ = 6.00, $p <0.05$), and retention test ($F_{1,17}$ = 41.30, $p <0.01$) of standard I higher level students and thereby shows that LRA was highly effective.
2. For standard 1 lower level LRA was effective in the development of total writing skills that significant mean difference exists between experimental and control groups in post test ($F_{1,16}$ = 7.33, $p<0.05$), and retention test ($F_{1,16}$ = 82.72, $p <0.01$). No significant mean difference exists in the parallel test ($F_{1,16}$ = 2.82, $p>0.05$).

3. For standard III effectiveness of LRA in the development of writing skills is seen in the retention test with a significant mean difference between experimental and control groups ($F_{1,16} = 5.39$, $p < 0.05$). No significant mean difference exists in post test ($F_{1,16} = 3.96$, $p > 0.05$) or parallel test ($F_{1,16} = 0.33$ $p > 0.05$).

Significance of mean difference in various pairs of experimental and control groups in writing scores

For standard 1 higher the repeated ANOVA and post hoc test of least significant difference for pair wise comparisons for experimental and control groups show significant mean difference between the following pairs – total writing scores of pre-post tests ($p<0.01$ for experimental and $p<0.05$ for control) with high mean score in post test, pre-parallel tests ($p<0.01$) with high mean score in parallel test, pre-retention tests ($p<0.01$) with high mean score in retention test. Also there is significant difference in the pairs post-parallel ($p<0.01$), post-retention ($p<0.01$) for experimental, and parallel-retention ($p<0.01$) for control group.

For standard 1 lower the repeated ANOVA and post hoc test of least significant difference for pair wise comparisons for experimental and control groups show significant mean difference between the following pairs – total writing scores of pre-post tests ($p<0.01$) with high mean score in post test, pre-parallel tests ($p<0.01$) with high mean score in parallel test, pre-retention tests ($p<0.01$) for experimental group only with high mean score in retention test. Also there is significant difference in the pairs post-parallel for experimental ($p<0.05$) and for control ($p<0.01$), post-retention for control ($p<0.01$) and parallel-retention for experimental ($p<0.05$) and for control group ($p<0.01$).

For standard III the repeated ANOVA and post hoc test of least significant difference for pair wise comparisons for experimental and control groups show significant mean difference between the following pairs – total writing scores of pre-post tests $p<0.01$) with high mean score in post test, pre-parallel tests ($p<0.01$) with high mean score in parallel test, pre-retention tests ($p<0.01$) with high mean score in retention test. Also there is significant difference in the pairs post-parallel ($p<0.01$) and, post-retention ($p<0.01$) for control group.

TENABILITY OF HYPOTHESES

Table 5.1: Tenability of first major hypothesis

Major Hypothesis I: There will be significant difference between the experimental and control groups in vocabulary development.		
Sl.No.	**Minor Hypothesis**	**Accepted/Rejected**
1.	There will be significant difference between the experimental and control groups in vocabulary development of standard 1 higher level students with intellectual disability in post test.	Accepted
2.	There will be significant difference between the experimental and control groups in vocabulary development of standard 1 higher level students with intellectual disability in parallel test.	Rejected
3.	There will be significant difference between the experimental and control groups in vocabulary development of standard 1 higher level students with intellectual disability in retention test.	Accepted
4.	There will be significant difference between the experimental and control groups in vocabulary development of standard 1 lower level students with intellectual disability in post test.	Accepted
5.	There will be significant difference between the experimental and control groups in vocabulary development of standard 1 lower level students with intellectual disability in parallel test.	Rejected
6.	There will be significant difference between the experimental and control groups in vocabulary development of standard 1 lower level students with intellectual disability in retention test.	Accepted
7.	There will be significant difference between the experimental and control groups in vocabulary development of standard III students with intellectual disability in post test.	Accepted
8.	There will be significant difference between the experimental and control groups in vocabulary development of standard III students with intellectual disability in parallel test.	Rejected
9.	There will be significant difference between the experimental and control groups in vocabulary development of standard III students with intellectual disability in retention test.	Accepted

The major hypothesis I is accepted in case of post tests and retention tests. However it is rejected in parallel tests.

Table 5.2: Tenability of second major hypothesis

Major Hypothesis II: There will be significant difference among vocabulary scores of children with intellectual disability of the experimental and control groups in pre, post, parallel and retention tests.		
Sl.No.	**Minor Hypothesis**	**Accepted/Rejected**
1.	There will be significant difference among vocabulary scores of standard I higher level children with intellectual disability of the experimental group in pre, post, parallel and retention tests.	Accepted
2.	There will be significant difference among vocabulary scores of standard I higher level children with intellectual disability of the control group in pre, post, parallel and retention tests.	Accepted
3.	There will be significant difference among vocabulary scores of standard I lower level children with intellectual disability of the experimental group in pre, post, parallel and retention tests.	Accepted
4.	There will be significant difference among vocabulary scores of standard I lower level children with intellectual disability of the control group in pre, post, parallel and retention tests.	Accepted
5.	There will be significant difference among vocabulary scores of standard III children with intellectual disability of the experimental group in pre, post, parallel and retention tests.	Accepted
6.	There will be significant difference among vocabulary scores of standard III children with intellectual disability of the control group in pre, post, parallel and retention tests.	Accepted

The major hypothesis II is accepted.

Table 5.3: Tenability of third major hypothesis

Major Hypothesis III: There will be significant difference between the experimental and control groups in reading comprehension development.		
Sl.No.	**Minor Hypothesis**	**Accepted/Rejected**
1.	There will be significant difference between the experimental and control groups in reading comprehension development of standard 1 higher level students with intellectual disability in post test.	Accepted
2.	There will be significant difference between the experimental and control groups in reading comprehension development of standard 1 higher level students with intellectual disability in parallel test.	Accepted
3.	There will be significant difference between the experimental and control groups in reading comprehension development of standard 1 higher level students with intellectual disability in retention test.	Accepted
4.	There will be significant difference between the experimental and control groups in reading comprehension development of standard 1 lower level students with intellectual disability in post test.	Rejected
5.	There will be significant difference between the experimental and control groups in reading comprehension development of standard 1 lower level students with intellectual disability in parallel test.	Accepted
6.	There will be significant difference between the experimental and control groups in reading comprehension development of standard 1 lower level students with intellectual disability in retention test.	Accepted
7.	There will be significant difference between the experimental and control groups in reading comprehension development of standard III students with intellectual disability in post test.	Rejected
8.	There will be significant difference between the experimental and control groups in reading comprehension development of standard III students with intellectual disability in parallel test.	Rejected
9.	There will be significant difference between the experimental and control groups in reading comprehension development of standard III students with intellectual disability in retention test.	Accepted

In the case of retention test the major hypothesis III is accepted whereas in post test it is partially rejected and in parallel test it is partially accepted.

Table 5.4: Tenability of fourth major hypothesis

Major Hypothesis IV: There will be significant difference among reading comprehension scores of children with intellectual disability of the experimental and control groups in pre, post, parallel and retention tests.

Sl.No.	Minor Hypothesis	Accepted/Rejected
1.	There will be significant difference among reading comprehension scores of standard I higher level children with intellectual disability of the experimental group in pre, post, parallel and retention tests.	Accepted
2.	There will be significant difference among reading comprehension scores of standard I higher level children with intellectual disability of the control group in pre, post, parallel and retention tests.	Accepted
3.	There will be significant difference among reading comprehension scores of standard I lower level children with intellectual disability of the experimental group in pre, post, parallel and retention tests.	Accepted
4.	There will be significant difference among reading comprehension scores of standard I lower level children with intellectual disability of the control group in pre, post, parallel and retention tests.	Accepted
5.	There will be significant difference among reading comprehension scores of standard III children with intellectual disability of the experimental group in pre, post, parallel and retention tests.	Accepted
6.	There will be significant difference among reading comprehension scores of standard III children with intellectual disability of the control group in pre, post, parallel and retention tests.	Accepted

Major hypothesis IV is accepted.

Table 5.5: Tenability of fifth major hypothesis

Major Hypothesis V: There will be significant difference between the experimental and control groups in phonological awareness development.		
Sl.No.	**Minor Hypothesis**	**Accepted/Rejected**
1.	There will be significant difference between the experimental and control groups in phonological awareness development of standard 1 higher level students with intellectual disability in post test.	Rejected
2.	There will be significant difference between the experimental and control groups in phonological awareness development of standard 1 higher level students with intellectual disability in parallel test.	Rejected
3.	There will be significant difference between the experimental and control groups in phonological awareness development of standard 1 higher level students with intellectual disability in retention test.	Rejected
4.	There will be significant difference between the experimental and control groups in phonological awareness development of standard 1 lower level students with intellectual disability in post test.	Rejected
5.	There will be significant difference between the experimental and control groups in phonological awareness development of standard 1 lower level students with intellectual disability in parallel test.	Rejected
6.	There will be significant difference between the experimental and control groups in phonological awareness development of standard 1 lower level students with intellectual disability in retention test.	Accepted
7.	There will be significant difference between the experimental and control groups in phonological awareness development of standard III students with intellectual disability in post test.	Rejected
8.	There will be significant difference between the experimental and control groups in phonological awareness development of standard III students with intellectual disability in parallel test.	Rejected
9.	There will be significant difference between the experimental and control groups in phonological awareness development of standard III students with intellectual disability in retention test.	Rejected

Major hypothesis V is rejected in post tests and parallel tests. It is partially rejected in retention tests.

Table 5.6: Tenability of sixth major hypothesis

Major Hypothesis VI: There will be significant difference among phonological awareness scores of children with intellectual disability of the experimental and control groups in pre, post, parallel and retention tests.

Sl.No.	Minor Hypothesis	Accepted/Rejected
1.	There will be significant difference among phonological awareness scores of standard I higher level children with intellectual disability of the experimental group in pre, post, parallel and retention tests.	Accepted
2.	There will be significant difference among phonological awareness scores of standard I higher level children with intellectual disability of the control group in pre, post, parallel and retention tests.	Accepted
3.	There will be significant difference among phonological awareness scores of standard I lower level children with intellectual disability of the experimental group in pre, post, parallel and retention tests.	Accepted
4.	There will be significant difference among phonological awareness scores of standard I lower level children with intellectual disability of the control group in pre, post, parallel and retention tests.	Accepted
5.	There will be significant difference among phonological awareness scores of standard III children with intellectual disability of the experimental group in pre, post, parallel and retention tests.	Accepted
6.	There will be significant difference among phonological awareness scores of standard III children with intellectual disability of the control group in pre, post, parallel and retention tests.	Accepted

Major hypothesis VI is accepted.

Table 5.7: Tenability of seventh major hypothesis

Major Hypothesis VII: There will be significant difference between the experimental and control groups in reading fluency development.		
Sl.No.	**Minor Hypothesis**	**Accepted/Rejected**
1.	There will be significant difference between the experimental and control groups in reading fluency development of standard 1 higher level students with intellectual disability in post test.	Rejected
2.	There will be significant difference between the experimental and control groups in reading fluency development of standard 1 higher level students with intellectual disability in parallel test.	Accepted
3.	There will be significant difference between the experimental and control groups in reading fluency development of standard 1 higher level students with intellectual disability in retention test.	Rejected
4.	There will be significant difference between the experimental and control groups in reading fluency development of standard 1 lower level students with intellectual disability in post test.	Accepted
5.	There will be significant difference between the experimental and control groups in reading fluency development of standard 1 lower level students with intellectual disability in parallel test.	Accepted
6.	There will be significant difference between the experimental and control groups in reading fluency development of standard 1 lower level students with intellectual disability in retention test.	Accepted
7.	There will be significant difference between the experimental and control groups in reading fluency development of standard III students with intellectual disability in post test.	Accepted
8.	There will be significant difference between the experimental and control groups in reading fluency development of standard III students with intellectual disability in parallel test.	Rejected
9.	There will be significant difference between the experimental and control groups in reading fluency development of standard III students with intellectual disability in retention test.	Accepted

Major hypothesis VII is partially accepted in the case of post, parallel and retention tests.

Table 5.8: Tenability of eighth major hypothesis

Major Hypothesis VIII: There will be significant difference among reading fluency scores of children with intellectual disability of the experimental and control groups in pre, post, parallel and retention tests.

Sl.No.	Minor Hypothesis	Accepted/Rejected
1.	There will be significant difference among reading fluency scores of standard I higher level children with intellectual disability of the experimental group in pre, post, parallel and retention tests.	Accepted
2.	There will be significant difference among reading fluency scores of standard I higher level children with intellectual disability of the control group in pre, post, parallel and retention tests.	Accepted
3.	There will be significant difference among reading fluency scores of standard I lower level children with intellectual disability of the experimental group in pre, post, parallel and retention tests.	Accepted
4.	There will be significant difference among reading fluency scores of standard I lower level children with intellectual disability of the control group in pre, post, parallel and retention tests.	Accepted
5.	There will be significant difference among reading fluency scores of standard III children with intellectual disability of the experimental group in pre, post, parallel and retention tests.	Accepted
6.	There will be significant difference among reading fluency scores of standard III children with intellectual disability of the control group in pre, post, parallel and retention tests.	Accepted

Major hypothesis VIII is accepted.

Table 5.9: Tenability of ninth major hypothesis

Major Hypothesis IX: There will be significant difference between the experimental and control groups in writing skill development.

Sl.No.	Minor Hypothesis	Accepted/Rejected
1.	There will be significant difference between the experimental and control groups in writing skill development of standard 1 higher level students with intellectual disability in post test.	Accepted
2.	There will be significant difference between the experimental and control groups in writing skill development of standard 1 higher level students with intellectual disability in parallel test.	Accepted
3.	There will be significant difference between the experimental and control groups in writing skill development of standard 1 higher level students with intellectual disability in retention test.	Accepted
4.	There will be significant difference between the experimental and control groups in writing skill development of standard 1 lower level students with intellectual disability in post test.	Accepted
5.	There will be significant difference between the experimental and control groups in writing skill development of standard 1 lower level students with intellectual disability in parallel test.	Rejected
6.	There will be significant difference between the experimental and control groups in writing skill development of standard 1 lower level students with intellectual disability in retention test.	Accepted
7.	There will be significant difference between the experimental and control groups in writing skill development of standard III students with intellectual disability in post test.	Rejected
8.	There will be significant difference between the experimental and control groups in writing skill development of standard III students with intellectual disability in parallel test.	Rejected
9.	There will be significant difference between the experimental and control groups in writing skill development of standard III students with intellectual disability in retention test.	Accepted

Major hypothesis IX is accepted in the case of retention tests. However it is partially accepted in post tests and partially rejected in parallel tests.

Table 5.10: Tenability of tenth major hypothesis

Major Hypothesis X: There will be significant difference among writing skill scores of children with intellectual disability of the experimental and control groups in pre, post, parallel and retention tests.		
Sl.No.	**Minor Hypothesis**	**Accepted/Rejected**
1.	There will be significant difference among writing skill scores of standard I higher level children with intellectual disability of the experimental group in pre, post, parallel and retention tests.	Accepted
2.	There will be significant difference among writing skill scores of standard I higher level children with intellectual disability of the control group in pre, post, parallel and retention tests.	Accepted
3.	There will be significant difference among writing skill scores of standard I lower level children with intellectual disability of the experimental group in pre, post, parallel and retention tests.	Accepted
4.	There will be significant difference among writing skill scores of standard I lower level children with intellectual disability of the control group in pre, post, parallel and retention tests.	Accepted
5.	There will be significant difference among writing skill scores of standard III children with intellectual disability of the experimental group in pre, post, parallel and retention tests.	Accepted
6.	There will be significant difference among writing skill scores of standard III children with intellectual disability of the control group in pre, post, parallel and retention tests.	Accepted

Major hypothesis X is accepted.

CONCLUSIONS AND SUGGESTIONS

The major conclusions that are arrived from the present investigation and suggestions made on the basis of the conclusions are given below.

The present study revealed that the experimental group in three levels (standard1 higher, standard 1 lower, and standard III) acquired (based on parallel test results), generalized (based on post test results), and maintained (based on retention test results) literacy skills (total reading and writing score) better than control group with the help of LRA. This shows the effectiveness of LRA in the language development of children with intellectual disability. Hence it can be concluded that children with mild intellectual disability are able to follow supplementary activities which give high motivation, creative experiences, and age appropriate exercises for literacy instruction and are definitely improved in their literacy skills.

Analysis of data revealed the gain of scores and differences between pre, post, parallel, and retention tests within experimental and control groups indicate that both groups in all levels improved a lot from pretest performance. This shows the effectiveness of systematic instruction followed in the conventional approach and Literacy-Rich Approach. The higher score of experimental group in three levels shows the superiority of LRA over conventional approach.

In the vocabulary development area, in all the three levels experimental group outperformed control group in generalizing and maintaining vocabulary skills whereas, both the groups performed similarly in the acquisition stage. Therefore it can be concluded that for initial acquisition of vocabulary skills systematic instruction using conventional approach is adequate. But for applying the acquired knowledge to a new material and for continuing the skills overtime literacy rich environment and Literacy Rich Approach is essential.

Analysis revealed that both experimental and control groups of the three levels gained scores from initial performance. This indicates the success of instruction in vocabulary area. The experimental group generalized and maintained the learned skills while control group's performance lowered in these stages.

Results of reading comprehension tests reveal that LRA was highly effective for standard I higher level students. The experimental group learned, generalized and maintained reading comprehension skills much better than control group. In the case of standard I lower level the effectiveness of LRA is seen in initial acquisition (based on parallel test results) and maintenance (based on retention test results). In the post test both groups performed similarly. For standard III, although effect of LRA was not shown in initial acquisition and generalization, it did show in maintenance of reading comprehension skills. Since reading comprehension is one of the hardest area of instruction for children with intellectual disability, the result of this study gives some guidelines for successful instruction in developing, generalizing and maintaining the skills.

Group wise analysis in this area shows both the groups-experimental and control-improved from the initial performance. Performance of experimental group is better than control group and it indirectly shows the influence of LRA in improving reading comprehension skills.

In phonological awareness area improvement of students can be seen at all levels. Literacy Rich Approach did not show its effect in this area.

In the area of reading fluency effect of LRA was shown predominantly by standard 1 lower level students. The results of post, parallel and retention tests illustrate this. These lower level students really benefited from various activities and experiences of LRA. Standard III students also exhibit the effect by generalizing and maintaining fluency skills. In standard

1 higher level the effectiveness was seen in acquisition stage. It can be concluded that three levels of students got benefit of LRA at different stages and therefore this approach is effective in reading fluency instruction.

Group wise analysis revealed that students at all levels have improvements in reading fluency skills from initial performance.

In writing skill development standard 1 higher experimental group shows the clear influence of LRA by exhibiting high performance in acquiring, generalizing and maintaining skills. Standard 1 lower level students' improvement due to LRA is seen in generalizing and maintaining stages. Standard III students' LRA effect is shown only in maintenance stage. From these results the following conclusion can be made. Systematic instruction using conventional approach may be adequate in the acquisition stages of writing instruction; but there is no doubt that instruction using Literacy Rich Approach is needed for generalizing and maintaining skills.

On the basis of the above conclusions the following suggestions are given:

1. Literacy instructional content for children with intellectual disability should be elaborated by skills in vocabulary, reading comprehension, reading fluency and writing skills. Always visualize the functional use of selected content in the life of students with intellectual disability.
2. Since literacy skills are fundamental to every day life, stress should be given for generalization and maintenance of selected literacy content.
3. Professional development is one of the key aspects of successful literacy instruction. Therefore teachers and other professionals should be trained effectively in imparting literacy instruction.
4. Instruction should be followed in a sequential order. Provide alphabet – word - sentence – paragraph order which will enable students to combine learned alphabets and make simple words, then combine learned words and make simple sentences, and finally combine sentences and make paragraph.
5. Context-based letter/word/sentence/paragraph instruction should be followed.
6. For developing and maintaining vocabulary, comprehension, fluency and writing skills literacy rich environment can be established in classrooms as well as in whole school.
7. Educational policy makers should provide encouragement and financial support to schools and child care centers to become literacy-friendly institutes.
8. Instructions provided in the classrooms should be clear and specific. Students should be under the control of literacy instructor, that is, instead of allowing them to read and write anything, instructor should keep specific goals and objectives for each student and let them move forward under the plan/guidance of the teacher.

9. Daily/weekly/monthly monitoring will help teachers, parents and students themselves to become aware of their performance in literacy skills. Based on this teachers can rearrange lessons.
10. Modern technological devices such as computers, CD Roms, tape recorders, language masters, etc. and other technological aids should be provided to classrooms and teachers should be properly trained in using these equipments and resources.
11. Literacy based low cost teaching/learning materials can be made by literacy instructor for day to day use.
12. Teachers should be careful on evaluating student's problems and remediate them correctly. Some of the literacy problems observed during the study are:
    - *(i)* Calling out individual letters, unable to combine them to make word and get meaning out of it.
    - *(ii)* Read words one by one and fails to combine them with adequate speed. Thus meaning is lost during the slow motion of reading. Without getting meaning from the text, students loose interest and motivation to read.
    - *(iii)* When reading material is not interesting and age appropriate, students will not improve in reading.
    - *(iv)* Those who lack background knowledge have difficulty in figuring out ideas and concepts. Therefore language experience may help to increase students' background knowledge and thereby reading comprehension.
    - *(v)* To improve reading comprehension ability, students should be taught to identify semantic, syntactic and contextual clues while reading the text.
    - *(vi)* While learning Malayalam literacy students may face additional problems, that is, many Malayalam letters have similar sounds. While it is difficult for normally developing children to learn these sounds correctly, intellectually disabled children's difficulty is even larger and they should be recognized and proper remedial measures should be followed. Activities to improve visual/auditory discrimination can be arranged.
    - *(vii)* Many mildly intellectually disabled students have spent years in regular school and followed regular education before starting special education. They may have experienced repeated failures and therefore may not have motivation to learn literacy skills. Therefore motivating them is an essential responsibility of literacy instructor.

13. Parents, family members and care givers should be given proper training and instruction on how to create a literacy rich environment at home and how it can be properly utilized.
14. To improve student's conceptual level and reading writing skills let them prepare literacy based projects.
15. Older students who have developed literacy skills can act as tutors for lower level students.
16. Grouping for literacy instruction is necessary. Students who are identical in functional level should be grouped together.
17. Reinforcers and rewards for literacy learning can be arranged by providing computer games based on literacy, story books etc.
18. Classroom based/school based/district based literacy competitions can be arranged.
19. For effective literacy instruction classroom/school library is essential. While setting library care should be taken to include books that match the mental age and ability of children with intellectual disability.
20. Measures should be taken by Department of Education of concerned state to prepare text books for literacy instruction for the benefit of students with intellectual disability in integrated and special education set ups.
21. Special educators should come forward to prepare literacy content for day to day instruction that match the functional level of students in their classroom.
22. Book companies are to be encouraged to publish text books and children's literature that suit to the mental ability of children with intellectual disability.
23. Curriculum content for teacher training courses (Diploma/degree/post graduate) that deal with literacy instruction of children with intellectual disability should be well planned including literacy rich approach.
24. State government should distribute literacy based materials free of cost to low income families and families having children with developmental disabilities.
25. A school wise or district wise literacy campaign can be organized to increase awareness of parents, siblings and community members on this subject.
26. The conventional approach, if implemented systematically, is proved to be effective to some extent for developing or acquiring the literacy skills. So effective mechanism should be there to ensure the implementation of the same scientifically.
27. Steps should be taken to give in-service training to special teachers in LRA.

28. Parents, special teachers and public should be made aware of the potential of children with mild intellectual disability to develop language skills. Thereby the underestimation of these children can be corrected.

IMPLICATIONS

When comparing the pretest and parallel test results it is obvious that conventional approach itself brought great improvement in literacy skills for both experimental and control groups at all three levels. This means conventional approach has not been applied systematically by teachers in literacy instruction. There may be several reasons for this:

Nowadays special school teachers of children with intellectual disability get very limited time to train academic skills since they have to train other domains of functional curriculum (e.g. social skill, self care, domestic skills etc.). Also they have to find time for various therapeutic activities (speech, physical and occupational), co curricular activities and competitions such as Special Olympics, very special arts etc. Above mentioned areas are essential when thinking of an integrated or cohesive development of children with intellectual disability. Therefore they utilize what ever time they get to train functional academics. It can be seen that like other subject areas the time allotted for literacy instruction is inadequate. While preparing time schedule for all other activities special teachers may not be able to organize literacy classes effectively or plan for additional activities for literacy instruction. Providing a literacy rich environment in classroom requires lot of time, energy and thinking from the part of the literacy instructor. Even though one can visualize the benefits, shortage of time and preoccupation with other activities prevent even the attempt to try for such situation. But the fact is that literacy rich environment once created, stay there throughout the year and students will get benefit from it each day. Another reason may be that special teachers are reluctant to prepare daily lesson plans and provide instruction systematically.

The results of the present study show that Literacy Rich Approach is highly effective in acquiring, generalizing and maintaining literacy skills of children with intellectual disability compared to the present conventional approach. These findings indicate several instructional implications in the field of special education to promote literacy development.

In the field of special education underestimation of children with intellectual disability especially to mild category exists. Conventional approach is being used in schools for literacy instruction. As it is seen from this research this approach is adequate for initial literacy acquisition. But what students learn will be forgotten soon since no effective measures are taken for generalization and maintenance. The usual conclusion made by special teachers parents and even professionals is children with intellectual disability are dull, they don't have long term memory, no hope for academic skills etc. The results of retention test, which was given six months after intervention, gave empirical evidence that students can and will learn if effective teaching approach is used. If teachers spend more time and effort for improving basic level skills, students will get a strong foundation for literacy skills and it will carry on throughout the instruction as well as throughout their life. Arrangement of literacy goals, objectives, daily lessons, and required instructional activities etc. are essential.

The concepts of mainstreaming, integration and inclusion are better practiced nowadays in the field of special education. Children with mild intellectual disability will be placed in regular schools where resource room facility is widely accepted and practiced. In these circumstances, the result of the present study has even more implications. Literacy instruction is always given top priority without considering whether students are in integrated set up or inclusive set up. Regular teachers as well as resource teachers can apply literacy rich approach to improve students' literacy skills. Also the knowledge and expertise students get through literacy instruction will be transferred to other school subjects such as mathematics, social sciences, value education etc. and they will learn these subjects effectively.

The wide practice among special educators to teach only vocabulary skills may be interpreted as follows: Conventional approach is adequate for acquiring vocabulary skills. But in the case of reading comprehension skills LRA is superior than conventional approach even in the stage of acquisition. Since teachers are not finding much improvement of reading comprehension skills, with conventional approach, they continue teaching of word level skills.

It can be stated that the application of each component of LRA contributed to the literacy improvement in the present study. Dividing students into small groups (same ability as well as mixed ability) benefited students and teacher. For example, this helped children to get help from others, contribute their literacy knowledge to group members, reduce teachers' responsibility, complete work in time etc. Daily story reading was really an entertainment for students. Without knowing the benefit of it, students of experimental group automatically improved literacy skills. Similarly classroom library was a privilege for them. Students became friends of books. It did not matter whether they read the allotted portion completely or partially, using library books was a chance, a requirement and something that improved their status as a student.

Writing center in the literacy rich classroom was not a pleasant factor in the beginning of the programme. But gradually students themselves experienced the benefit of it. Written document was a permanent record and therefore students could see their work at a later time.

The ongoing monitoring, positive feedback and continuous reinforcement were the components that kept student- teacher relationship, improve students' self esteem, maintain the quality of their work, and formed their total behaviour in and out of classroom. All these components aided the success of the programme.

The result of the study has several implications with respect to the personal development of children with intellectual disability.

1. Students will be able to read current matters (newspaper, magazines etc) and procure information and thus improve general knowledge.
2. Students will become readers of literary materials such as stories, novels, dramas, comics and cartoons. These are reading materials for entertainment. Thus students with intellectual disability will be able to spent their free time more fruitfully. No doubt leisure time activities will help them to reduce problem behaviours.
3. Persons who are proficient in literacy skills are considered as intellectually superior to those who cannot and thus these persons will be treated well by teachers, peers, school authorities and family members and they will be assigned to do more responsible duties.
4. Those who can read and write well will automatically become personally independent, have more self concept and this self growth will help them to open several areas of involvement.
5. In the family students with proficient literacy skills will be helpful for parents and others. They can also involve in day to day responsibilities at home situation. Family members can help children to maintain the learned literacy skills by providing literacy rich environment at home.
6. As observed during the study, the experimental group showed remarkable changes in their behaviour patterns. Development of leadership qualities, improved maturity, quick response to instructions, punctuality, improvement in reading habits, oral language comprehension, perseverance, are some of the noticeable changes. Since the level of these qualities is not pretested, the intensity of the development cannot be established. Still it can assume that application of LRA will bring these changes.

Educational research findings are meant to contribute to educational theory as well as educational practice. The current research provides empirical data to guide researchers and literacy instructors in special education as well as regular education. Review of the earlier research work done in the field of special education especially in intellectual disability revealed that programmes for children with intellectual disability give due importance in teaching skill areas such as social, self care and vocational. Majority of the research done in literacy instruction concentrate mainly on teaching of sight vocabulary of functional words. This trend is seen in international and national level researches. As many investigators (e.g. Katims 1991, 1994, 1996) stated children with intellectual disability can move toward more advanced literacy if presented with opportunities to interact with words in context, and construct meaning from text. Special educators will attend to various components of literacy if they get adequate information based on scientific research to impart these skills.

The present study gives importance to an elaborate content as well as one method to impart the content, that is, Literacy Rich Approach (LRA). Findings of this study is hoped to inspire and motivate researchers to do further research in this topic. Research works can be focused on each main component (e.g. reading comprehension, reading fluency, writing skill) and do independent study. The beginning researchers can also refrain from the shortcomings and limitations occurred in the present study while conducting scientific research.

The valuable experience gained from the present research and the findings of the study provoke the researcher to think about many issues: (i) whether general intelligence of children with intellectual disability increase with improvement in literacy, (ii) factors contributing to the enhancement of mental processes, an essential component in reading comprehension, (iii) involvement in literacy works and corresponding decrease in problem behaviours as well as increase in other subject areas, and (iv) possibility of involving high functioning students in literacy as teacher assistants to tutor low functioning students. All these issues deserve attention of special education researchers.

Since LRA has improved response generalization and maintenance skills of literacy, it can be assumed that same kind of generalization will occur in all areas of teaching.

In short, the present study very convincingly proved the effect of LRA in the literacy skill development of students with intellectual disability. Also findings of the present study have very much applications in general and in daily special education practices and research in particular.

LIMITATIONS OF THE STUDY

Even though the investigator tried very hard to make the present study as scientific as possible, certain limitations could not be avoided. The limitations of the present study are the following:

1. Intervention time was inadequate. Since the content area was vast, long period of intervention might have brought better results.
2. The size of the sample studied was only 60 and they are taken from one school. Larger sample would have brought more generalizable results. The difficulty to get students of identical functional level forced the investigator to limit the sample. Creating a similar experimental condition in various schools was also difficult.

3. If literacy-rich environment was provided throughout the day, children in experimental group would have been experienced high level influence and lot of changes would have occurred.

SUGGESTIONS FOR FURTHER RESEARCH

In the light of the findings that have emerged from the present study and the valuable experiences gained, the following suggestions are listed for future research.

1. The same study can be conducted with larger sample drawn from many schools so that more generalizable results could be obtained.
2. A similar study can be arranged with sample of students with moderate and severe intellectual disability or having clinical syndromes such as Down syndrome.
3. This study can be replicated as a school level project including more teachers, providing more instructional time and evaluating the effectiveness of each component of LRA separately.
4. An attempt may be made to conduct a study in a research setting where literacy rich environment is provided whole day.
5. A study may be conducted to get information on the experimental group of students' improvement in interpersonal skills, leadership qualities, other subject areas, punctuality, perseverance, and self-discipline that may be developed as byproducts during the intervention of Literacy Rich Approach.
6. Further studies may be conducted to investigate on the reading comprehension skills of students with intellectual disability including textually implicit and scriptually implicit materials.
7. An investigation may be conducted to get information on relationship between phonological awareness and literacy development.
8. An attempt may be made to study the role of parents in the implementation of LRA.
9. Effectiveness of parent training in the development of literacy skills among students with intellectual disability through LRA can be studied.
10. A more specific study may be conducted to identify the effectiveness of LRA on the development of sub skills of various literacy domains.

References

Afacan, K., Wilkerson, K.L. & Ruppar, A.L. (2018). Multicomponent Reading Intervention for Students with Intellectual Disability. *Remedial and Special Education, 39, (4)229-242. Eric number: EJ 1185472*

Alberto, P., Jones, N., Sizemore, A. & Doran, D. (1980). A Comparison of Individual and Group Instruction Across Response Tasks. *Journal of the Association for the Severely Handicapped, 5, 285-293.*

Alberto, P.A. & Troutman, A.C. (1995). *Applied Behaviour Analysis for Teachers.* Prentice-Hall, Inc., New Jersey, USA.

Alig-Cybriwsky, C., Wolery, M., Gast, D.L. (1990). Use of Constant Time-delay Procedure in Teaching Preschoolers in a Group Format. In J.A. Farmer, D.L. Gast, M. Wolery,. & V. Winterling. Small Group Instruction for Students with Severe Handicaps: A Study of Observational Learning. *Education and Training in Mental Retardation, 26(2), 190-201.*

Algozzine, B. & Wood, K.D. (1994). Reading and Special Education in the Twenty-first Century. In D.S. Katims Literacy Instruction for People with Mental Retardation: Historical Highlights and Contemporary Analysis. *Education and Training in Mental Retardation and Developmental Disabilities, 35 (1), 3-15.*

Allington, R.L. (1981). Sensitivity to Orthographic Structure in Educable Mentally Retarded Children. *Cotemporary Educational Psychology, 6 (2), 135-139.*

Allington, R.L. (1984). Oral Reading. In T.G. Gunning, *Assessing and Correcting Reading and Writing Difficulties.* Allyn and Bacon MA, USA.

Allor, J.H., Mathes, P.G., Roberts, J.K., Jones, F.G. & Champlin, T.M. (2010). Teaching Students with Moderate Intellectual Disabilities to Read. An Experimental Examination of a Comprehensive Reading Intervention. *Education and Training in Autism and Developmental Disabilities, 45(1), 3-22.*

Alnahdi, D.H. (2015). Teaching Reading for Students with Intellectual Disabilities: A Systematic Review. *International Education Studies 8*, 79-87.

Alston, J. & Taylor, J. (1987). *Handwriting: Theory, Research and Practice.* Nichols, New York).

Anderson, R.C., Wilson, P.T. & Fielding, L.G. (1988). Growth in Reading and how Children Spend their Time out side School. *Reading Research Quarterly, 23, 285-303.*

Anderson, R.C. (1977). Schema-directed Processes in Language Comprehension. In S. McCormic, *Instructing Students who have Literacy Problems* (2nd ed.). Prentice Hall, Inc. New Jersey.

Barker, R.M., Sevcik, R.A., Morris, R.D., Romski, M. (2013). A model of Phonological Processing, Language, and Reading for Students with Mild Intellectual Disability. *American Journal on Intellectual and Developmental Disabilities, 118(5), 365-380.*

Baker, S.K., Simmons, D.C., & Kame'enui, E.J. (1998). Vocabulary Acquisition: Research basis. In A.K. Jitendra, L.L. Edwards, G. Sacks, & L.A. Jacobson, What Research says about Vocabulary Instruction for Students with Learning Disabilities. *Exceptional Children, 70 (3), 299-322.*

Ball, E.W. & Blachman, B.A. (1991). Does Phoneme Awareness Training in Kindergarten make a difference in Early Word Recognition and Developmental spelling? In S. McCormic, *Instructing Students who have Literacy Problems* (2nd ed.). Prentice Hall, Inc., New Jersey.

Barr, R. & Dreeben, R. (1991). Grouping Students for Reading Instruction. In S. Vaughn, C. S. Bos, & J.S. Schumm. *Teaching Mainstreamed, Diverse, and at-risk Students in General Education Classroom.* Allyn & Bacon, MA, USA.

Bartlett, F.C. (1932). Remembering. In S. McCormic, (1995). *Instructing Students who have Literacy Problems* (2nd ed.). Prentice Hall, Inc., New Jersey.

Barudin, S.I. & Hourcade, J.J. (1990). Relative Effectiveness of Three methods of Reading Instruction in Developing Specific Recall and Transfer Skills in Learners with Moderate and Severe Mental Retardation. *Education and Training in Mental Retardation, 25, (5), 286-291.*

Berends, I.E., & Reitsma, P. (2007). Orthographic analysis of Words during Fluency Training Promotes Reading of New Similar Words. *Journal of Research in Reading, 30 (2), 129-139.*

Best, J. W. & Kahn, J.V. (1999). *Research in Education* (7th ed.). Prentice Hall of India, New Delhi.

Bigler, J.K. (1984). Increasing Inferential Comprehension Scores of Intermediate Age Mildly Retarded Students using Two different Teaching Procedures. *Education and Training of Mentally Retarded, 19 (2), 132-140.*

Bloom, B.S. (1984). The 2 Sigma Problem: The Search for methods of Group Instruction as Effective as One-to-one Tutoring. *Educational Researcher, 13 (6), 4-17.*

Bos, C.S. & Vaughn, S. (1994). *Strategies for Teaching Students with Learning and Behavior Problems.* Allyn & Bacon, Massachusetts, USA.

Brace, N., Kemp, R., & Snelgar, R. (2003). *SPSS for Psychologists* (2nd ed.). Palgrave Macmillan, New York.

Bradley, L. & Bryant, P. (1985). Children's Reading Problems. In T.G. Gunning *Assessing and Correcting Reading and Writing difficulties*. Allyn & Bacon, MA, USA.

Brophy, J.E. & Good, T.L. (1970). Teacher Communication of differential Expectations of Children's Classroom Performance: Some Behavioral Data. *Journal of Educational Psychology, 61, 365-374.*

Browder, D.M., Hines, C., McCarthy, L.J. & Fees, J. (1984). A Treatment Package for Increasing Sight Word Recognition for use in Daily Living Skills. *Education and Training of the Mentally Retarded, 19, 191-200.*

Browder, D.M., Huyyetters, D., & Karol, K. (1998). An Evaluation of Transfer of Stimulus Control and of Comprehension in Sight Word Reading for Children with Mental Retardation and Emotional Disturbance. *School Psychology Review, 17 (2), 331-342.*

Browder, D.M. & Minarovic, T.J. (2000). Utilizing Sight Words in Self-instruction Training for Employees with Moderate Mental Retardation in Competitive Jobs. *Education and Training in Mental Retardation and Developmental Disabilities, 35(1), 78-89.*

Browder, D.M., Trela, K., Gibbs, S.L., Wakeman, S. & Harris A.A. (2007). Academic Skills: Reading and Mathematics. In S.L. Odom, R.H. Horner, M.E. Snell, & J. Blacher (Eds). *Handbook of Developmental Disabilities*, New York: Guilford Press.

Brown, F., Holvoet, J., Guess, D., & Mulligan, M. (1980). The Individualized Curriculum Sequencing Model (III): Small Group Instruction. *Journal of the Association for the Severely Handicapped*, 5, 352-367.

Bryant, B.R. & Wiederholt, J.L. (1991). *Gray Oral Reading Tests – Diagnostic*. Pro-ed, Austin, Texas, USA.

Burns, M.K., Dean, V.J., and Foley, S. (2004). Pre Teaching unknown key words with Incremented Rehearsal to Improve Reading Fluency and Comprehension with Children Identified as Reading Disabled. *Journal of School Psychology, 42 (4), 303-314.*

Bus, A. & Van Ijzendoorn, M. (1999). Phonological Awareness and Early Reading: A Meta-analysis of Experimental Training Studies. In H.W. Catts & A.G. Kamhi *Language and Reading Disabilities* (2nd ed.). Pearson Education inc., MA, USA.

Butler, D. (1975). Cushla and her Books. In D.S. Katims, Literacy Instruction for People with Mental Retardation: Historical Highlights and Contemporary Analysis. *Education and Training in Mental Retardation and Developmental Disabilities, 35 (1), 3-15.*

Bysteveldt, A.K.V. (2006). Enhancing Phonological Awareness and Letter Knowledge in Preschool Children with Down Syndrome. *International Journal of Disability, Development, and Education, 53 (3), 301-329.*

Cannella-Malone, H.I., Konrad, M., & Pennington, R.C. (2015). ACCESS! Teaching Writing Skills to Students with Intellectual Disability. *Teaching Exceptional Children, 47(5), 272-280 Eric number EJ 1061466.*

Channell, M.M., Loveall, S.J. & Conners, F.A. (2013). Strenghts and Weakness in Reading Skills of Youth with Intellectual Disabilities. *Research in Developmental Disabilities: A Multidisciplinary Journal, 34 (2), 776-787 Eric number: EJ1006113*

Carlton, M.B. (1985). The Effect of Inter Class Peer Tutoring Programme on the Sight word Recognition Ability of Students who are Mildly Mentally Retarded. *Mental Retardation, 23, 74-78.*

Carney, J.J. (1979). What Research says about Reading for the Mentally Retarded Child. *A Paper Presented at the Annual Meeting of International Reading Association,* Atalanta, Georgia, on April 23-27, 1979. *Eric ED 176458.*

Carter, J.L. (1975). Intelligence and Reading Achievement of EMR in Three Educational Settings. *Mental Retardation, 13 (5), 26-27.*

Catts, H.W. & Kamhi, A.G. (2005). *Language and Reading Disabilities.* (2nd ed.). Pearson Education Inc., M A, USA.

Cazzell, S Browarnik, B., Skinner, A., Skinner, C., Cihak, D., Ciancio, D., McCurdy, M. & Forbes, B. (2016). Extending Research on a Computer-based Flashcard Reading Intervention to Post Secondary Students with Intellectual Disabilities. *School Psychology Forum* 10(2), 191-206. Eric number: EJ 1149033

Chard, D.J., Vaughn, S. & Tyler, B. (2002). A Synthesis of Research on Effective Interventions for Building Reading Fluency with Elementary Students with Learning Disabilities. *Journal of Learning Disabilities*, 35, 386.

Clarke, T. (2001). *Developing and Supporting Literacy-rich Environments for Children.* Retrieved October 2009 from http:// www.google.co.in search –literacy Rich Environments for Children –read pdf.

Clinton, L. & Boyce, K. (1975). Acquisition of Simple Motor Imitative Behaviours in Mentally Retarded and near Mentally Retarded Children. In P.A. Alberto & A.C. Troutman, *Applied Behaviour Analysis for Teachers.* Prentice-Hall, Inc., New Jersey, USA.

Collins, B.C., Gast, D.L., Ault, M.J. & Wolery, M. (1991). Small Group Instruction: Guidelines for Teachers of Students with moderate to Severe Handicaps. *Education and Training in Mental Retardation, 26(1)18-32.*

Conners, F. (1992). Reading Instruction for Students with moderate Mental Retardation: Review and Analysis of Research. In R. Didden, S.D.

Graaff, M. Nelemans, M. Vooren, & G. Lancioni, Teaching Sight Words to Children with Moderate to Mild Mental Retardation: Comparison between Instructional Procedures. *American Journal on Mental Retardation, 3 (5), 357-365.*

Conners, F. (2003). Reading Skills and Cognitive Abilities of Individuals with Mental Retardation. In R. Didden, S.D. Graaff, M. Nelemans, M. Vooren & G. Lancioni, Teaching Sight Words to Children with Moderate to Mild Mental Retardation: Comparison between Instructional Procedures. *American Journal on Mental Retardation, 3 (5), 357-365.*

Cunningham, A.E. & Stanovich, K.E.(1998). What Reading does for the Mind. In A.K. Jitendra, L.L. Edwards, G. Sacks & L.A. Jacobson, What Research says about Vocabulary Instruction for Students with Learning Disabilities. *Exceptional Children, 70 (3), 299-322.*

Dennis, L.R., Lynch, S.A., & Stockall, N. (2012). Planning Literacy Environments for Diverse Preschoolers. *Young Exceptional Children, 15 (3), 3-19 Eric Number: EJ 976955.*

Dessemontet, R.S., de Chambrier, A., Martinet, C., Moser, U., Bayer, N. (2017). Exploring Phonological Awareness Skills in Children with Intellectual Disability. *American Journal on Intellectual and Developmental Disabilities, 122(6), 476-491.*

Didden, R., Graaff, S.D., Nelemans, M., Vooren, M., & Lancioni, G. (2006) Teaching Sight words to Children with Moderate to Mild Mental Retardation: Comparison between Instructional Procedures. *American Journal on Mental Retardation*, 3 *(5), 357-365.*

Didden, R., Prinsen, H., & Sigafoos, J. (2000). The Blocking Effect of Pictorial Prompts on Sight Word Reading. In R. Didden, S.D. Graaff, M. Nelemans, M. Vooren, & G. Lancioni. Teaching Sight Words to Children with Moderate to Mild Mental Retardation: Comparison between Instructional Procedures. *American Journal on Mental Retardation, 3 (5), 357-365.*

Dixon, R.C., Carnine, D., and Kameenui, E. (1994). Tools for Teaching Diverse Learners: Using Scaffolding to Teach Writing. In T.G. Gunning, *Assessing and Correcting Reading and Writing Difficulties*. Allyn and Bacon, MA, USA.

Dorry, G. & Zeaman, D. (1975). Teaching Simple Reading Vocabulary to Retarded Children: Effectiveness of Fading and Nonfading Procedures. *American Journal of Mental Deficiency, 79, 711-716.*

Ediger, M. (1999). Reading and Vocabulary Development. *Journal of Instructional Psychology, 26 (1), 1-12.*

Ehri, L.C. (1998). Grapheme-phoneme knowledge is Essential for Learning to Read Words in English. In H.W. Catts & A.G. Kamhi, *Language and Reading Disabilities*. (2nd ed.). Pearson Education inc., MA, USA.

Ehri, L.C., Nunes, S.R., Willows, D.M., Schuster, B.V., Yaghoub-Zabeh, Z. & Shanahan, T. (2001). Phonemic Awareness Instruction helps Children to Read: Evidence from the National Reading Panel's Meta–analysis. In H.W. Catts & A.G. Kamhi . *Language and Reading Disabilities* (2nd ed.). Pearson Education inc, MA, USA.

Elbaum, B.E., Schumm, J.S., & Vaughn, S. (1995). Students Perceptions of Grouping formats for Reading Instruction. In S. Vaughn, C.S. Bos & J.S. Schumm, *Teaching Mainstreamed, Diverse, and at-risk Students in General Education Classroom*. Allyn & Bacon, MA, USA.

Farmer J.A., Gast, D.L., Wolery, M. & Winterling, V. (1991). Small Group Instruction for Students with Severe Handicaps: A Study of Observational Learning. *Education and Training in Mental Retardation, 26 (2) 190-201.*

Fernald, G.M. (1943). Remedial Techniques in basic School Subjects. In C.S. Bos, & S. Vaughn, *Strategies for Teaching Students with Learning and Behavior Problems*. Allyn & Bacon, Massachusetts, USA.

Fernald, G.M. (1988). Remedial Techniques in basic School Subjects. In C.S. Bos & S. Vaughn, *Strategies for Teaching Students with Learning and Behavior Problems.* Allyn & Bacon, Massachusetts, USA.

Fink, W.T. & Sandall, S.R. (1978). One-to-one versus Group Academic Instruction with Handicapped and Non Handicapped Preschool Children. *Mental Retardation, 16, 236-240.*

Fowler, G.L. & Davis, M. (1985). The Story Frame Approach: A Tool for Improving Reading Comprehension of EMR Children. *Teaching Exceptional Children, 17 (4), 296-298.*

Frederickson, N. & Wilson, J. (1996). Phonological Awareness Training: A New Approach to Phonics Teaching. *Dyslexia – an International Journal of Research and Practice, 2, (2), 101-120.*

Fuchs, L.S., Fuchs, D., & Compton, D.L. (2004). Monitoring Early Reading Development in First Grade: Word Identification Fluency versus Nonsense Word Fluency. *Exceptional Children, 71 (1), 7-21.*

Fuchs, L.S., Fuchs, D., Hosp, M.K., and Jenkins, J.R. (2001). Oral Reading Fluency as an Indicator of Reading Competence: A Theoretical, Empirical, and Historical Analysis. In B. Gunn, K. Smolkowski, A. Biglan, C. Black, & J.Blair, Fostering the Development of Reading Skill through Supplemental Instruction: Results for Hispanic and non-Hispanic Students. The *Journal of Special Education, 39 (2), 66-85.*

Fuchs, L.S., & Deno, S.L. (1991). Curriculum-based Measurement: Current Applications and Future Directions. In B. Gunn, K. Smolkowski, A. Biglan, C. Black, & J.Blair, Fostering the Development of Reading Skill through Supplemental Instruction: Results for Hispanic and Non-Hispanic Students. The *Journal of Special Education,* 39 (2), 66-85.

Fuller, R. (1991). The Primacy of Story. *In context, 27, 26-28.*

Gay, L.R. (1996) *Educational Research: Competencies for Analysis and Application* (5th ed). Prentice-Hall, Inc., New Jersey.

Gillon, G. (2002) Phonological Awareness Intervention for Children: From the Research Laboratory to the Clinic. *A S H A Leader, 7, 4.*

Graham, S. (1992). Helping Students with LD Progress as Writers. In T.G. Gunning,. *Assessing and Correcting Reading and Writing Difficulties.* Allyn and Bacon, MA, USA.

Graham, S. & Miller, L. (1980). Handwriting Research and Practice: A Unified Approach. *Focus on Exceptional Children, 13 (2), 1-16.*

Graves, D.H. (1983). Writing: Teachers and Children at Work. In C.S. Bos & S. Vaughn,. *Strategies for Teaching Students with Learning and Behavior Problems.* Allyn & Bacon, Massachusetts, USA.

Graves, D.H. (1994). A Fresh New Look at Writing. In E.A. Polloway & J.R. Patton, *Strategies for Teaching Learners with Special Needs.* Prentice-Hall, Inc., New Jersey, USA.

Griffith, P.L. & Olson, M.W. (1992). Phonemic Awareness helps beginning Readers Break the Code. In S. McCormic, *Instructing Students who have Literacy Problems* (2nd ed.). Prentice Hall, Inc., New Jersey.

Gunning, T.G. (1998). *Assessing and Correcting Reading and Writing Difficulties.* Allyn & Bacon, Massachusetts, USA.

Guthrie, J.T., Seifert, M. & Kline, L.W. (1978). Clues from Research on Programmes for Poor Readers. In T.G. Gunning, *Assessing and Correcting Reading and Writing Difficulties.* Allyn and Bacon, Massachusetts, USA.

Guzel – Ozmen, R. (2006). The Effectiveness of modified Cognitive Strategy Instruction in Writing with Mildly Mentally Retarded Turkish Students. *Exceptional Children, 72 (3), 281-297.*

Haigh, M. (2007). Sustaining Learning through Assessment: An Evaluation of the Value of a Weekly Class Quiz. *Assessment and Evaluation in Higher Education, 32 (4), 457-474.*

Hanley-maxwell, C. (1982). A Comparison of Vocabulary Learning by Moderately Retarded Students under Direct Instruction and Incidental Presentation. *Education and Training of the Mentally Retarded, 17 (3), 214-221.*

Hansen, J. (1981). The Effects of Inference Training and Practice on young Children's Comprehension. In S. McCormic, *Instructing Students who have Literacy Problems* (2nd ed.). Prentice Hall, Inc., New Jersey.

Hedrick, W.B., Katims D.S., & Carr, N.J. (1999). Implementing a Multimethod, Multilevel Literacy Programme for Students with Mental Retardation. *Focus on Autism and Other Developmental Disabilities, 14, 231-239.*

Hiebert, E.H. (1994). A Small-group Literacy Intervention with Chapter I Students. In T.G. Gunning, *Assessing and Correcting Reading and Writing Difficulties.* Allyn and Bacon, Massachusetts, USA.

Helf, S., Cook, N.L. & Flowers, C.P. (2009). Effects of Two Grouping Conditions on Students who are at Risk for Reading Failure. *Preventing School Failure, 53 (2), 113-128.*

Henk, W.A., Helfeldt, J.P. & Platt, J.M. (1986). Developing Reading Fluency in Learning Disabled Students. *Teaching Exceptional Children, 18 (3), 202-206.*

Hua, Y. Woods-Groves, S., Ford, J.W. & Nobles, K.A. (2014). Effects of the Paraphrasing Strategy on Expository Reading Comprehension of Young Adults with Intellectual Disability. *Education and Training in Autism and Developmental Disabilities, 49, 429-439.*

Hurst, M. & Joliyette, K. (2006). Effect of Private versus Public Assessment on the Reading Fluency of Middle School Students with Mild Disabilities. *Education and Training in Developmental Disabilities, 41 (2), 185-196.*

Idol, L. (1987). A Critical thinking Map to Improve Content Area Comprehension for Poor Readers. *Remedial and Special Education, 8 (4), 28-40.*

Jayachandran, P. & Vimala, V. (1992). *Madras Developmental Programming System.* Vijay Human Services, Chennai.

Johnson, M.S., Kress, R.A., & Pilkulski, J.J. (1987). Informal Reading Inventories (2nd ed.). In T.G. Gunning, *Assessing and Correcting Reading and Writing Difficulties.* Allyn and Bacon, Massachusetts, USA.

Jones, K.M. (1987). Using Computer Guided Practice to Increase Decoding Fluency in Learning Disabled Children: A Study using the Hint and Hunt I programme. *Journal of Learning Disabilities, 20 (2), 122-128.*

Joseph, L.M. & Seery, M.E. (2004). Where is the Phonics: A Review of the Literature on the use of Phonetic Analysis with Students with Mental Retardation. In K.J. Saunders & A. Defulio, Phonological Awareness and Rapid Naming Predict Word Attack and Word Identification in Adults with Mental Retardation. *American Journal on Mental Retardation, 112 (3), 155-166.*

Joseph, L.M. & Konrad, M. (2009). Teaching Students with Intellectual or Developmental Disabilities to Write. *Research in Developmental Disabilities, 30 (1), 1-19.*

Juel, C. (1991). Beginning Reading. In S. McCormic, *Instructing Students who have Literacy Problems* (2nd ed.). Prentice Hall Inc., New Jersey.

Kamps, D., Abbot, M., Greenwood, C., Wills, H,. Veerkamp, M. & Kauffman, J. (2008). Effects of Small Group Reading Instruction and Curriculum Differences for Students most at Risk in Kindergarten: Two Year Results for Secondary and Tertiary – Level Interventions. *Journal of Learning Disabilities, 41 (2), 101-114.*

Katims, D.S. (2001). *Literacy Assessment of Students with Mental Retardation. Education and Training in Mental Retardation and Developmental Disabilities, 36 (40), 363-372.*

Katims, D.S. (2000 a). Literacy Instruction for People with Mental Retardation: Historical Highlights and Contemporary Analysis. *Education and Training in Mental Retardation and Developmental Disabilities, 35 (1), 3-15.*

Katims, D.S. (2000). The Quest for Literacy: Curriculum and Instructional Procedures for Teaching Reading and Writing to Students with Mental Retardation and Developmental Disabilities. In D.S. Katims, Literacy Instruction for People with Mental Retardation: Historical Highlights and Contemporary Analysis. *Education and Training in Mental Retardation and Developmental Disabilities, 35 (1), 3-15.*

Katims, D.S. (1996). The Emergence of Literacy in Elementary Students with Mental Retardation. *Focus on Autism and Other Developmental Disabilities, 11 (3), 147-157.*

Katims, D.S. (1991). Emergent Literacy in Early Childhood Special Education: Curriculum and Instruction. *Topics in Early Childhood Special Education, 11(1), 69-84.*

Katims, D.S. (1994). Emergence of Literacy in Preschool Children with Disabilities. *Learning Disability Quarterly, 17, 58-71.*

Katims, D.S., & Pierce, P.L. (1995). Literacy-rich Environments and the Transition of Young Children with Special Needs. *Topics in Early Childhood Special Education, 15(2), 219-234.*

Kauffman, J.M., & Hung, Li-Yu. (2009). Special Education for Intellectual Disability. Current Trends and Perspectives. *Current Opinion in Psychiatry, 22(5), 452-456 htt:// dx.doi.org/10.1097/YCO.0b013e32832eb5c3*

Khan, J.A. (2007). *Research Methodology.* APH Publishing Corporation, New Delhi.

Kimmel, M.M. & Segal, E. (1988). *For Reading out Loud.* Delacorate, New York.

Koppenhaver, D.A. & Yoder, D.E.(1993). Classroom Literacy Instruction for Children with Severe Physical Impairments (SSPI): What is and what might be ? In D.S. Katims,. *Literacy Assessment of Students with Mental Retardation. Education and Training in Mental Retardation and Developmental Disabilities, 36 (40), 363-372.*

Lalli, J. & Browder, D. (1993). Comparison of Sight Word Training Procedures with Validation of the most Practical Procedure in Teaching Reading for Daily Living. *Research in Developmental Disabilities, 14(2), 107-127.*

Lally, M. (1981). Computer-assisted Teaching of Sight word Recognition for Mentally Retarded School Children. *American Journal of Mental Deficiency, 85 (4), 383-388.*

Langone, J. (1986). *Teaching Retarded Learners – Curriculum and methods for Improving Instruction.* Allyn & Bacon, USA.

Leung, C.B. (1992). Effects of Word Related Variables on Vocabulary Growth through Repeated Read-aloud Events. In S. McCormic, *Instructing Students who have Literacy Problem* (2nd ed.). Prentice Hall, Inc., New Jersey.

Lomax, R.G. & McGee, L.M. (1987). Young Children's Concepts about Print and meaning: Toward a Model of Word Reading Acquisition. In S. McCormic, *Instructing Students who have Literacy Problem.* (2nd ed.). Prentice Hall, Inc., New Jersey.

Lundberg, I & Reichenberg, M. (2013). Developing Reading Comprehension among Students with Intellectual Disabilities - An Intervention Study. Scandinavian Journal of Educational Research, Vol. 57, No. 1 89-100.

Mackay, C. (2007).Why do I learn to read. Retrieved March 29, 2019 from http://ezinearticles.com/ why-Do-I-Need-To-Learn-To-Read &id=897851

Mann, P.H., Suiter, P.A., & McClung, R. (1992). *A Guide for Educating Mainstreamed Students.* Allyn and Bacon, Massachusetts, USA.

Maria, K. (1990). *Reading Comprehension Instruction: Issues and Strategies.* Parkton, MD: York.

McCormic, S. (1995). *Instructing Students who have Literacy Problems* (2nd ed.). Prentice Hall, Inc., New Jersey.

McCormic, S. & Hill, D.S. (1984). An Analysis of the effects of Two Procedures for Increasing Disabled Readers' Inferencing Skills. In S.McCormic, *Instructing Students who have Literacy Problems* (2nd ed.) Prentice Hall, Inc., New Jersey.

Mcguire, P. (1986). Social Skill Training for Health Professionals. In P.J. Schloss, M.A. Smith & C.N. Schloss, *Instructional Methods for Adolescents with Learning and Behaviour Problems* (2nd ed.). Allyn & Bacon, Massachussets, USA.

Merimee, S.N. (2017). Addressing Reading Fluency of Students with Intellectual Disabilities using a Multiple Probe Design. *Kentucky Teacher Education Journal, 4 (1),1-20.*

Mihai, A., Friesen, A,. Butera, G. Horn, E., Lieber, J. & Palmer, S. (2015). Teaching Phonological Awareness to all Children through Story Book Reading. *Young Exceptional Children, 18(4), 3-18.*

Mims, P.J., Browder, D.M., Baker, J.N., Lee, A. & Spooner, F. (2009). Increasing Comprehension of Students with Significant Intellectual Disabilities and Visual Impairments during Shared Stories. *Education and Training in Developmental Disabilities, 44 (3),409-420.*

Moody, S.W., Vaughn, S., Hughes, M.T. & Fischer, M. (2000). Reading Instruction in the Resource Room: Set up for Failure. *Exceptional Children, 66 (3), 305-316.*

Myreddi, V. & Narayan, J. (1998). *Functional Academics for Children with Mental Retardation – A Guide for Teachers*. National Institute for the Mentally Handicapped, Secunderabad.

Narayan, J. (1997). *Grade Level Assessment Device for Children with Learning Problems in School*. National Institute for the Mentally Handicapped, Secuderabad.

National Reading Panel. (2000). Teaching Children to Read: An Evidence-based Assessment of the Scientific Research Literature on Reading and its Implications for Reading Instruction. In K.J. Saunders & A. Defulio, Phonological Awareness and Rapid Naming Predict Word Attack and Word Identification in Adults with Mental Retardation. *American Journal on Mental Retardation, 112, (3), 155-166.*

NIMH (1994). *Functional Assessment Checklist for Programming (FACP).* National Institute for the Mentally, Handicapped, Secundrabad.

Noble, T. & Merrill, J. (1989). Teaching Sight Vocabulary to Children with Developmental Disabilities. *Australia and New Zealand Journal of Developmental Disabilities, 15 (1), 27-39.*

Oliver, P.R. (1983). Effects of Teaching different Tasks in Group versus Individual Training Formats with Severely Handicapped Individuals. *The Journal of the Association for the Severely Handicapped, 8 (2), 79-91.*

Orelove, F. (1982). Acquisition of Incidental Learning in Moderately and Severely Handicapped Adults. *Education and Training of the Mentally Retarded, 17, 131-136.*

Payne, J.S., Polloway, E.A., Smith, J.E. & Payne, R.N. (1981). *Strategies for Teaching the Mentally Retarded* (2nd ed.). Charles E. Merrill Publishing Company, Columbus, OH.

Pennington, R., Flick, A., & Smith-Wehr, K. (2018). The use of Response Prompting and Frames for Teaching Writing to Students with Moderate Intellectual Disability. *Focus on Autism and other Developmental Disabilities, 33(3), 142-149. Eric number:EJ1187670*

Perfetti, C.A. (1985). Reading ability. In D.J. Chard, S. Vaughn & B. Tyler, A Synthesis of Research on Effective Interventions for Building Reading Fluency with Elementary Students with Learning Disabilities. *Journal of Learning Disabilities, 35, 386-392.*

Peshawaria, R. & Venkatesan, S. (1992). *Behavoural Assessment Scales for Indian Children with Mental Retardation*. National Institute for the Mentally Handicapped, Secunderabad.

Pikulski, J.J. (1994). Preventing Reading Failure: A Review of Five Effective Programmes. *The Reading Teacher, 48, 30-39.*

Polloway, E.A. (1986). Corrective Reading Programme: An Analysis of Effectiveness with Learning Disabled and Mentally Retarded Students. *Remedial and Special Education, 7 (4), 41-47.*

Polloway, E.A. & Patton, J.R. (1997). *Strategies for Teaching Learners with Special Needs*. Prentice-Hall, Inc., New Jersey, U.S.A.

Rabren, K., Darch, C. & Eaves, R. (1999). The Differential Effects of Two Systematic Reading Comprehension Approaches with Students with Learning Disabilities. *Journal of Learning Disabilities, 32 (1), 36-47.*

Rankhorn, B., England, G., Collins, S.M., Lockavitch, J.F. & Algozzine, B. (1998). Effects of the Failure Free Reading Programme on Students with Severe Reading Disabilities. *Journal of Learning Disabilities, 31 (3), 307-312.*

Raphael, T.E. & Englert, C.S. (1990). Writing and Reading: Partners in Constructive meaning. *The Reading Teacher, 43, 388-400.*

Rasinski, T.V. (1990). Investigating measures of Reading Fluency. In C.S. Bos, & S. Vaughn, *Strategies for Teaching Students with Learning and Behavior Problems.* Allyn & Bacon, Massachusetts, USA.

Reddy, L.G., Malini, S. & Kusuma, A. (2004). *Special Education Series – Mental Retardation: Education and Rehabilitation Services.* Discovery Publishing House, New Delhi.

Rousseau, M.K. & Foshee, J.G. (1981). Increasing Reading Comprehension of Direct Care Trainees. *Mental Retardation, 19 (4), 169-172.*

Rousseau, M.K. (1993). Syntactic Complexity in the Writing of Students with and without Mental Retardation. *American Journal on Mental Retardation, 98 (1), 113-120.*

Rubin, R. (1997). *Diagnosis and Correction in Reading Instruction* (3rd ed.). Allyn & Bacon, Massachusetts.

Rumelhart, D.E. (1981). Schemata: The Building Blocks of Cognition. In S. McCormic, *Instructing Students who have Literacy Problems* (2nd ed.). Prentice Hall, Inc., New Jersey.

Samuals, S.J. (1987). Information Processing Abilities and Reading. *Journal of Learning Disabilities, 20 (1), 18-22.*

Samuals, S.J. (1979). The method of Repeated Readings. *The Reading Teacher, 32, 403-408.*

Saunders, K.J. & Defulio, A. (2007). Phonological Awareness and Rapid Naming Predict Word Attack and Word Identification in Adults with Mental Retardation. *American Journal on Mental Retardation, 112 (3), 155-166.*

Sax, G. (1980). *Principles of Educational and Psychological Measurement and Evaluation* (2nd ed.). Belmont, CA: Wadsworth.

Schalock, R.L., Borthwick - Duffy, S.A., Bradley, V.J., Buntinx, H.E., Coulter, D.L., Craig, E.M. (.....), Yeager, M.H., (2010). Intellectual Disability: Definition, Classification, and Systems of Supports (11th ed.) American Association on Intellectual and Developmental Disabilities, Washington D.C.

Schloss, P.J., Smith, M.A . & Schloss, C.N. (1995). *Instructional methods for Adolescents with Learning and Behavior Problems*. (2nd ed.). Allyn & Bacon, Massachussets, USA.

Sedlak, R.A. & Sedlak, D.M. (1985). *Teaching the Educable Mentally Retarded*. State University Press, New York, USA.

Sella, A.C., Tenorio, J.P., Bandini, C.M, & Bandini, H.M. (2016). Games as a measure of Reading and Writing Generalization after Computerized Teaching of Reading Skills. *Psychology Research and review* http://dx.doi.org/10.1186/s41155-016-0039-3 Retrieved on 20-03-2019.

Share, D.L. & Stanovich, K.E.(1995) Cognitive Processes in Early Reading Development: Accommodating Individual Differences into a Model of Acquisition. In B. Gunn, K. Smolkowski, A. Biglan, C. Black & J.Blair, Fostering the Development of Reading Skill through Supplemental Instruction: Results for Hispanic and Non-Hispanic Students. *The Journal of Special Education, 39 (2), 66-85.*

Shavelson, R.J. (1988). *Statistical Reasoning for the Behavioural Sciences* (2nd ed.). Allyn and Bacon, Inc., Boston.

Shurr, J.& Taber-Doughty, T. (2017). The Picture Plus Discussion Intervention: Text Access for High School Students with Moderate Intellectual Disability. *Focus on Autism and Developmental Disabilities, 32 (3)198-208 Eric number: EJ1152445*

Singh, N.N. & Singh, J. (1986). Reading Acquisition and Remediation in the Mentally Retarded. In D.S. Katims (2000). Literacy Instruction for People with Mental Retardation: Historical Highlights and Contemporary Analysis. *Education and Training in Mental Retardation and Developmental Disabilities, 35 (1), 3-15.*

Singh, N., & Solman, R. (1990). A Stimulus Control Analysis of the Picture-word Problem in Children who are Mentally Retarded: The Blocking Effect. In R. Didden, S.D. Graaff, M. Nelemans, M. Vooren & G. Lancioni, Teaching Sight Words to Children with Moderate to Mild Mental Retardation: Comparison between Instructional Procedures. *American Journal on Mental Retardation*, 3 (5), 357-365.

Slavin, R.E. (1987). Ability Grouping and Student Achievement in Elementary Schools: A best Evidence Synthesis. *Review of Educational Research, 57 (3), 293-336.*

Smith, M.R. (1968). *Clinical Teaching - Methods of Instruction for the Retarded* (2nd ed.). McGraw – Hill Book Company, New York.

Snow, CE. (2002). Reading for Understanding. Towards R & D Programme in Reading Comprehension. In A.K. Jitendra, L.L., Edwards, G. Sacks & L.A. Jacobson, What Research says about Vocabulary Instruction for Students with Learning Disabilities. *Exceptional Children, 70 (3), 299-322.*

Snow, C.E., Burns, M.S. & Griffin, P. (1998). Preventing Reading Difficulties in Young Children. In D.J. Chard, S. Vaughn, & B. Tyler, A Synthesis of Research on Effective Interventions for Building Reading Fluency with Elementary Students with Learning Disabilities. *Journal of Learning Disabilities, 35, 386-392.*

Stahl, S.A. (1986). Three Principles of Vocabulary Instruction. In A.K. Jitendra, L.L., Edwards, G. Sacks & L.A. Jacobson, What Research Says About Vocabulary Instruction for Students with Learning Disabilities. *Exceptional Children*, 70 (3), 299-322.

Stahl, S.A. & Shiel, T.G. (1999). Teaching meaning Vocabulary: Productive Approaches for Poor Readers. Read about it! Readings to Inform the Profession. In A.K. Jitendra, L.L., Edwards, G. Sacks, & L.A. Jacobson, What Research says about Vocabulary Instruction for Students with Learning Disabilities. *Exceptional Children, 70 (3), 299-322.*

Steel, R.G.D and Torrie, J.H. (1980). *Principles and Procedures of Statistics* (2nd ed.). MC Graw – Hill Book Co. London.

Stevens, E.A.,Walker, M.A., Vaughn, S. (2017). The effects of Reading Fluency Interventions on Reading Fluency and Reading Comprehension Performance of Elementary Students with Learning Disabilities: A Synthesis of the Research from 2001-2014. *Journal of Learning Disabilities, 50(5), 576-590.*

Stone, J.P., Rivera, C.J., & Weiss, S.L. (2018). Literacy-rich Environments for Students with Significant Developmental Delays. *Young Exceptional Children 21 (4), 191-203 Eric number: EJ1197305.*

Sukumaran, P.S. (2000). *Parental Involvement in the Education of Mentally Handicapped Children.* Discovery Publishing House, New Delhi.

Sulzby, E. & Teale, W. (1991). Emergent Literacy. In S. McCormic, *Instructing Students who have Literacy Problems* (2nd ed.). Prentice Hall, Inc., New Jersey.

Sweet, A.P. (1993). State of the Art: Transforming Ideas for Teaching and Learning to Read. In S. McCormic, *Instructing Students who have Literacy Problems* (2nd ed.). Prentice Hall, Inc., New Jersey.

Swinson, J. & Knight, R. (2007). Teacher Verbal Feedback Directed towards Secondary Pupils with Challenging Behaviour and its Relationship to their Behavior. *Educational Psychology in Practice, 23(3), 241-255.*

Taylor, B.M., Strait, J. & Medo, M.A. (1994). Early Intervention in Reading: Supplimental Instruction for Groups of Low-achieving Students provided by First-grade Teachers. In T.G. Gunning, *Assessing and Correcting Reading and Writing Difficulties.* Allyn and Bacon, Massachusetts, USA.

Trelease, J. (1989a). Jim Trelease Speaks on Reading Aloud to Children. In C.S. Bos & S. Vaughn, *Strategies for Teaching Students with Learning and Behavior Problems.* Allyn & Bacon, Massachusetts, USA.

Uhry, J.K. (1993). Predicting Low Reading from Phonological Awareness and Classroom Print. In S. McCormic *Instructing Students who have Literacy Problems* (2nd ed.). Prentice Hall, Inc., New Jersey.

Vaughn, S., Bos, C.S., & Schumm J.S. (1997). *Teaching Mainstreamed, Diverse, and at-risk Students in General Education Classroom.* Allyn & Bacon, MA, USA.

Vellutino, F.R. & Denckla, M.B. (1991). Cognitive and Neuropsychological Foundations of Word Identification in Poor and Normally Developing Readres. In S. McCormic (1995). *Instructing Students who have Literacy Problems* (2nd Edn.). Prentice Hall, Inc., New Jersey.

Vygotsky, L.S. (1978). Mind in Society: The Development of Higher Mental Process . In D.S. Katims, Literacy Instruction for People with Mental Retardation: Historical Highlights and Contemporary Analysis. *Education and Training in Mental Retardation and Developmental Disabilities, 35 (1), 3-15.*

Westling, D.L. (1986). *Introduction to Mental Retardation.* Prentice Hall, Engle Wood Cliffs, New Jersy.

Whalen, C., Schuster, J.W. & Hemmeter, M.L. (1996). The use of Unrelated Instructive Feedback when Teaching in a Small Group Instructional Arrangement. *Education and Training in Mental Retardation and Developmental Disabilities, 31(3),188-202.*

Whiteley, H.E., Smith, C.D. & Conners, L. (2007). Young Children at Risk of Literacy Difficulties: Factors Predicting Recovery from Risk Following Phonologically based Intervention. *Journal of Research in Reading, 30 (3), 249-269.*

Williams, J.P. (2005). Instruction in Reading Comprehension for Primary-grade Students: A Focus on Text Structure. *The Journal of Special Education, 30(1), 6-18.*

Winterling, V. (1990). The Effects of Constant Time Delay, Practice in Writing or Spelling and Reinforcement in Sight Word Recognition in a Small Group. *Journal of Special Education, 24, 101-116.*

Wood, L., Browder, D.M., & Flynn, L. (2015). Teaching Students with Intellectual Disability to use a Self Questioning Strategy to Comprehend Social Studies Text for an Inclusive Setting. *Research and Practice for Persons with Severe Disabilities, 40,* 275-293.

Yopp, H.K. (1998). The Validity and Reliability of Phonemic Awareness Tests, *Reading Research Quarterly, 23, 159-177.*

Yopp, H.K. (1995). A Test for Assessing Phonemic Awareness in Young Children. In T.G. Gunning, *Assessing and Correcting Reading and Writing Difficulties.* Allyn and Bacon, MA, USA.

Zihyun, L. & Suk-Hyang, L. (2019). Effects of an Interview Article Writing Intervention using Lass Wide SNS on Writing Abilities and Self-esteem of Students with Intellectual Disabilities and Peers' Attitudes. *Journal of Special Education Technology, 34 (1), 27-40 Eric number: EJ 1204422.*

Index

❖ ❖ ❖ ❖ ❖